Unlock Your Mind to Academic and Life Success©

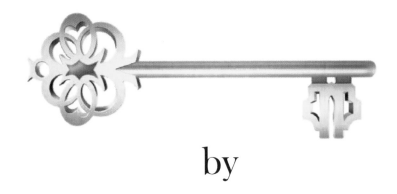

by

Dr. Tuesday S. Hambric

QPOR®
Publications
Quality Protected Open Resources

Published in the United States by *Quality Protected Open Resources®*, an imprint of *Higher Order Teaching & Learning Institute® LLC,* Texas

Library of Congress Cataloging-in-Publications Data

Control Number: 1-784-533

Tuesday S. Hambric

Book Designed by Tuesday S. Hambric

For Book Orders: www.hotlinstitute.org; email: tshambric@hotlinstitute.org

To My Immediate Family,

I would like to dedicate this body of work to…

- ♥ My husband, Anthony "Tony" Hambric. Thank you for supporting me through all the long hours and brainstorming sessions.
- ♥ My oldest son, Anthony Eugene Hambric. Thank you for trying some of my study methods and providing me with good critiques.
- ♥ My youngest son, Chyphes Jatory Hambric. Thanks for helping me think through some of my concepts and for helping me develop realistic examples.

I Love You…

To My Students,

Thank you. Thanks to each and every one of you who cared enough about yourself to have the will to learn and try new things. Your efforts keep me motivated and pressing forward in order to give all that I have to help you help yourself. Much love, always.

To the Learning Framework/Student Success Faculty,

Myesha Applewhite, Giantonio-Jonathan Michelon, Ana Rodriguez, S. Ke'shun Walker, Patrice Johnson, Anita Perry, Cherrender Brown, Kristen Carroll, Pamela McNulty, Tanesha Gant, Carole Stinson, Shirley Kaczka, Gale Karuth, Kathleen McGann, Demetrius Peters, Derrick Thomas, Alicia Muhammad … Wow! I could not have asked for a better team between the years of 2010 through 2017. When I was tired, you lifted me up; when I was too demanding, you pressed forward anyway, embracing my every standard and goal. I love you and appreciate you more than you may know. Thank you for being an honest and great team and a caring work family.

To the Extended Eastfield College Family,

Myesha Applewhite, S. Ke'shun Walker, Giantonio-Jonathan Michelon, Patrice Johnson, Kevin Giles, Tim Lo, Larissa Pierce, Eges Egedigw , Selena Alexander, Liz Nichols, Bret Wilkinson, Laura Carr, Mike Walker, Leticia Escobar, Regina Brown, Glynn Newman, Amy Dennis, Nick Vera, Kendra Wallis, Marques Washington, Tammy Oliver, Johnathon Verwys, Dora Saucedo-Falls, Erika Glaser, Lauren Shafer, and Ashley Martinez. You all may not be aware of this, but when I needed instructors to share classroom assignments or grant me access to their classes so that I could learn, develop, and integrate my writings, you were willing to do that *without hesitation.* Your humbleness allowed me to see things from the perspective of other disciplines. Some of you took time to review the material and offered discipline-specific expertise. Thank you. In essence, all of you helped me to strengthen my knowledge and advance my teaching applications. Without the benefits of your humility and hospitality, my writings would be wisdom from yesteryears. Instead, the information is real and relevant for students of today. ☺ Thank you for being such great colleagues without even trying. ☺

Thanks to my production team:

- The content editor: Elizabeth Zack of BookCraftersLLCc.com
- The line editor: Max Edwards of ServiceScape.com
- The graphics artist: Sherilyn Jones of www.TheConceptMediaGroup.com
- The cover designer: Jennifer Givner of AcapellaBookCoverDesign.weebly.com
- The layout and technical design team: Matthew Bourchier of PublishingSolutionsGroup.com
- The print production: Voom Group Printing Solutions
- The Web developers: G4 Design House of www.g4designhouse.com

Table of Content

III: *CHOP®* ACADEMICALLY — 83–154

AN IMPORTANT NOTE FROM THE AUTHOR...

Hello, Everyone,

Welcome to College!

I am excited about the information in this book. I am excited because I've been given an opportunity to revive, modify, synthesize, and expand upon some the greatest educational works since Socrates. And believe this or not, I have been gifted with an idea that will help you gain or maximize success in all aspects of your life. This idea is called *Customized Higher Order Processing (CHOP®)*.

CHOP® is a process by which **you** get to choose from several cognitive-behavioral frameworks, "chop them up," and integrate them in any manner that you like, and then use them in order to produce a systemized way of thinking that will maximize your chances for success. It's that easy.

So, wait ... Let's pause and think about this for a second ... In this book, I will teach you a couple of different ways to think critically. Then, you can use those critical thinking tools in any way you want, in order to produce <u>your</u> best chances for success.

The cool part about *CHOP®* is that *you* get to define the success *you* want, not me. So, however *you* define success—regardless of the situation, industry, or level of difficulty—*CHOP®* is applicable and designed to bring you greater success.

Remember what I stated earlier, "Believe this or not..." Well, that's because what I introduce in this book tends to have one of two effects on students. So, before I tell you what those two effects are, know that *more than 94%* of the people who use *CHOP®* report afterward that they have been positively and significantly impacted in their academic and their personal lives (Hambric, 2013a). In fact, here are two reactions students display once exposed to *CHOP®*:

- **Reaction #1:** Ninety-four percent of students exposed to *CHOP®* were excited about the opportunity *to take ownership of their lives through strategic critical thinking.* In addition, they were also excited about the potential success that thinking strategically brings to their futures.
- **Reaction #2:** Six percent of students exposed to *CHOP®* rejected the idea of being in charge of their own life outcomes. While they expressed this criticism through different explanations, what was common among their different reasons was *fear*—the fear of exposing their own flaws. You see, in order to embrace *CHOP®*, people will have to explore their current way of thinking, accept any flaws that they might find, and then work hard to make the needed adjustments.

But a great part about *CHOP®* is that *you*, not me nor the teacher, get to decide what exactly needs changing, if anything. Also, *you* get to choose what cognitive-behavioral tools you will use to make the needed changes, thus maximizing your potential for success.

Are you thinking, "Well this all sounds great, but I have heard it before? Thinking and learning … it's all the same." Or are you thinking, "Really? You're going to teach me how to *think?* Uhm, I've ONLY been doing that since I was born."

Well, here is the difference: You know how we think success depends on motivation and hard work? Well, that's true … *but from where does this motivation spring?* There is a certain kind motivation that is needed—a motivation resulting from the unique interaction between brain and mind (Siegel, 2015). This motivation is *Motivation 3.0*. **Motivation 3.0** *Motivation is the act of consciously or subconsciously, assessing, applying, and sometimes altering one's own beliefs to stimulate actions and reactions.*

So, what does this mean for you? Well, instead of you having to learn the depth of success one class at a time (or one life lesson at a time), I have sorted through an abundance of work in psychology, neurobiology, education, and critical thinking to share ideas from some of the most brilliant minds of yesterday and today.

In this book, I will mention influential works from philosophers and researchers such as Socrates, Dr. Benjamin Bloom, Drs. Richard Paul and Linda Elder, Dr. Albert Ellis, Dr. Abraham Maslow, and neurologist Dr. Daniel Siegel.

But wait! Don't let me oversell (or undersell) those names. I feel strongly about giving those heavy hitters credit, but, just as the cover reveals, this book is written as, and should read as, **a conversation,** in order that you, the reader, can easily understand and apply its concepts. The idea behind the laid-back, conversational style is to convey relaxation. My writing voice and tone are inspired by my personality and tons of research—research that asserts that people learn better when they are in a "happy place" (Sharot, 2011). For me, that means a happy place in our minds and our physical environments. I want you to engage and reason with me, feel good about pondering the material as you read, and then write down your questions for your teacher to explore in class or online. When you do this, you, your teacher, and I will have together raised the bar for success.

It is my prayer and hope (whichever you choose) that this style of writing will encourage you to actually *read* this book *before* you go to class. Moreover, I want you to be prepared to have a lively discussion and application of the concepts learned. Therefore, I apologize upfront if my tone is not what you expect for higher education; but make no mistake about it, the content is significant, and it works well when put into action. So, give it a chance and *Unlock Your Mind to Academic and Life Success.*

P.S. For you heavy hitters, there is a *Recommended Reading* page that follows the last chapter in this book. That *Recommended Reading* page will lead you to some of the works from the aforementioned pioneers and their contributions that aided me in my thinking and ultimately this book.

Signed Sincerely,

Dr. Tuesday S. Hambric
a.k.a. Mrs. Tuesday

Chapter I

Welcome to College!

Come Reason with Me

(Rationale and Buy-In)

Chapter I is designed to provide you with this book's rationale, in the hope that you will easily relate to the stories and information I share, become skeptics where things are rigid or obscure, and eventually reason your way to trusting the process. The most important topics in this chapter are *ownership and accountability* and *generating success your way.* Also, it is important to commit to memory the *Student Learning Outcomes* and to be willing to work hard when applying them.

WELCOME TO COLLEGE!

Are you excited, nervous, or both? Did you know that the first day of class and graduation day are probably the two most stimulating days you will experience in your academic career? Well, believe it or not, those two days are the most exhilarating days for us educators as well.

As stated in my letter on page one, I am excited. I personally want you to know that you are in the right hands for both academic and life success. Now, this may sound boastful, so know that this claim is supported by students just like you: first-time-in-college students, students returning from the workforce (including active duty and veteran military), community college students, and university students. The list goes on and on.

It's true that each and every one of you has a unique circumstance. However, in general, students just like you have encountered this material, and, based on their testimonies, you are in the right hands for both academic and life success.

Allow me to explain. The materials in this course and the application of the material have been evaluated through both qualitative and quantitative research. First, there is the qualitative proof. According to the data analysis report, *In Their Own Voices* (Hambric, 2017), 94% of former *First-Time in College* students expressed, in written statements, how the "Learning Framework material significantly changed their lives both academically and socially."

To further support what the students expressed in writing, the quantitative measures revealed that students entered this course with an average of 46% of the critical thinking skills needed to ensure academic and life success. However, those same students graduated from the course with an average of 86% of the critical thinking skills needed to ensure success both academically and socially. To state this differently, students on average began the course with an unacceptable amount (46% = F) of the critical thinking skills needed to ensure academic success. However, by the end of the term, students left the course with an above-average (86% = B) level of critical thinking skills needed to ensure academic success. (This information was collected and analyzed through the use of a pre- and post-test.)

With all of that being true, I think it is safe to say that this is one of the most important classes you will ever take during your academic career. So many blessings or good luck to you on this first day of the rest of your academic career.

Why A Student Success Class?

Almost every institution of higher education today has a course that is designed to help students succeed in college. The idea to design such a course was and still is a great idea. The problem is that, initially, *students* don't seem to think so. This is a problem because if you (the student) are upset about taking the course (vs. being happy about taking the class and the possibility of learning new ideas), then you will struggle throughout the course and learn very little, if anything at all. Remember, research says that people learn best when they are in a happy place (Sharot, 2011).

Now, with that stated, I *do* "get it." I really do understand why some of you would be upset that you have to take this course. Then, to add insult to injury, you find out that the class covers topics that you were exposed to in high school—you know, the old faithful ones, like how to take notes, manage your time, and utilize readily available resources.

Now at this point you might also be thinking, "Wait, Dr. Hambric just contradicted herself. Because she just indicated that she understands why some students would be hesitant about taking this course. But then in an earlier paragraph she says the class, '…was and still is a good idea.' Now that is a contradiction if I've ever seen one."

Well now, hold on and hear me out ☺. I do think the class is a great idea, and I believe some of the topics like time management and note-taking are important, too. But I also think we educators need to modernize our teaching to include new technologies and new ways to deliver information. We educators need to shake things up and learn to utilize learning preferences that best fit today's students. By doing so, we help you get to that happy place where significant learning is achieved. In other words, we educators need to embrace today's approach to learning. We need to turn our proven old faithful topics and our approach to student success classes on their heads—and I hope the visuals and interactive readings will be a good start. ☺

Why The "Old Faithful" Topics?

Student Success courses were and still are classes designed to help students be successful in college. Now, this didn't happen because someone thought, "Hey, the college can make a lot of money by offering such courses." Nooo … Student success classes were developed in response to an alarming number of students dropping out of college. Years ago, students said that the primary reasons why they quit college were because they themselves

- were academically unprepared;
- experienced culture shock due to the differences between high school expectations and college expectations;
- were made to feel like a minority and as a result felt unwelcomed and discouraged;
- lacked motivation and time-management skills;
- lacked funding (money).

And guess what? Each one of those roadblocks still exists for new students TODAY—in addition to the age-old excuse, "School just isn't for me." So now when you think about it, there is a logical explanation as to why the old faithful topics still exist. They exist because some of the past reasons for leaving college are still the primary reasons why new-to-college students drop out of school today (Tinto, 2012). With that said, though, because we teach the old faithful topics with a twist, more students are now choosing to stay in school and to graduate.

Let's Reflect A Bit.

So, what kind of roadblocks might you have? Here is a *Quick Help* reference list of the academic roadblocks mentioned earlier and their corresponding topics/solutions within this resource. The topics/solutions are designed to help you resolve or better manage such roadblocks. So, please, take a minute or two to examine the list.

REASONS FOR LEAVING COLLEGE	TOPICS/SOLUTIONS
Unprepared intellectually	*Study Skills, Bloom's Taxonomy*
Culture shock & increased expectations	*Ownership and Accountability, Stage Theory*
Felt unwelcomed and/or discouraged	*Emotional Intelligence, ABCD Theory*
Lack of motivation and procrastination	*Motivation Theory, Mottos, ABCD Theory*
Lack of time management	*Steven Covey's Quadrant Theory*
Minimal funding	*Money Management, The Elements of Thought*
Obligations and the stress of family life	*Resiliency, the Three Domains of Learning*

Now that you've had a chance to review some of the primary reasons why students quit school and a few of their corresponding solutions, were there any reasons listed that you can relate to, or were there one or more topics you think you might need to explore? Finally, are there other reasons that may cause you to quit college that are *NOT* listed?

Well, once I looked closer at the primary reasons why students quit school, I began to notice one really important theme, i.e., the concept of *resiliency*—or a lack thereof.

Resiliency actually serves as THE KEY to not only academic success—but all success. So, what is resiliency? **Resiliency** *is the ability to intentionally see things from more than one perspective and to create or to find opportunities to achieve success* (Hambric, 2011). No matter the problems or how the problems may present themselves, *resiliency creates alternatives and opportunities to take charge, overcome, and succeed.* So, a well-designed *student success* course—this course—gives you all the tools you need to discover such resiliency and to uniquely design your own system of thinking and demonstrated actions.

Ownership and Accountability

Have you ever heard a person say, "Things are true if you believe they are true?" Or have you ever heard a person say, "Nothing in this world has meaning unless the individual gives it meaning?" Well, the implication of those statements is that we have control over our thoughts (within reason that is). To take this idea further, Dr. Albert Ellis states that, by having control over our thoughts, we have control over our behavior; therefore, we have control over our life successes (Ellis, 1973, 2001). Do you believe this conclusion? Yes or no? Why?

**Please note that, at this point, it is important you think this through. Share your thoughts pertaining to this conclusion with your instructor because what you think and believe will determine whether or not you <u>fully</u> experience and embrace success. Your thoughts on this subject will determine if you are among the 94% of students who are excited about taking ownership and control of their lives through CHOP®—or if you are among the 6% of students exposed to CHOP® who reject the idea of being in charge of their own life outcomes.

If you are unfamiliar with the acronym *CHOP*ᴿ, then go back to *An Important Note from the Author* to find out more. I explain it there in detail. I also use and refer to *CHOP*ᴿ throughout this entire resource. So it's important to gain a clear understanding of *CHOP*ᴿ right away, so you can completely appreciate the rest of the material as it integrates the concepts using *CHOP*ᴿ.

Let's get back to the flow of things: control over our thinking and our lives…

- Do you believe we have control over our behaviors and, thus, control over our life successes? Explain and support your answer below.

  _____

  _____

  _____

What did you conclude? Let's discuss your answer briefly here (hopefully, you will discuss it in detail with your teacher and peers). Now, if you said, "No, I do not believe I have control over my thinking, behaviors, or my life outcomes," and you are not open to the idea of having control over these things, then this class might be a bit vexing … because this class and all the literature cited in it proclaims just that: that you <u>do</u> have control over your thinking, behaviors, and life successes—<u>within reason</u>, of course.

Notice I keep stating, "within reason…" That's because the truth of the matter is that there are a few exceptions to having control over your thoughts, behaviors, and outcomes. For example, some people may have certain cognitive or medical deficiencies or chemical dependencies that will not allow them to control their thinking without some form of help (David, 2014). Plus, there is the argument that relates to the degree of control that we might have over our thinking. This naturally leads to my final point here: Neither I nor the other experts mentioned in this book can claim that individuals have control over their thinking, behaviors, and life outcomes without acknowledging the fact that some people believe that God is in control.

Now, although each of these arguments I've identified has its own valid points from one perspective or another, undoubtedly you can reasonably identify different times in your life when you had to make choices—choices that were sometimes in your best interest and sometimes not. Well, didn't all those choices require you to undergo a bit of contemplation (thinking) first? So, within reason, can we *cautiously agree* we all have *some* control over our thinking and, therefore, *some* control over our behaviors and life successes? If you said yes, then you believe we have control over our thinking *within reason*. Enough said.

Moving On...

Generating Success Your Way...

Now, before you can generate success for yourself, you must first *define* success for yourself. Let's do that now. First, I want you to define success for yourself using the questions below. When you finish the exercise that follows, I want you to remain focused on *your* definition of success as you move through the rest of this course. So again … jump right in! The questions below serve as a brainstorming exercise. You are to use your answers to the questions to help you craft your definition of success.

1. Does having academic goals somehow fit within your ideas of success? If yes, how?
2. Does having career goals somehow fit within your ideas of success? If yes, how?
3. Does having family goals somehow fit within your ideas of success? If yes, how?
4. Does having healthy relationships somehow fit within your ideas of success? If yes, how?
5. Does having a spiritual foundation somehow fit within your ideas of success? If yes, how?
6. What character traits would you like for others to witness when they encounter you?
7. What core behaviors would you like to consistently display?
8. How would you describe your quality of thinking now, and how would you like to describe it five years from now?
9. Where do you see yourself five years from now?
10. Does giving back to society somehow fit in your ideas of success? If yes, how?

Now, using your answers to the aforementioned questions, write out your definition of success by finishing this statement: *Success is...*

_____

_____

_____

At this point, you may already have a clear idea about my hypothesis and the direction in which it will lead. If not, let me be clear: My premise for this resource is founded in the belief that if we, the faculty, help you, the students, use *CHOP*[R] to strengthen your intellectual abilities to customize your higher-order processing skills, then you will gain the self-confidence and self-control needed to make a positive impact on the different events that present themselves as roadblocks to your academic and life successes. In order to use *CHOP*[R], you must first learn how to maneuver your brain's way of processing information, and then you must learn how to intentionally use those maneuvers and processes to your *humble* (e.g., unpretentious) advantage.

As an example of getting past a roadblock using *CHOP*[R], let's use the idea of a dysfunctional home environment. You may now notice that I didn't cite *The Dysfunctional Home Environment* as a roadblock in the *Quick Help* reference list. But that's only because students often are too embarrassed to mention it during an open and general research interview. However, when I conducted more intimate research interviews and during one-on-one conversations with students, many students became comfortable enough to mention things like "family problems" and "criminal offenses" as reasons they struggled to remain in college.

Okay, let's see how a change in your thinking can change your home environment and ultimately *change your pathway to success*. By the way, whether it is the change in this *story* or a change in *real life*, the change that I speak of can be a *physical* change or simply a change *in how you perceive* your different experiences. Either way, both can ultimately change the reality in which you live.

After we explore *The Dysfunctional Home Environment* factor, we will examine how real-life experiences can generate excuses for dropping out of college and how taking mindful ownership of your thinking can generate success and resiliency, thus giving you a humble advantage.

Insights: Penetrating Below the Surface; Application of Theories...

The Dysfunctional Home Environment

Juan Martinez is a 20-year-old college student whose parents recently divorced. Juan lives with his mother and 15-year-old sister, while his father remarried and started a new family in another state. Juan hates the fact that his parents got a divorce.

To make matters worse, Juan and his mother never agree on anything, and their every conversation is fueled with anger and frustration. Juan's mother often accuses him of having a "bad attitude" and disrespecting her authority. Juan, on the other hand, thinks his mother is disrespecting him and being too lenient with his sister. All of this is stressing Juan out and is just the right combination of events for Juan to make bad decisions. Consequently, he spends most of his time focusing on matters at home and spending very little time on his studies. Needless to say, Juan is failing his classes.

One day after another huge fight with his mother, Juan goes in his room and reflects on the argument. He asks himself a couple of strategic questions. These questions help Juan explore the possible reasons as to why his mother so often accuses him of being disrespectful.

In processing the matter, Juan comes to recognize his *belief* that he has to take his father's place as head of the household. Additionally, Juan realizes he's angry at his father and that he holds a *belief* that his dad is not "man enough" to carry out his fatherly commitments. Finally, because of these reflections, Juan suddenly understands why he has been taking on more responsibility around the house: *He wants to show his mom and sister that he will <u>never</u> be like his father.*

After intentionally searching his thoughts for deeper explanations, Juan concludes that his beliefs about being head of household and his anger toward his father are causing him to make decisions that place him in a position of superiority over his mother. Juan quickly identifies his proper place, i.e., as a young man who is financially supported by his mother and still living under her roof.

Juan thinks differently now and appreciates his mother's strength, which enables her to endure the hardships that often comes hand-in-hand with divorce. He now knows that his mom is doing the best she can to raise him and his sister well.

Juan reflected on how his mother has adapted financially and how she involved her children in every decision that was made. Because Juan *changed* the way *he perceived* his life circumstances at home, he now has a new respect for his mother.

Juan then spoke with his mother about his thoughts, both old and new. To his surprise, she thanked him and told him that she, too, wanted to apologize for not recognizing the stress that the divorce placed on him. Needless to say, life for Juan suddenly became quite a bit better.

Because he perceived his personal circumstances differently, Juan changed his reality. His home environment was no longer filled with stress. Less stress at home meant that Juan was better able to concentrate in other areas of his life and, thus, be better able to focus on schoolwork and his actions toward success.

- How did Juan's dysfunctional home environment affect his schoolwork?

  _____
  _____
  _____

- What did Juan do to make his life less stressful?

  _____
  _____
  _____

- Using the story to support your answer, explain how Juan took ownership, accountability, and reasonable control over his thinking.

  _____
  _____
  _____

Juan's story may or may not mirror your own personal story, but, through it, can you see how, to a certain degree, people have control over their own thinking? I want you to think about the implied beauty of such a statement:

> *If you can deliberately restructure your thinking, then, within reason, very few impeding factors or roadblocks will be able to delay or stop your progress.*

Checking In…

Remember how I said I wanted to turn the information and our approach to student success classes on their heads? Well, all of that starts with **creating resiliency through critical thinking.** Critical thinking allows us to see things from more than one perspective; by doing so, opportunities are revealed and creativity is born. It may not seem like it, but that is HUGE!

Now, instead of us, the professors, seeing things our way and our way only, are now seeing things *your* way, from the *students'* perspective. Students say they want to be more engaged. Well, that is exactly what this resource and this class will provide: In this course, you will be more involved with projects, interactive assignments, and collaborations.

Also, the assignments will not be the run of the mill. These assignments will be grounded in relevant and real-life situations (like the situations presented earlier) as roadblocks to students' success. These up-to-date scenarios or practical applications are called *Insights: Penetrating Below the Surface* and will allow you to develop and exercise your own critical thinking skills. These practice scenarios will help you to apply the course materials and to reason in ways that will create alternative solutions and opportunities for you to succeed.

Now yes, there *will* be some lecturing. (How else will your instructors be able to check your intellectual clarity and understanding?) Nonetheless, the lectures will involve *all* of us. They will allow all of us to have a *conversation* with one and other. You see, any time you read the textbook, then discuss the book from my perspective, add your own perspective, and mix in your professor's and peers' viewpoints, *then* you will have an interactive dialogue from which everyone can engage, enjoy, and learn. As a matter of fact, to prove that we are engaging more and utilizing more technology, some of you may already be taking advantage of the digital version of this book right now. For those of you who are choosing the paperback format, you will need to have digital access via a smart phone, tablet, or computer in order to fully experience all the technological innovations that this resource has to offer.

Reading Check…

How is this style of writing and reading working for you so far? Did you know that, across the United States, some colleges have lowered their entry-level reading requirements? Well, by lowering the reading requirements, more students have a greater chance of taking college-level classes like this one during their first semester of school. That means students get an opportunity to avoid developmental reading and writing all together.

With that said, however, the implication of such collegiate actions is that you must be honest with yourself about your reading level. *You can really hurt your chances of college success if you do not assess your reading abilities accurately and honestly and then further work to improve your reading level if needed.* So, let's do that now. Let's assess your reading level. I can do so through asking just one question: Are you reading and still not fully understanding what you are reading? If your answer to this question is, "Oh no, I understand very well," then that's great. You can move on to the next section (the *Welcome Back* section).

However, if your answer is, "Yes, I am a bit confused by this conversational style of reading," then let's stop here and conduct a reading exercise. I want you to go back to the beginning of your reading and try reading the text **analytically.** (This may sound confusing, but it's not.) Just read one or two sentences or phrases at a time, <u>pausing every time you see a comma and stopping at every period.</u> By doing so, you will better understand the conversation's flow, my tone, and my attempt to place emphases on different words or phrases.

Now, after reading a few words or reading one or two sentences at a time, stop and ask yourself, "What did I just read?" If you can't answer that question, then it probably means that there is one or more words in the reading that you do not understand—and that's no problem. Just…

- First, identify words in your reading that are unfamiliar and for which you do not know the definition.
- Second, place a thin line through the words that are unfamiliar. Next, use your phone or tablet to Google the unfamiliar words, searching for their synonyms. Finally, replace all unfamiliar words with familiar words you use every day. In other words, use synonyms. For example, *Professor Joiner had to make a decision that required <u>contemplation</u>.* Insert: *careful thinking.* (*contemplation* is the same as careful thinking.)
- Finally, reread the material one or two sentences at a time using the new words. For example, *Professor Joiner had to make a decision that required careful thinking.*
- Then, ask yourself, "What did I just read?" Having just changed out the unfamiliar words with your everyday words, you should be able to appropriately answer this question now. Follow these instructions several times throughout your reading, moving along one paragraph at a time.

Once you are finished reading an entire section, ask yourself, "Do I agree with the author?" Whatever your answer, be it yes or no, you should then dialogue (*talk it out*) in your mind or with your classmates, specifying the reasons you agree or disagree with what you've read. If you prefer writing things down, no problem then; write your thoughts down. Use whatever makes you comfortable.

Now, once you are finished reading and understanding the material, move on to this next section: The *Welcome Back* section.

Welcome Back…

Why do you think I took the time to check your reading skills? Do you think it is only because of the changes to the college entry-level reading requirements? Well, yes, that is one of the obvious reasons. But the nonapparent reason is because I also want you to learn how to read at in-depth levels. This will serve you well not only in your classes but in all areas of your life where reading is required.

Most importantly, I want you to develop *intrinsic motivation*; in other words, *your own reasons for wanting to know more.* Remember, I said *you* get to decide what is important to *you*—not us. We—your professors and I—are challenged with orchestrating the material in ways that evoke critical thinking. You, the student, is charged with examining the material *and expanding it from there.* Any questions or thoughts you might develop from your reading, please take them to class. Or, if you are taking the class online, add your questions to the discussion board, or wherever it is appropriate to pose questions to your teacher and the others in your class. By doing these things, you add to the live discussion and make learning that much more fun.

Rounding Out the Course: Student Learning Outcomes (SLOs)

Throughout this course, you will learn practical cognitive skills that lead to behavioral skills. These behavioral skills are also known as *Student Learning Outcomes* (SLOs) and workforce skills. **Student Learning Outcomes** *are abilities you are asked to demonstrate as a result of your learning; they are proposed academic tasks that can later be used as effective workforce skills.* Student learning outcomes are typically used as a way of holding you, your teachers, and your institution accountable for producing desirable and much needed skills. **Workforce skills** *are abilities or talents that bring forth or contribute to significant economic value.*

Now, following this passage, you will find SLOs and listed workforce skills for the *Unlock Your Mind...Success Program*. The SLOs are written both in higher education jargon and in laymen terms. I did this to reinforce the idea of analytical reading. That way, you can see how easy it is to take something that is written using industry-specific verbiage and restate it in more concise and practical terms. Now you might be thinking, "Why not simply present the material only in laymen's terms?" Well, in college, the professors expect you and your vocabulary to improve as you get closer to graduation. In the professional world, both industry-specific jargon and laymen communication are expected; therefore, I want you to be prepared for both.

The workforce skills are listed at the bottom of the SLO chart. These are key soft skills that most if not all employers are looking for in their employees. Learn how to demonstrate these skills as well as the SLOs, and you will do well.

Unlock Your Mind...Student Success Program:
<u>Student Learning Outcomes</u>

By the end of this book and as a result of your learning, you <u>should</u> be able to

1. *CHOP®:* Construct a synthesized theoretical approach to learning that leads to mindful developments and deductions in academia via *reading, notetaking, dissecting instructions, communication, and empirical & quantitative reasoning.*
   - Use theories to create a way to demonstrate learning and different skill sets.

2. BE "INFORMATION-SAVVY": Research and assess a variety of resources for their credibility, utility, and appropriate applications.
   - Find different resources and decide if they are useful or not and why.

3. USE VALUES-BASED REASONING: Communicate via oral, visual, and/or written means a self-developed values system that ethically frames your personal decisions.
   - Illustrate how your values and beliefs explain your perceived thoughts and behaviors.

4. SELF-MANAGE & WORK AS PART OF A TEAM: Use meta-cognitive skills and *The Elements of Thought* to achieve individual and/or team cognitive, emotional, and behavioral success.
   - Weigh the pros and cons of how you think and use that thinking to assist you and/or the team in succeeding emotionally and behaviorally.

5. DETERMINE RESPONSIBILITY: Use your *Values-Based Motto* and one or more points of view to articulate and justify your personal and social responsibilities.
   - Use your values and beliefs to help you think through and explain your contributions to self and society.

6. TRACK STEAM TRENDS: Research and evaluate one science, technology, engineering, art, and/or math trend (a.k.a. "STEAM") as a current or future career choice.
   - Find and learn about different STEAM developments and choose one or more as your career path.

7. INTEGRATE LEARNING SKILLS: Markedly express how learned academic skills transfer to industries and personal success.
   - Clearly show how skills learned in college can help you in your personal life and in business.

WORKFORCE SKILLS Are the abilities or talents that bring forth or contribute to significant economic value, e.g., critical reasoning, information discernment, analysis, planning, development, and implementation; effective communication, creativity, and multitasking; quantitative reasoning, self-motivation, self-regulation, goal-oriented teamwork and interpersonal problem-solving, and humility.

Back to the original focus … the following illustration will be your student learning outcomes for the *Unlock Your Mind…Success Program*. Now, your instructor may or may not require these SLOs. However, by reading this book and doing the exercises, you will make attempts at demonstrating and/or mastering the given student learning outcomes. Keep in mind *you have to **engage** in order to get the most out of this class.*

Please, take your time and examine the SLOs for yourself. In fact, here is your **first challenge***: I challenge you to find at least one valuable reason why you should learn to demonstrate each SLO in other classes and in the workforce.* So, let's do that here.

- List at least one reason why you should be able to demonstrate each student learning outcome in future classes and throughout your career.

  _____
  _____
  _____

Let's do a final exercise before we close out the chapter. Look at Figure 1.01. I want you to interpret this visual image both literally and figuratively. Then, once you have composed your thoughts and applied meaning to the image, I want you to write down your interpretation within the space provided. Also, as a heads up, the letters *TP* stand for *theory processed*, *TA* stands for *theory applied*, and *SLOs* stand for *student learning outcomes*.

Figure 1.01: *Visual Course Design*

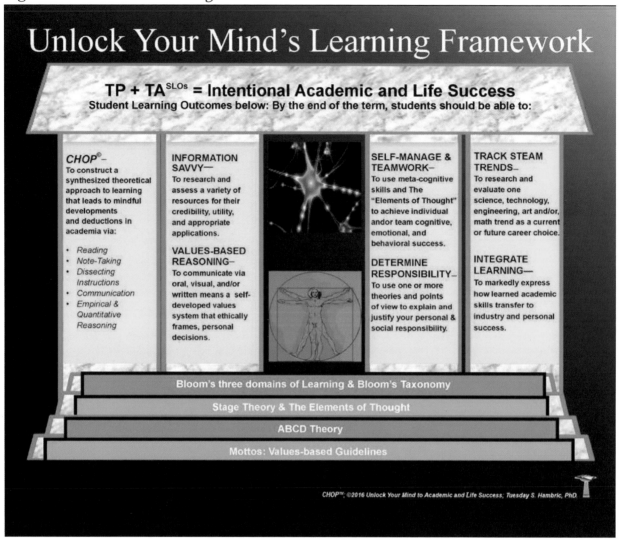

- Now that you are finished analyzing this visual, write down what message or messages you think this image is communicating.

  _____

  _____

  _____

So how did you do? What did you conclude from the image?

Now let's look at one of many ways in which the image *could have been* interpreted. While we are doing that, I want you to *compare and contrast your conclusion with that of the following explanation.* Again, the explanation that follows is only one of many ways in which the picture could be interpreted.

Okay, first I want you to notice the figure's title and then the title of the image. The title of the image, *Unlock Your Mind's Learning Framework,* is simply the name that represents the words, *"Visual Course Design"* in the figure's title. It also tells us that there is a framework in which to learn.

Next, find the SLOs. Where are they located in this image? As you can see, the SLOs are located on the pillars *holding up the roof.* Notice that the roof displays a formula that reads: TP + TA^{SLOs} = Intentional Academic and Life Success. When stated, the formula reads:

Theory Processed (TP) plus Theory Applied (TA) that is powered by skillfully demonstrated SLOs equals Intentional Academic and Life Success.

Now look again at the SLOs. Note that the pillars (the SLOs) are being made steady by *a solid foundation.* The foundation represents the *Super Six Theories* that you will be exploring shortly; the names of these theories are specifically placed as the foundation for the overall structure. If you take away the pillars, the roof/formula falls (i.e., your success falls). If you remove the foundation—the *Super Six Theories*—your skills may waver. But if you have *both* the foundation and the pillars together, you have a STRONG framework in which to grow and learn.

In the center of the image, you have a neuron and a picture of Leonardo da Vinci's *Vitruvian Man.* Both pictures, along with their location in the image, communicate that YOU and the ways in which you THINK are the central focus of this book and student success program. Thus, you have a learning framework in which to *unlock your mind to academic and life success.*

Chapter Conclusions

Earlier in the chapter, I spoke of resiliency and how students who possess that character trait are typically successful in college and in life. Well, I want *you* to mindfully possess that trait as well. So, here's the key and the formula you need to unlock the door of resiliency, thus success. The key to intentional academic and life success *is* resiliency, and the formula to unlock resiliency is *CHOP*^{R}. The success formula, illustrated, looks like this: **TP + TA^{SLOs} = Intentional Academic and Life Success.**

By the end of this book, I want you to feel confident in knowing that you are able to demonstrate these highly favored and much needed academic and workforce skills. But remember, *your attitude toward learning these cognitive and behavioral skills will determine whether or not you retain the information for life-long success or simple short-term gain.* So, be prepared and willing to ENGAGE. Success starts with YOU. If *you* learn to use *CHOP*^{R}, then *you* will increase *your* ability to make insightful choices. ***Insightful choices*** *are choices that are reasoned and filtered through your core beliefs.* By increasing your ability to make insightful choices through *CHOP*^{R}, you gain the ability

- to strategically assess and manage your own thinking, feelings, and behaviors; and
- to successfully function in spite of the environment around you.

Ultimately, you become resilient and, in essence, a ***healthy autonomous learner****—a learner who is self-directed and yet interdependent.* Within reason, you control your academic and life success as you define it.

So now let me give you your **second challenge**. *I challenge you to apply these concepts to all areas of your life in order to achieve complete success.* In other words, you are expected to use what you learn in this class *to learn in other classes—and in your life as well.*

Moving On...

Hopefully at this point, you are a bit more fired up about college and somewhat more curious about this course and its material. Hopefully, after reading all of this, you are sold on, or at least open to, the idea of controlling your own life outcomes (within reason, that is ☺). After all, I have shared with you the definition of a student success course, the opinions of former students, and how the course benefited those students in the hopes that you will temporarily trust the judgments of your fellow students and keep an open mind.

In good faith, try NOT to write off the course until you can make an educated assessment about the course's material and your ability to use the information to motivate yourself. Now let's take a break to get organized and after that, take a break for fun (if you need it).

Break: Let's Get Organized...

Before we dive into this next chapter and the rest of our classes with all of their assignments, **PLEASE STOP TO GET ORGANIZED.** I strongly suggest that you do not ignore this message.
One of many approaches to get organized is to do the following:

- First, use one (if you can) three-ring zip-around binder for all of your classes. Be sure this binder has two pens, two pencils, and then dividers, pocket folders, and loose-leaf paper for each section. Each section is to represent a different class. Again, try to put all of this into one three-ring zip-around binder so that everything you need *is in one place.* I also recommend having a paper calendar located in the front of the binder for dates at-a-glance and for quickly recording date changes that professors sometimes spontaneously make.
- Next, take out all of your syllabi out, and, one at a time, record or add in your paper calendar, electronic calendar, or both:
  - *All* of your assignments *and* estimated preparation and completion times for each assignment.
  - Your study times. In other words, set aside times to study and *commit to them!*
  - Your work schedule (if you work).
  - Your practice schedule and game schedule (if you play organized sports).
  - Your spiritual and/or reflection times.
  - Your fun/social times. Yes, *schedule* your social times. This means discipline yourself to only *so many minutes* of social media and so many days of partying and fun. For example, you could schedule and then set your cellphone to airplane mode or quiet time for about 60 minutes each day, broken down into three 20-minutes sessions (morning, lunch, and evenings after you are completely finished with all studying and work). Also, you could designate, say, Mondays through Thursdays to be all of your school, work, and/or business

days; Fridays and Saturdays can be your fun social days; and then Sunday can be your reflection day, e.g., the day you regroup for the upcoming week.

- Once you have planned, scheduled and set your activities and schoolwork, you can then simply follow through governing yourself according to your allotted times, i.e., your self-management framework.

Great work so far. Now, if you need to take a break from all of this, do so. At this point in the class, most students who fully engage in the previous reading and exercises like to take a break before they start the next chapter.

So … maybe stop and reflect, and/or watch 10 or 15 minutes of a TV show. Perhaps play a game or listen to a song or two. (These are just a few examples of things many students do to relax.) Once you are ready, then you can start reading Chapter II. There, you will start building or adding to *your* cognitive-behavioral foundation.

Moving On…

Chapter II

The Essentials!

Knowing, Understanding, Analyzing, and Evaluating the *Super Six Theories*: The Foundation That Generates Success

Chapter II: The Essentials

This chapter serves as a *brief* introduction to the six major theories we'll use to construct your cognitive-behavioral foundation or critical thinking/doing profile. In later chapters, we will further analyze these theories for deeper cognitive understanding and in-depth applications.

It is important that you pay close attention to what you see and read and pay close attention to what's being implied by what you see and read. This is significant because both the apparent and nonapparent wisdoms will be used throughout all the chapter readings, lectures, online discussions, applicable exercises, and assigned work.

MENTAL NOTE

Please keep the following in mind as you turn the page to continue your reading:

- You will now *engage* in **constructing your cognitive-behavioral foundation or critical thinking/doing profile.**
- The first step is to become familiar with the *Super Six Theories* used to CHOP®.
- Learn how each part of each *Super Six Theory* works alone and then interdependently.
- Make note of your favorite theories and master them.

The Super Six Theories: The Essentials of Success

As I stated earlier, success, be it academic, personal, or both, depends entirely upon our ability to customize our thinking within each situation. In order to do this, we must know and understand what I call the *Super Six Theories*. The **Super Six Theories** *are essential cognitive-behavioral theories that reflect human existence (in particularly, your existence) and can be used to monitor, assess, change, and maintain human thoughts, emotions, and behaviors.*

With these essential theories, you are going to build *your critical thinking profile.*

The *Super Six Theories* are...

- *Bloom's Taxonomy:* used primarily for mindful academic critical thinking.
- *Bloom's Three Domains of Learning:* employed to differentiate and understand the three areas of information-processing.
- *Stage Theory* (or *Meta-Cognitions*): used primarily to pinpoint current levels of social or intellectual thinking abilities, and to plan further cognitive advancements and growth.
- *The Elements of Thought:* utilized to systematically identify and assess the different components or "parts" of thinking.
- *ABCD Theory:* used primarily to assess and transform faulty thinking in order to strengthen emotional and behavioral management.

- *Values-Based Mottos:* An acronym or set of sentences made up of a person's chosen values and beliefs, used as guidelines to maintain a state of homeostasis or balanced living.

Now, let me be honest with you (as always ☺): Constructing a cognitive-behavioral platform is *not* an easy task. As a matter of fact, it may be one of the hardest challenges you will ever face. You see, in order to construct a cognitive-behavioral foundation, you will have *to convince yourself to change* **whenever change is needed** and then convince yourself **to stick to** *this act of changing.*

So, here is my **third challenge** to you: *By the end of this class, I want you to be able to appropriately select, synthesize, and use often any two (or more) of these aforementioned theories in order to create values-based thinking that leads to successful behaviors.*

Now, you might like to know that former students deemed the *Super Six Theories* "urgent" and "important," and they expressed a desire to have learned the *Super Six* much sooner in their academic term rather than later. That's why I'm introducing all the *Super Six Theories* in this early chapter. Then will give them much more analytical attention in later chapters.

The analytical attention that I speak of may come in the form of lectures, online discussions, exercises, and assignments. In fact, you will not be able to accurately complete the assignments without thinking deeply about the material and applying it in in-depth ways. I will try to elicit most of that thinking throughout the textbook in the form of thought-provoking questions. So, to do this course, you are going to have to commit to the act of *engaging.* As I pose the questions to you, STOP, THINK, and actually ANSWER these questions. Pretend that I am standing right there in front of you and guiding you through these inquiries.

Bloom's Taxonomy

BLOOM'S TAXONOMY: NUMBER ONE OF THE SUPER SIX

In 1956, Dr. Benjamin Bloom and his team of educators claimed that there are *only six* levels of thinking and dialogue in which any human being can learn and demonstrate such learning (Bloom & Krathwohl, 1956). To further solidify Dr. Bloom's levels of thinking and dialogue claim, he and his team of educators categorized and then fashioned the six levels of thinking into one of the most influential tools used in Western education to date (David, 2014). This essential tool, which is closely aligned with *The Socratic Method* of dialectic or dialogue (which I will define later) is known as *Bloom's Taxonomy* (see Figure 2.01).

Bloom's Taxonomy is a six-level illustrated hierarchy of learning, where each progressive level of thinking uses specific verbs to provoke action. (These actions words or verbs are located to the right of each level of thinking in Figure 2.01.)

Figure 2.01: *Bloom's Taxonomy (the Original Order)*

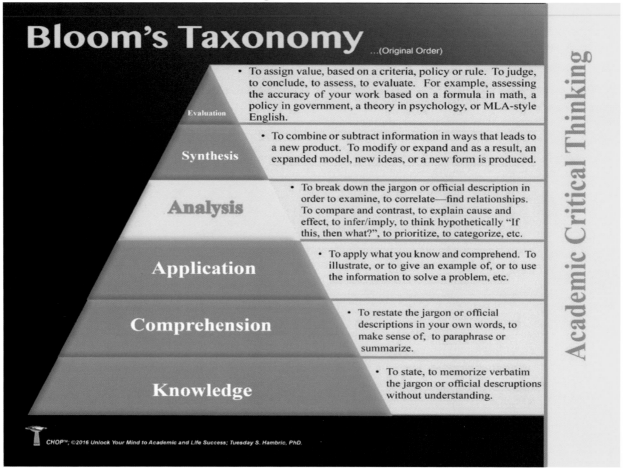

Let's observe and examine together. In Figure 2.01, you should see six levels of thinking, each one labeled and identified by one of the following major terms or nouns: knowledge, comprehension, application, analysis, synthesis, and evaluation. Although each level of thinking or information processing is identified or labeled by a noun, if you look to the right of each respective noun in Figure 2.01, you will see that *each level of thinking* is *determined by or driven by specific thinking or actions that can be identified with or motivated by one or more specific verb(s) or action word(s).*

For example, let's start with the level of knowledge, which is the very first level of thinking or communicating. Now look to the right of the noun knowledge, there you should see the action words used to think or to communicate information at the level of knowledge. These verbs are *state* and *memorize*. Next, I want you to notice that the action words used to process information or to communicate information at the level of comprehension are *restate*, *make sense of*, *paraphrase*, and *summarize*.

Now it's time for you to *engage*...

- What are the action words/verbs used to process information or to communicate information at the level of application?

They are _____, _____, or give an _____ of; or _____ the information in order to _____ a problem.

- What verbs are used to help you think or communicate information at the level of analysis?

They are _____, _____, _____, _____ and _____, to explain _____ and _____, to _____/_____, to _____ think, (e.g., _____ this _____ what?), to _____, to _____.

We might as well keep going and finish the last two:

- Again, using Figure 2.01, what are some of the action words or verbs used to guide your thinking or to communicate information at the level of synthesis? To _____ or _____, to _____ or _____.

- What about the level of evaluation? What phrase and/or action words are used to help process information or to think at the level of evaluation? To _____, _____, _____, _____ or _____.

So, let's check to see how many you got correct—and this is not about if you were perfect or terribly wrong. ☺ This exercise is to get you involved with the literature and better prepared for your classroom discussion. So, let's see what you now know and understand.

For the level of application, did you decide that the words *apply, illustrate,* and *solve* were the driving verbs or key action words?

What about the level of analysis? Did you choose to *break down, examine, correlate, compare & and contrast, cause & and effect, infer/imply, to think hypothetically (if this, then what), prioritize,* and *categorize*?

For the level of synthesis, were the driving action words *combine, subtract, modify,* and *expand*?

And finally, the level of evaluation used the driving words or action words *assign value, judge, conclude, assess,* and *evaluate.*

Hopefully, this exercise helped you become a bit more familiar with the six different levels of thinking in *Bloom's Taxonomy* and some of the actions that need to take place in order to demonstrate learning within specific levels of *Bloom's Taxonomy.*

Connecting the Dots…

You should know that progressive thinking, or the *Taxonomy of Learning*, was not an original idea from 1956. As a matter of fact, more than 2,000 years ago, one of the greatest philosophers to date actually established the foundation of progressive thinking around 399 B.C. (Before Christ, or Before Common Era) (Jowett, 2011). Nevertheless, by further establishing this foundation many years later, Dr. Bloom and his team of educators were given credit and praise for defining the concepts of progressive thinking in concrete and measurable ways.

Following in their footsteps, I use *Bloom's Taxonomy* as a tool to measure different levels of thinking as well. In this book, there are several *Student Learning Outcomes* (SLOs) and attainable workforce skills that are designed to produce concrete thinking within the specific levels of *Bloom's Taxonomy*. When demonstrated properly, students' present cognitions that are perceived and measured according to the *Student Learning Outcome* outlined in Chapter I (see Figure 1.01).

In the meantime, let's see how closely you are connecting the dots while you're reading. *Question:* Have you contemplated or wondered who the great philosopher might be, the one who established the foundation for progressive thinking? Well, it's Socrates. I mentioned him in the beginning of this section to give you yet another opportunity to be aware, to check for full analytical engagement, and to adjust your reading if needed. If you already knew which philosopher I mentioned, then outstanding. Keep it up!

Now back to our main focus. Socrates was the first to investigate and coin the concept of progressive thinking (Jowett, 2011). He developed this concept through his method of teaching— *The Socratic Method*, which is still widely used today (David, 2014; Whiteley, 2006). Remember I stated earlier that *The Socratic Method* and *Bloom's Taxonomy* were closely aligned and that I would define it later? Well, later is now.

The Socratic Method *is a style of teaching where Socrates used progressive questioning, inspired by specific verbs, to arouse deep and insightful thinking from his students* (Jowett, 2011). Does that sound familiar? Socrates did so with the intention of challenging his students to think deeply and to help them discover the answers to life's questions on their own, from their own perspective (Jowett, 2011).

Connecting More Dots…

So, tell me what you think so far. First, analyze what you've read about *Bloom's Taxonomy*, do a re-examination of Dr. Bloom's illustration of *Bloom's Taxonomy*, and consider the fact that there are ONLY six levels in which any human being can think. *Please do this and then* **DRAW A CONCLUSION**.

Consider adding to your conclusion the fact that progressive teaching and learning endured over a very long time: from 399 B.C. to 2018 and beyond. Consider how the two, Socrates and Benjamin Bloom, intellectually came together over time to create one important, time-sustaining, and relevant tool—*Does that information somehow add more credibility to the importance of progressive thinking?* Compile your thoughts and answer the following questions:

- What collective conclusions can you draw about *Bloom's Taxonomy* and its usefulness for learning?

  _____

  _____

  _____

- How can you use *Bloom's Taxonomy* to help you *construct a cognitive-behavioral platform or critical thinking framework*? In other words, how can you use *Bloom's Taxonomy* to help you process information and/or to communicate what you've learned at the different levels of thinking?

  _____

  _____

  _____

Using those same questions that I presented to you, here are a few conclusions that I've drawn:

- If there are ONLY six levels of thinking in which any human being can process or communicate information, then my instructors are using one or more of those levels of thinking to teach me and to test me.
  - With that being the case, then I should learn how to think on <u>all</u> levels. I should take notes and study at all levels of thinking as well. By doing each of these mentioned, my success in school should be a sure thing. But, how do I do that? How do I get started?
- If Socrates started using specific verbs back before Christ or before Common Era to help himself and others process information **and** his method of teaching is still being actively used today, then his teaching has to be important.
  - With that being said, then Bloom's Taxonomy is worth me exploring further with the intention of developing deliberate and mindful thinking as a skill set. But again, how do I do that? How do I get started?
- And so-on and so-forth.

There are so many different and yet correct conclusions you can draw from reading and analyzing the information. As a matter of fact, you can draw both negative and positive conclusions. However, what conclusions can you draw that would bring you *a greater probability (chance) of success?* In other words, anyone can perceive things negatively—and sometimes negative thoughts prove to be the best thoughts, like when your safety is in question. But, in this case, what *positive* conclusions can you draw that will lead you to having an open mind and being ready to develop critical thinking as a mindful skill set and framework?

Learning a Lot from a Little...

At this point, we've already defined *Bloom's Taxonomy* and also gathered that *Bloom's Taxonomy* is an illustration of *The Socratic Method* and primarily used to highlight the six ways in which people think academically. Well, so far, we have only scratched the surface. There are some other things we can do with *Bloom's* as well.

You see, as a student, you can use this taxonomy to help you read, write, take notes, study, do math, AND get this … you can use *Bloom's Taxonomy* to make a class more intellectually challenging and to help your teachers stay on task. Yes, you can help us professors, teachers, and instructors (whatever the title) stay on task. Do you see where I am going with just this one theory? This is YOU taking charge of YOUR education and becoming a *healthy autonomous learner.*

Let's *engage.* Now using the same *Bloom's Taxonomy* figure as before, Figure 2.01, I will ask you a series of questions. Except this time, the questions will be a bit more structured and will increase in their level of difficulty.

Figure 2.01: *Bloom's Taxonomy (the Original Order)*

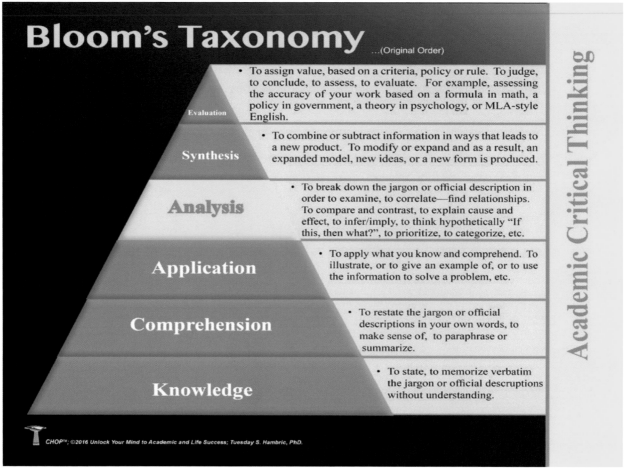

Exploring Bloom's Taxonomy Through a Series of Instructions or Questions

- *Let's Gather Information & Facts:* Using Figure 2.01, list what you see. For example, I might write, "I see a triangle with different size sections." Take *30 seconds only* to list everything you see.

  _____

  _____

  _____

- *Let's Understand the Information & Facts:* Explain what you understand from Figure 2.01. In other words, define and make sense of what you just listed under the prior bullet and/or what you see in Figure 2.01. For example, I might write, "I see a triangle that is divided up into sections that have different lengths. As a result of these different lengths, the sections might mean one level is harder than the other." Take *about 60 seconds* to define or give meaning to the things you see.

  _____

  _____

  _____

- Let's *Analyze and Draw a Few Conclusions*:
    a. Examine each of the different levels of thinking in Figure 2.01 and tell me which level requires the most complex and/or difficult thinking and why? Explain your answer.

    _____

    _____

    _____

    b. Which level do you think is the most important—not the most difficult necessarily—but most important level and why? Explain your answer.

    _____

    _____

    _____

    c. Six levels of thinking are presented in Figure 2.01. Do you think that everyone thinks in the exact same order as what is presented? Yes or no? Why?

    _____

    _____

    _____

    d. Finally, putting your best effort forward, I want you to observe the following list of eight *Practical Uses of Bloom's Taxonomy for Students*. They are different ways in which *Bloom's Taxonomy* can help you:
        1. Read
        2. Write papers
        3. Refine my notes
        4. Optimize the way I study
        5. Better understand and apply math concepts and do math problems
        6. Help me to make class more intellectually challenging
        7. Help me keep "off-topic teachers" on task
        8. Set and achieve my goals

Now, pick only <u>one</u>, and use it to **explain** or **demonstrate** just <u>one</u> possible way you could use *Bloom's Taxonomy*. Use the following statement to help you:

- *I could use Bloom's Taxonomy to help me* _____ *, and here is how I would do it:*

    _____

    _____

    _____

What have you learned so far about *Bloom's Taxonomy*? Did you notice that I used *The Socratic Method* of dialogue to help you examine *Bloom's Taxonomy* and to gain deeper insights? Did you notice that each question got progressively more difficult to answer? Or better stated, did you notice that each question required more thinking on your part and mine? If you noticed at least one of these two questions, you are doing excellently. It means *you are developing a comprehensive or analytical picture by connecting the dots*. In other words, you are linking information from one section of the reading to another and possibly applying some of the concepts to your life as well. (We will expand upon this shortly.)

If you did not answer yes to either of these questions, that's okay, too. That is okay because now we know, and, k*nowing is half the battle.* ☺ With all pun intended, of course: I am an army veteran, so I *had* to throw that in there. ☺ (Did you see how easy it is for me to get off-track?) Okay, back to my earlier point ... You are fine if you did not recognize that I was using *Bloom's Taxonomy* and *The Socratic Method*. However, that means you are going to have to set aside more time for reading because *reading actively and analytically with high levels of concentration are required*. At this point, I would say to go back to employing the reading techniques that I taught you in Chapter I under the *Reading Check* section. If you are using those techniques already, then again, *slow down to concentrate and contemplate while you read.*

Okay, I just stated a lot of "stuff," but hidden in that "stuff" are *the benefits to active and analytical reading.* So, here's a question for you:

- Do you think it's important to learn to read actively and analytically? Yes or no and why?

  _____
  _____
  _____

- What advice can you give to someone who struggles with reading insightfully?

  _____
  _____
  _____

Thanks for engaging! Now, that is *Bloom's Taxonomy* in a nutshell.

It's now time to move on to the *Three Domains of Learning*; however, if you need to take a break, this would be a good time to do so. If this is your first time being exposed to *Bloom's Taxonomy* or analyzing and applying *Bloom's Taxonomy*, then take 15 minutes or so before you start the next section. The reason for this is to give your brain time to relax and to place all the new information in its appropriate places within the brain. This also allows for easy recall when this information is needed in later chapters.

If you took the break, welcome back! If you did not, that is fine, too. Either way, you're communicating that it's time to move on to the *Three Domains of Learning*. With that said, keep *Bloom's Taxonomy* in mind because we will continue to refer back to it and learn more about it throughout the next couple of chapters. So, here is a quick request before moving on.

Without looking back in the book, list and explain all six levels of *Bloom's Taxonomy*.

_____
_____
_____

Did you answer the question? Good. If you couldn't answer the question, please go back and commit the answers to your memory. Now, let's move on.

Bloom's Three Domains of Learning

THE THREE DOMAINS OF LEARNING: NUMBER TWO OF THE SUPER SIX

Dr. Bloom and his team of educators were not only developing *Bloom's Taxonomy*, but prior to that development, they also discovered that learning takes place in, yes, you've guessed it—the *Three Domains of Learning*.

The **Three Domains of Learning** *is an academic tool divided into three categories where learning is demonstrated and used as a means for measuring cognitive skills, affective skills, and psychomotor skills* (see Figure 2.02) (Bloom & Krathwohl, 1956; Clark, 2010). The **cognitive domain** refers to the six levels of progressive thinking (i.e., *Bloom's Taxonomy*), the **affective domain** refers to a person's emotions or attitude, and the **psychomotor domain** refers to a person's observable behaviors (Clark, 2010).

Now, by researching *The Socratic Method* of teaching, *Bloom's Taxonomy*, and the *Three Domains of Learning*, I learned that *The Socratic Method* and *Bloom's Taxonomy* both rely on lower-order thinking skills (LOTs) and higher-order thinking skills (HOTs) (Bloom & Krathwohl, 1956; Jowett, 2011). This concept of LOTs and HOTs is well illustrated in most *Bloom's Taxonomy* diagrams, where the lower levels of thinking are represented by knowledge, comprehension, and application, and the higher levels of thinking are represented by analysis, evaluation, and synthesis (Clark, 2010). Further, I learned that *The Socratic Method* and *Bloom's Taxonomy* are truly like father and son to each other, as both fall under the cognitive domain within the *Three Domains of Learning*, and both can be used to assess student learning outcomes, thus placing them in the psychomotor domain as well.

Therefore, if your plan is to have lasting learning and lasting success, you must really think about *both* the *Three Domains of Learning* and *Bloom's Taxonomy*, for this integration of information is critical to helping you build your cognitive platform.

A Deeper Look...

Follow me here. After careful analysis and integration of other theories (like the *ABCD Theory*), I discovered that skills learned in each of the domains—cognitive, affective, and psychomotor—are all developed by the cognitive domain itself, and that each of the three domains have two categories of demonstration—a.k.a., *demonstrated learning*—within them. So, you might be saying, "How's it possible for the cognitive domain to develop itself?" That's easy. It's called *meta-cognitions,* and the process was laid out by Richard Paul and Linda Elder.

Throughout this process of thinking about your thinking, you are consistently checking your thinking for flaws and accuracy (Elder & Paul, 2013b). I will explain a bit more about meta-cognitions later—it is theory number three of the *Super Six*—but, for now, just understand that this is how the cognitive domain (the mind and the brain) develops and shapes itself. With that, it's also important to know that the mind and brain work hard to improve themselves with or without conscious help (Siegel, 2015). And, according to the *ABCD Theory* and a slew of similar theories, the brain and the mind also control affective skills/emotions and your psychomotor skills/behaviors (Ellis, 2001; Siegel, 2015; Sharot, 2011). In essence, **what we think is what we do.** (THIS IS SUPER IMPORTANT! And yes, I know we established this in Chapter I, but like other things in this book, important things bear repeating.)

Now, if you will recall, I stated that each of the *Three Domains of Learning* has two categories of demonstration—or demonstrated learning. For these, I've coined the terms *mimicked demonstrations* and *coherent demonstrations.*

Importantly, if you are striving to achieve lasting learning and consistent success, then you should make sure that you're learning and processing information through coherent demonstrations—not mimicked demonstrations, and here is why. **Mimicked demonstrations** *are learning that is unable to be explained or completed beyond the act of repeating or memorizing exactly what someone else has already said or done.* It is a form of modeling without insightful understanding.

Coherent demonstrations or learning is just the opposite: **Coherent demonstrations** *are learning that demonstrates reason and discernment.* It is learning that is, at the very least, paraphrased and can go beyond what someone else has already articulated or completed.

For example, I could stand and give a stellar performance mimicking one of Maya Angelou's famous readings. Here, I simply would have copied what I saw Ms. Angelou do at a previous performance, but it would *appear* during my recital that I had fully understood the emotions, the behaviors, and the thinking of Ms. Angelou's during her previous recital. The audience judging my performance as excellent thus would be fooled into thinking that my mimicked performance was one filled with understanding and passion, when in fact, *I understood only to do (mimic or copy) what she did.*

Should that be your goal, too? Do you want to go through life *pretending* to live and learn? Do you want to be that person in a conversation who is simply pretending to have substance? I hope not.

Now let's get specific and look at things academically: Have you ever taken a class and *pretended* to comprehend the information by nodding in agreement or answering questions in class by repeating the professor's exact words? Well, this would be the same as *mimicking* Maya Angelou's famous recital without understanding the reading. You see, when you mimic learning, your learning does not last too much beyond the asked question and could be perceived as fake or temporary learning. Here, you might memorize key words for testing purposes and use them to pass the tests (sometimes with high scores)—but you end up walking away from the testing without having acquired the necessary information to be successful in future classes, your career, or in life in general.

Let's use the Maya Angelou example again. Sure, I could do that same kind of performance—but this time, I also could have examined and conceptualized prior to my recital the meaning of Ms. Angelou's movements, feelings, and thinking at the time of her performance. This would make my recital performance further come alive, and the audience would be better able to connect cognitively and emotionally with me (and me with them). I would have given them a *coherent* performance that established its intended meaning *and* took the audience to new heights. As a result of this, I would not only *remember* what I deemed important information—what I learned would actually *last.*

This example therefore shows how coherent demonstration or coherent learning engages all *Three Domains of Learning*. Also, the fact that the information was deemed important enough to remember increases the probability for successful information recall when it's needed to advance in life or in other classes.

Let's Engage…

- If we were to use the Maya Angelou example to help a friend better connect with his or her instructors and to perform well on assignments, what would you suggest that your friend examine and conceptualize? Would it be
    a. The instructor's words?
    b. The instructor's emotions?
    c. The meaning of the instructor's behavior?
    d. All of the above?
    e. A and C only?

    The answer is D. But why? Why would that be the best way to connect to instructors and their lessons?

    _____

    _____

    _____

- Using *Bloom's Taxonomy* to help guide your friend with classroom success, what level(s) of thinking would you choose to help him or her practice thinking and learning and why?

    _____

    _____

    _____

Let's reflect a bit because I know I am asking you to do a lot of cognitive multitasking. But it's necessary, as we are discussing the *Three Domains of Learning* through the integration of *Bloom's Taxonomy* and how within each domain of learning you can demonstrate mimicked or coherent learning. So, here's a refresher:

- What are the *Three Domains of Learning*?

    _____

    _____

    _____

- What are the two categories of demonstration apparent in each domain?

    _____

    _____

    _____

- If seeking clarity of thought helps develop the cognitive domain, then how would your thinking about your thinking help develop the other two domains?

So, why is all of this so important? Here are a couple of reasons:

- You learn to *take ownership of your learning.* If you know that lasting learning and consistent success comes from learning holistically (e.g., within all *Three Domains of Learning*), then why would you approach success any other way?

- If you find that *coherent learning* is difficult for you, then assess yourself using each of the *Three Domains of Learning* and each of the six levels of *Bloom's Taxonomy* to see where you need to improve.

- Because no questions fall outside of *Bloom Taxonomy's* six levels of thinking, and because those levels of thinking can be demonstrated within a person's thinking (cognition), emotions (affective), and behaviors (psychomotor), then it would be wise for you to ensure that you're learning in *coherent* ways within all the levels of *Bloom's Taxonomy* and each of the *Three Domains of Learning.*

- If you master processing and demonstrating information using all six levels of *Bloom's Taxonomy,* and if you manage those skills in all three areas of the *Three Domains of Learning,* then you would have, in fact, mastered not only academia but most of your life as well.

As an educator and life-long student myself, I can say that an overwhelming majority of your and your children's academic careers will be determined by how well you know, understand, use, analyze, evaluate, and synthesize information.

Let's wrap up with an exercise that solidifies your understanding of the *Three Domains of Learning* through analyzing and applying it.

Figure 2.02: *The Three Domains of Learning with Corresponding Theories*

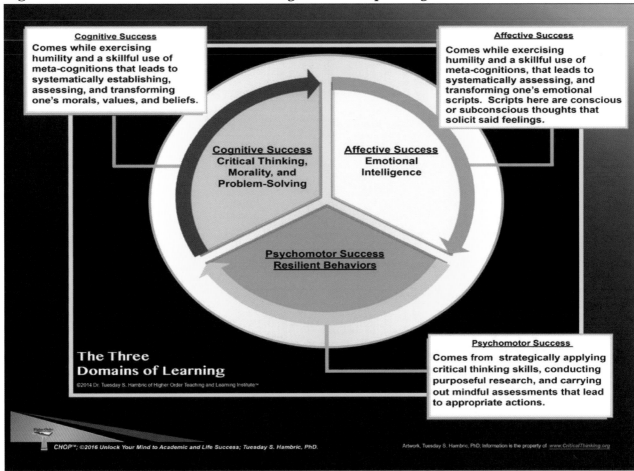

Let's engage…

Ponder for a moment Figure 2.02, *The Three Domains of Learning.* Now answer the following questions:

- According to the chart, what domain(s) would you use to assess and control your emotions?

  _____

  _____

  _____

- According to the chart, what domain(s) would you focus on in order to demonstrate successful resilient behaviors? Explain why.

  _____

  _____

  _____

Switching Gears…

- Recall your earlier definition of success and record it here.

  _____

  _____

  _____

- How does Figure 2.02 support or not support your definition of success? Please explain.

  _____

  _____

  _____

- After examining Figure 2.02 and considering all that you have read so far, do you think your definition of success needs revising? If yes, do so on the lines that follow. If not, then continue on—but remember, these exercises are about you taking ownership and being held accountable for generating *your* success. So, if you are thinking about moving on without contemplation, DON'T. *Don't be intellectually lazy. Engage.* The course questions are designed to help you create and use *your* definition of success as a life compass.

- IF your idea of success needs to be revised, do so here.

  _____

  _____

  _____

While exploring success through the eyes of the *Three Domains of Learning*, what did you discover? You don't have to write down your answer for that question. I just wanted you to think about it.

Now, if you decided to engage in the questions and answers portion of this section, most of you probably focused only on the task at hand. If you did, then that is exactly what I asked, and that is no problem. As a matter of fact, I commend you for engaging because some students chose to simply move on.

So, let's see what you've accomplished so far in this section … Basically you were using *Bloom's Taxonomy* to think at the levels of knowledge, comprehension, application, analysis, synthesis, and evaluation. How so? I'm glad you asked. Again, if you *engaged* in the exercise, you were able to gather and understand further the *Three Domains of Learning* and how they relate to success. You did this at the level of knowledge and comprehension. Then you explored success and the *Three Domains of Learning* a little deeper. You analyzed the information and compared it to your own thoughts, feelings, and behaviors toward success. Finally, you created an explanation that supported your conclusion and definition of success. YES, that's right. You I did all of that. In one exercise, you thought at all six levels of *Bloom's Taxonomy*—and did it well, I might add. ☺

Concluding Thoughts…

It is my belief (and was that of Dr. Albert Ellis prior to his departure in 1992) that our cognitions control not only our thinking but our behaviors and attitudes as well. Therefore, it will be obvious from the *Three Domains of Learning* that I've placed a lot of apparent emphasis on the cognitive and psychomotor domains and less apparent emphasis on the affective domain. Nonetheless, by the end of this course, it is important that you use the *Super Six Theories* to acquire the necessary skills to be balanced in all three areas.

You see, we as human beings engage less in meta-cognitions and more in recognizing our behaviors and our expressed emotions. Well, *in order to be successful "on purpose," we must develop the necessary skills to control our thinking, attitudes, and behaviors most of the time. We must recognize that our behaviors and emotions are a direct reflection of our thinking* … and this brings us back full circle to *Customized Higher Order Processing—CHOP*[R]. Once you are able to engage in in-depth thinking—in which you can mindfully recognize, assess, change, and monitor your own desired and undesired cognitions, attitudes, and behaviors—then you will be able to masterfully customize and use the *Super Six Theories* to your humble advantage.

In later chapters, I will focus more directly on the psychomotor and affective domains. But for now, we will continue to work within the cognitive section of the *Three Domains of Learning* where I will introduce *Stage Theory* and *The Elements of Thought*—theories number three and four of the *Super Six*. Stage theory and *The Elements of Thoughts* will be used to teach you the art of **meta-cognitions,** *which is thinking about your thinking.*

Hopefully, through the readings and exercises, you are quickly learning the difference between simply *"Talking about it"*—success, that is—and *"Being about it!"* Now keep your *Bloom's Taxonomy* frames ☜ on and your *Three Domains of Learning* frames ☜ on as you learn about *Stage Theory* and *The Elements of Thoughts*.

Moving On…

We have discussed critical thinking primarily from an academic perspective, yet earlier I stated that we, the professors, want to help you succeed both academically and personally, right? Well, no problem! ☐☐ Just as it is important to direct your own thinking while in school, it is also important to direct your own thinking in your social life as well.

According to one of the most notable student success authors to date, thousands and thousands of students graduate every year without experiencing real change and doing nothing more than *temporary* learning (Downing, 2012). ☹ Echoing that same sentiment, two of the leading scholar–practitioners on critical thinking, Linda Elder and Richard Paul, proclaimed that a large number of students who graduate from college are still unaware of the impact of quality thinking (2013b).

So, to maximize your chances at success and to ensure that you leave college not only *aware of* the thinking process but also *very well versed* in it, I have relied on the experts—Elder and Paul. I have chosen their theories, *Stage Theory* and *The Elements of Thoughts*, to not only help with awareness and articulation but to help you become skilled at assessing your thinking. When used well, these theories ultimately *lead you to managing your own thinking*, which in turn will aid you in *managing your emotions and behaviors*.

Stage Theory (www.criticalthinking.org)

STAGE THEORY: NUMBER THREE OF THE SUPER SIX

Stage Theory is a theory of intellectual development in which critical reasoning is improved by systematically subjecting it to intellectual self-assessment (Elder & Paul, 2013b). In other words, *Stage Theory* lays out six intellectual stages of development that one must pass through in order to develop as a critical thinker. These six stages are *unreflective thinker, challenged thinker, beginning thinker, practicing thinker, advanced thinker,* and *accomplished thinker* (Elder & Paul, 2013b).

In an effort to cut down on confusion and to express the distinct stages, I will cut back tremendously on Elder and Paul's (2013b) original work and attempt to align our thinking with that of the authors. We will do this by understanding the authors' premise; however, to fully grasp their theory's foundation, concepts, assumptions, inferences, and conclusions, please visit Elder and Paul at www.criticalthinking.org. To access a direct link to the article referenced in this chapter and to gain greater insights, please visit www.criticalthinking.org/pages/critical-thinking-development-a-stage-theory/483. Once accessed, you will notice that Elder and Paul's original work was intended for faculty only. With this in mind, I have taken the liberty of refocusing their sections on *Implications for Instructions* to *Implications for Self-Application*. In this way, students can become active learners by supplementing or adding to the teaching and learning process.

By using the suggested steps within the *Implications for Self-Application* section, you will not only improve your chances of achieving the success in all six levels of *Stage Theory*, you also progress towards becoming a *healthy autonomous learner*. These practices allow you to actively participate in the teaching and learning process (regardless of how inspiring or uninspiring the environment might be).

Aligning with the Authors of Stage Theory

Stage Theory works from a set of operating assumptions (Elder & Paul, 2013b). These assumptions are: *In order for a person to develop as a critical thinker, he or she must...*

1. Advance through and master lower levels of development before reaching higher levels.
2. Agree that regression in thinking is possible.
3. Commit to systematic self-assessment.
4. Understand that subconscious intellectual advancements are not likely to happen without conscious practice.
5. Understand that a critical thinker, in the fullest sense of the word, is one who displays *accomplished-*level thinking in most of the domains of his or her life.
6. Success is directly connected to a person's intellectual quality and work efforts.

From this point forward, I will explain each of the six stages of intellectual development. So now, as stated by Shawn Ludwick, one of my former students, let's "DO WORK!"

The Unreflective Thinker

Unreflective thinkers are those who do not consciously understand that thinking drives their behaviors and that there is a natural process to thinking (Elder & Paul, 2013b; www.criticalthinking.org). *Unreflective* thinkers spend the majority of their time reacting to life's situations and are unaware of the flaws in their thinking.

Successes for the *Unreflective* thinkers are random and unskillfully managed. Because there is a lack of true awareness and strategic control, their thinking goes unchecked, and their flawed sense of intellectual security creates all kinds of problems, such as prejudices and misconceptions (Elder & Paul, 2013b).

Some Implications for Self-Application: You want to build your cognitive platform by adding intellectual tools that are relevant and easily integrated to your critical thinking toolbox. Here's how:
1. To change from being an *Unreflective* thinker and from experiencing random success to experiencing planned success, your first step is to **recognize** that there is a *natural process* to thinking and that by managing that natural process, you increase your chances of success *on purpose*.

With that written, it's time to practice *CHOP*®. Remember, I advised at the beginning of this section to keep your *Bloom's Taxonomy* glasses on? Well, that was just another way of saying that you need to continue to think using *Bloom's Taxonomy* as you process the rest of this book and the rest of your life experiences. So, as we polarize, or make obvious, the integration of *Bloom's Taxonomy* and *Stage Theory*, you will in essence use *CHOP*® to chop one theory up to understand another.

Let's check for comprehension:

Using your everyday vocabulary, how would you define the *Unreflective* thinker

_____

_____

_____

Let's analyze, assess, and conclude:

- Can you relate to the *Unreflective* thinker, or do you know of others who display unreasoned behaviors like those of an *Unreflective* thinker? Explain.

_____

_____

_____

Let's evaluate and conclude:

According to the *Stage Theory's* creators, thinking has a natural process that humans go through. Elder and Paul (2013a) stated that the natural process of thinking has eight elements, which is the foundation for basic thinking. Together, these elements are called *The Elements of Thought*.

The eight elements or parts to thinking are
- Purpose   Questions   Information   Assumptions
- Concepts   Inferences   Implications   Points of view*

*Feel free to skip ahead to see the visual in Figure 2.03 but return when done.

This thinking process flows naturally as people gather information and gain insights. Unfortunately, however, this process can naturally flow with *accurate* information *or* it can naturally flow with distorted or *incorrect* information.

- Using what you now know about the *natural thinking* process (a.k.a. *The Elements of Thought*), do you employ any of these eight elements when you are processing information (i.e., thinking about things)?

  _____

  _____

  _____

- How does being aware of *The Elements of Thought* move you past the stage of being an *Unreflective* thinker? (Be sure to use your definition of the *Unreflective* thinker to justify your answer.)

  _____

  _____

  _____

You're doing a great job thinking so far. As you read further, see if how what you thought matches or fits what Elder and Paul identified as the *natural process* of thinking and learning.

The Challenged Thinker

*If you understand that thinking actually plays a role in your life's outcomes, yet you do not try to use that information to improve your chances of success; you are, at the very least, a **Challenged Thinker.***

Challenged thinkers move from the *Unreflective* stage to the *Challenged* stage when they initially become aware of their own positive and negative thinking and also become aware that thinking plays a role in all their successes and their failures. *Challenged* thinkers realize that positive thinking is more likely to lead to positive outcomes and that negative thinking is more likely to lead to negative outcomes. *Challenged* thinkers may or may not be aware of the mistakes in their own thinking, although they are aware that high-quality thinking requires *deliberate* meta-cognitions.

Challenged thinkers also may or may not be aware of the *natural thinking* process, and they may or may not believe that they have control over their own thinking. Either way, they are not able to clearly identify the flawed elements within their natural thinking process.

Nor are they willing to assess their thinking by checking for clarity, accuracy, precision, relevance, logicalness, etc. You see, *Challenged* thinkers are not willing to commit to the effort and hard work it takes to change. Like *Unreflective* thinkers, *Challenged* thinkers have developed *some* thinking skills, but their skills are inconsistent and can be deceiving (Elder & Paul, 2013b; www.criticalthinking.org).

Implications for Self-Application: In order to move out of the *Challenged* thinker stage, you must *employ authentic humility* and *commit to self-assessment*. You must challenge yourself. But, as I stated earlier—and yes, I am reiterating it—***this challenge is probably one of the most difficult challenges you will face this early in your life***. You see, you have to admit that you have flaws in your thinking. Yes, I wrote that: You have flaws in your thinking! Guess what, though? I have flaws in my thinking, your teachers have flaws in their thinking, your parents have flaws in their thinking—and yes, *you* have flaws in *your* thinking.

For you to move on to the *Beginning* thinker stage, you must *embrace authentic humility* and *commit to self-assessment*. It is my opinion these are the most important skills that transcend across all the other stages of critical thinking.

In summary, if you want to move from the *Challenged* thinker stage to the *Beginning* thinker stage, you must

1. Humble yourself (for real ☺, in all *Three Domains of Learning*) by admitting that you have flaws in your thinking. Therefore, you may very well have flawed emotional and flawed behavioral responses to life's experiences. (Note: Here we are linking past information to present information for *coherent learning*.)

2. Understand and believe that you have control over your thinking.

3. At the very least, randomly commit to self-assessment and self-management by attempting to assess *the ways in which you think* as well as *what you are thinking*. This is important because a lot of people think so much that they take no productive action … and meta-cognitions become a burden instead of a blessing.

To conclude, a *Challenged* thinker is aware that thinking plays a part in his or her successes and failures; however, this person may or may not be willing to admit to flaws in his or her thinking—and this person has not committed to meta-cognitive change. *Challenged* thinkers, however, are familiar with, or becoming familiar with, the *natural process* of thinking—but again, they are not trying to make *positive changes* in their thinking. If this is you and you want to move from this stage into the *Beginning* thinker stage, read again the *Challenged* thinkers' *implications for self-application*—and engage.

Let's check for comprehension:

-   Using your everyday vocabulary, how would you define the *Challenged* thinker?

    _____

    _____

    _____

Let's analyze:

-   Compare and contrast the *Unreflective* thinker to the *Challenged* thinker. Write your analysis below.

    _____

    _____

    _____

Let's draw a conclusion:

-   Using the information and facts you've gathered from the *Unreflective* and *Challenged* thinker stages, how can being a *challenged* thinker personally hurt you? I am not asking you about others, but about *you* personally.

_____

_____

_____

_____

The Beginning Thinker

Beginning thinkers are those who are aware that thinking drives behaviors, thus thinking drives their successes and their failures. But, unlike the Challenged thinker, Beginning thinkers have embraced authentic humility and self-assessment; however, they have no systematic way of evaluating meta-cognitive practices (e.g., thinking about thinking). *Beginning* thinkers believe that they have control of their thinking, and they are aware of the natural thinking process (i.e., thinking through concepts, assumptions, inferences, implications, points of view, etc.) (Elder & Paul, 2013a).

However, *Beginning* thinkers are not able to clearly identify the flawed element or elements within their own natural thinking process—and, as a result, their conscious efforts to try and control their thoughts and behaviors mostly go in vain. Consequently, *Beginning* thinkers notably have more successful experiences than *Unreflective* thinkers as well as *Challenged* thinkers. Still, there are fewer successful experiences when compared with the number of failed experiences and the number of quality or substantial outcomes (Elder & Paul, 2013b; www.criticalthinking.org). The problem with this stage of thinking is that *Beginning* thinkers have not identified and/or mastered a systemic way of assessing their thoughts—nor have they mastered the ability to make valuable changes.

Some Implications for Self-Application: To master the *Beginning* thinker stage, you must maintain authentic humility and commitment. Even when you are discouraged by your failures, you must use your successes to build your self-confidence and then to seek out a reliable way of assessing your thinking. To propel forward to the *Practicing* stage, you must follow at least <u>one</u> systematic way of assessing your thinking and then apply change to that assessment, where it is needed. So, for example, pairing *The Elements of Thought* with the *Intellectual Standards* and/or the *ABCD Theory* will work well for this. (The *ABCD Theory* will be introduced shortly.)

Both the *ABCD Theory* and *The Elements of Thought* will give you greater insights as to what you are thinking and how well you are thinking. So, in order to change from a *Beginning* thinker to a *Practicing* thinker, you need to do the following:

1. Build up your intellectual confidence without evoking egocentrism. In other words, be willing to listen, understand, and value not only your thoughts, actions and feelings, but the thoughts, actions and feelings of others as well.

2. Commit to at least one type of systematic, meta-cognitive self-assessment and applied change that can be used in a variety of contexts.

3. Compare and contrast your thinking with that of the *natural thinking* process. Do this by asking yourself the following questions:

   o Does your thinking logically draw conclusions that originate from the initial inquiries?

- o Does your thinking lead to knowledge and further understanding, which eventually leads to true and appropriate conclusions? (*The word* true *in this book means* based on your belief system.)

- o Do these conclusions lead to concepts, which lead to implications and consequences that lead to further assessments and final actions?

If your answers to these questions are "no" then make a commitment to begin actively assessing your thinking *within at least one area of your life.* As you gain more skills, you can commit to assessing additional areas of your life. I suggest one at a time until you become comfortable with the process of assessing your thinking.

Resist intellectual laziness and understand completely that thinking about your thinking (meta-cognitions) and actually acting on it can be *exhausting.* You must prepare, in advance, healthy ways to recharge. For example, enjoy a movie with entertainment being your only intention—no analyzing the film for its character development, intriguing plot, etc. Or simply take a long walk on a nature trail enjoying its beauty not pondering how it came into existence. ☺

Let's check for comprehension:

- Using your everyday vocabulary, how would you define the *Beginning* thinker?

_____

_____

_____

Let's Engage…

Insights: Penetrating Below the Surface; Application of Theories…

When in Rome, do as the Romans do, but not Always

Stephanie loves school. She quickly learned from watching her peers that taking good notes in her history class was the key to earning an easy grade of A. *So, when in Rome…*

Stephanie, too, started taking good notes. She wanted to earn the grade of A like many of her classmates. Stephanie wrote down everything the professor said in class and compared her notes with those of her classmates. By doing this she also captured notes she may have overlooked. As a result, Stephanie's notes were equal to those of her peers. Unfortunately, though, Stephanie still did poorly on her next history exam.

Stephanie's efforts had failed her, and she became depressed. Then one day Stephanie just took a deep breath and began to think strategically about what she learned regarding *Bloom's Taxonomy,* the *Three Domains of Learning,* and *The Elements of Thought.* As a result of her thinking, Stephanie discovered that she had simply *mimicked* her peers' note-taking and that she still needed to examine and contemplate her notes to gain a deeper understanding of the material—*and so she tried…*

Before her next test, Stephanie studied what she captured in her notes by reciting them aloud because she was an auditory learner. (If anyone had asked, Stephanie could have recited the entire paper of notes with her eyes closed.) Stephanie took the test and received better results this time but nowhere near the grade of A that she desired. Stephanie then realized she forgot to *contemplate* and *examine* her notes.

Now using a systematic way of assessing her thinking, Stephanie applied *The Elements of Thought* and *Bloom's Taxonomy* to assess her thoughts and her behaviors. Using *The Elements of Thought*, Stephanie learned that she was studying with the wrong *purpose* in mind; Stephanie realized she needed to understand from within her notes the different historical characters' *point of views*, the different *cause and effects, the implications* of the cause and effects, the *assumptions*, and so on. Stephanie looked back in her book at *Bloom's Taxonomy* and discovered that she needed to study at the level of *analysis* in order to gain deeper understanding. Armed with this new information, Stephanie studied accordingly and passed all future history tests with the grade of A.

- At the beginning of this story, what stage of thinking is Stephanie exhibiting: *unreflective, challenged, beginning,* or *practicing,* **and why**? Think carefully and support your answer.

  _____

  _____

  _____

- By the middle of this story, what stage of thinking is Stephanie exhibiting: *unreflective, challenged, beginning,* or *practicing,* **and why**? Think carefully and support your answer.

  _____

  _____

  _____

- By the end of this story, what stage of thinking is Stephanie exhibiting *unreflective, challenged, beginning,* or *practicing,* **and why**? Think carefully and support your answer.

  _____

  _____

  _____

Great work engaging, guys! Let's continue on…

The Practicing Thinker

Thinkers at the Practicing stage possess the same great qualities of the *Beginning* thinkers with an additional layer of commitment to meta-cognitions. ***Practicing thinkers*** *believe they have control over their thinking, and they've embraced the idea of intellectual humility. But, they've also committed to at least ONE way of systematically assessing the quality of their thinking.* As a result of their meta-cognitive assessment and commitment to quality changes, *Practicing* thinkers have more meaningful successes and a greater quantity of successes than failures (Elder & Paul, 2013b; www.criticalthinking.org).

Practicing thinkers gain more control over their life outcomes through consistent, logical, and rational self-assessments. They do this by analyzing the meaning of their behaviors and emotions, thus recognizing that both are simply symptoms of their thinking—be it conscious thinking or subconscious thinking. *Practicing* thinkers usually experience high levels of success in only one area of their life and inconsistent success across the others.

Practicing thinkers' intellectual skills are strengthened every day due to their diligence and commitment to succeed intellectually. This repetition prepares *Practicing* thinkers to succeed in most areas of their lives. Finally, *Practicing* thinkers are aware of the global impact their thinking has on society, but they are not actively pursuing this (Elder & Paul, 2013b; www.criticalthinking.org).

Some Implications for Self-Application: The *Practicing* thinker stage is ***the gate-keeper*** to the last two stages of intellectual self-assessment. Consistent hard work is involved here: practice, practice, practice. But, hey, it's worth it because *you* are worth it. To fully embrace the *Practicing* thinker stage, you have to

1. Understand and believe that you have control over your thinking.

2. Possess authentic humility.

3. Be persistent and committed to deliberately engaging in systematic thinking using *The Elements of Thought* and/or the *ABCD Theory* (Elder & Paul, 2013a).

If all the above is applied and integrated with *Bloom's Taxonomy*—and catch this: applied and integrated *within all Three Domains of Learning*—you will slowly become not only a social or intellectual critical thinker but an academic critical thinker as well. So, you will learn to transfer and apply your comprehension and understanding from one class to another class—and then to your life (e.g., you would use *CHOP*ᴿ to chop up these theories and use them in your math class, government class, etc.).

Checking In. Now, before we move to the final two stages of intellectual thinking—the highest two stages—let's stop and process. Here is what I want you to do: *ponder the following questions, and then write your answers on the lines below.* I want to become aware of what you're thinking right now.

-   There are six stages of intellectual development. You've been introduced to four of them. List the four stages and then summarize collectively your reaction to each stage below.

    _____

    _____

    _____

-   Have you personally identified with any of those stages? If you have, write that stage down here.

    _____

    _____

    _____

-   If you personally identified with one of the four types of thinkers, what will it take for you to personally master the next stage? Write your answer below.

    _____

    _____

    _____

Good, good, good! Now, so far, you've read about the lower stages of intellectual development. There are two stages left. At this point, you might be asking yourself, "What exactly is systemic thinking?" and "How do you use *The Elements of Thought* and the *Intellectual Standards* as a system of assessing and changing thinking, thus changing emotions and behaviors?" I'm glad you asked. ☺ *The Elements of Thought*, number four of the *Super Six Theories*, is considered a systematic way of thinking. Examine Figure 2.03.

Now together, let us pause to look at number four of the *Super Six Theories*. I am purposefully plugging this theory here because this is exactly where it fits within *Stage Theory*. So, let us pause for this insertion and discuss *The Elements of Thought*. Once finished, we will return to the last two stages of *Stage Theory*.

The Elements of Thought (www.criticalthinking.org)

THE ELEMENTS OF THOUGHT: NUMBER FOUR OF THE SUPER SIX THEORIES

The Elements of Thought is the natural process of thinking broken down into its individually labeled parts (Elder and Paul, 2013a). Accompanying *The Elements of Thought* are *the Intellectual Standards* (see below). Together, these theories help you to clarify not only your thinking, but to better understand the thoughts and conversation of others.

Figure 2.03: *The Elements of Thought and Intellectual Standards*

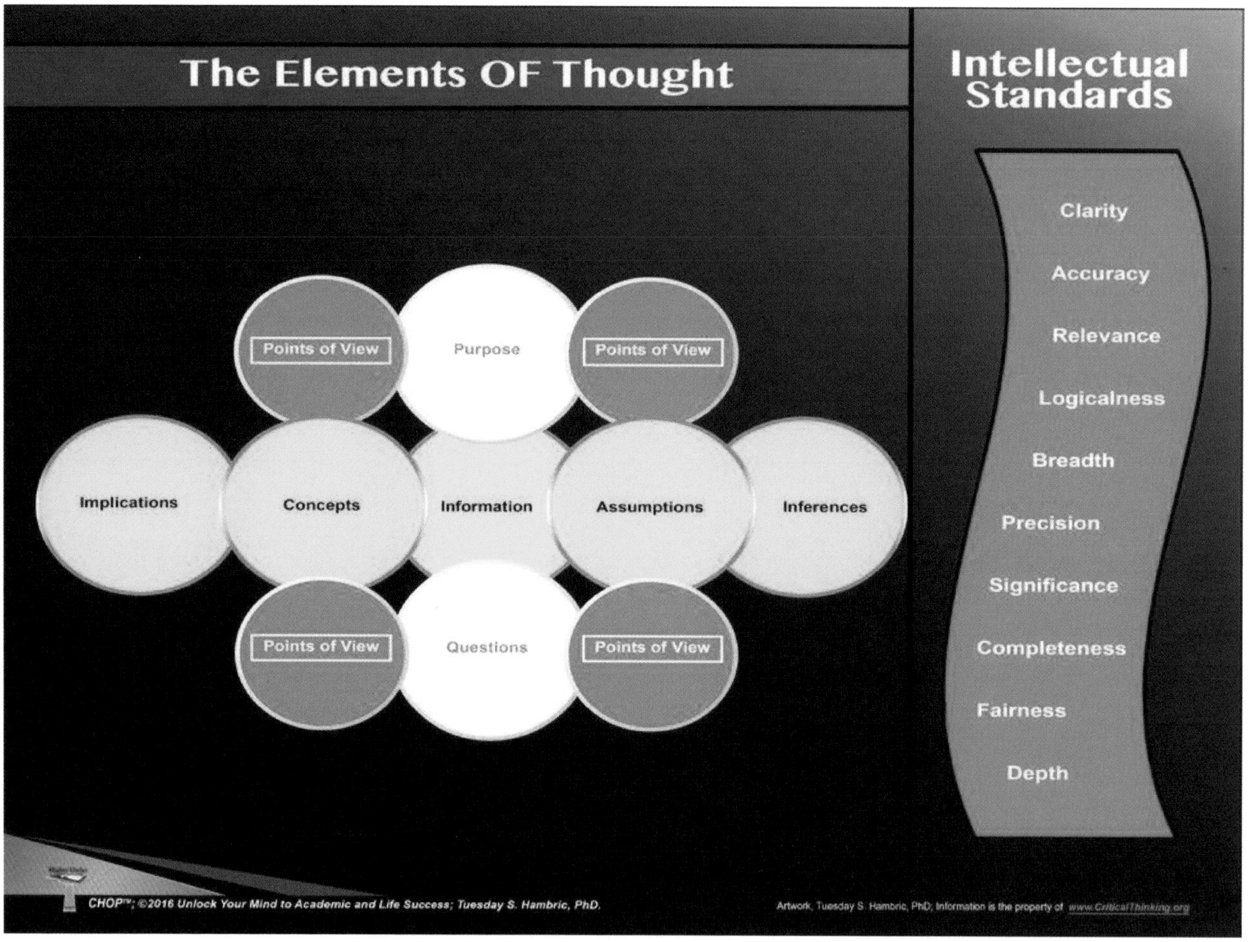

Paul and Elder labeled the eight parts or elements to thinking as:

- Purpose   Questions   Information   Assumptions
- Concepts   Inferences   Implications   Points of view

In my opinion, *The Elements of Thought* would be nothing without *Bloom's Taxonomy* or the *Intellectual Standards*. The **Intellectual Standards** *are a reasoned approach to examining and assessing knowledge and wisdom by seeking to find*

- Clarity   Accuracy   Relevance   Logicalness   Breadth
- Precision   Significance   Completeness   Fairness   Depth of information

So, let's think about that for a moment … I want you to understand that the natural process in which we humans think can be *well-ordered* and *intentionally used* as an actual system of thinking or systemic thinking.

Now to answer that earlier question you may have had when you learned about the *practicing thinker,* "What is systemic thinking?" **Systemic thinking** *is when you intentionally break down, examine, clarify, and reason through yours or someone else's elements of thinking.* As a result of such systemic thinking, your thoughts will more than likely lead you to a valuable flow of precise information and successful outcomes. However, without this type of meta-cognitive examination, your natural thinking process could lead you to a flow of distorted information and less successful outcomes. As an example, let's use Vanessa's writing dilemma to further understand *The Elements of Thought* and the *Intellectual Standards* when applied.

Insights: Penetrating Below the Surface; Application of Theories…

Yesterday's Woes Dictating Today's Learning

Vanessa, a college freshman, hates writing. When Vanessa was in elementary school, her fifth and sixth-grade teachers often expressed their distaste for her writing, and so, by the time Vanessa made it to middle school, she felt defeated. Conversely, Vanessa's seventh and eighth-grade instructors worked consistently and lovingly to successfully improve Vanessa's writing. Now five years later, Vanessa is now faced with her first college paper, but she still gets stressed out at the very idea of writing. Her attitude towards writing makes the writing process—even for a short essay—difficult.

How would you use *The Elements of Thought* and *Intellectual Standards* to assess, identify, and resolve Vanessa's problem? I want you to think it through aloud and then review my suggestion.

Be sure to note that *The Elements of Thought* are in bold and in italics. Also note that the *Intellectual Standards* are in bold, italic, and underlined. And again, my suggestion that follows is just one of many ways you could use these theories to help you or others in real-life situations:

- *Orient Yourself*
  - Seek *clarity* by stating the task.
    - For example, "My purpose is to assess, identify, and help resolve Vanessa's problem."

- o   Remember to use the theory(ies) and the task to guide your thinking.
- *Assess*
  - o   Read the given facts surrounding Vanessa and take note of significant and ***relevant information and facts*** given and how those facts could have helped Vanessa formulate accurate and or faulty ***concepts***.
    - ▪   For example, because Vanessa was told as a child that her writing was not good enough, she uses only that activating event to define her ability to write.
- *Problem Identified*
  - o   State your ***conclusion***
    - ▪   For example, Vanessa hates writing, and, because of her attitude toward writing, the act of getting started is grueling.
- *Resolution*
  - o   After careful analysis, use ***logic*** to help Vanessa see things from more than one ***point of view***. Help her to realize that she is ignoring her more successful script (her successful seventh- and eighth-grade writing experience) only to hold on to an outdated, negative script (her fifth- and sixth-grade writing experience).
  - o   Use ***accuracy*** to help Vanessa consider the truth behind all of her writing successes over the years and to use those positive ***concepts*** (scripts) as her new way of defining her writing abilities.

Well now, just like that you have explored *The Elements of Thought* and the *Intellectual Standards* to experience guided and systematic thinking. I hope you are able to realize that, if you are *not* using this type of meta-cognitive examination, then your natural thinking process could lead you to a flow of distorted information and less successful outcomes. In addition, I hope you are able to understand how, by using meta-cognitive examination, you increase your chances for success.

So, as you can see, advancing to the higher levels of thinking takes practice, practice, and more practice of high-quality systemic thinking using both *The Elements of Thought* and the *Intellectual Standards* (Elder and Paul, 2013a; www.criticalthinking.org).

Checking In...

- Using *The Elements of Thought* and the *Three Domains of Learning* as your sources of information, how does having a flawed system of thinking affect the three domains? In other words, how might flawed thinking affect your cognitions, your emotions, and your behaviors?

  _____

  _____

  _____

- Here is a throwback question for you: What are the six levels of thinking in *Bloom's Taxonomy*?

  _____

  _____

  _____

It is imperative that you become familiar with *The Elements of Thought* and that you master the use of its *Intellectual Standards*. By synthesizing your comprehension of *The Elements of Thought* with the *Intellectual Standards* and then mastering your ability to apply them both, you will increase your intellectual abilities to make and follow through using sound decisions. Such insightful decision-making tends to lead you to the last two stages of *Stage Theory*. Like the *practicing* level thinker, both the final stages of *Stage Theory* require systemic thinking. However, the last two stages yield even greater probabilities of success across all areas of your life. Let us reconnect with the *Practicing* lever thinker and then move on to the other two stages.

Stage Theory Returns (www.criticalthinking.org)

THE PRACTICING THINKER (continued)

Do you see how the *Practicing* thinker stage is the gate-keeper stage? Understand that, without a system of thinking, you will NEVER reach the *Advanced* or *Accomplished* stages of thinking. That makes the *Practicing* stage, *The Elements of Thought*, and the *Intellectual Standards* (systematic thinking) *critical*.

Now according to Elder and Paul (2013a), *The Elements of Thought* and the *Intellectual Standards* combined are *the* foundation for assessing thinking. However, *Bloom's Taxonomy* and the *ABCD Theory* is another great complement to *The Elements of Thought* and its *Intellectual Standards* when thinking and acting on purpose. Again, I will explain the *ABCD Theory* shortly. But, for now, we will finish elaborating on *Stage Theory* and its last two stages of intellectual development, i.e., the *Advanced* thinker and the *Accomplished* thinker.

The Advanced Thinker

Advanced thinkers *possess the same qualities as the Practicing thinker, except the Advance thinkers are constantly and consistently refining their thinking across domains, leading to successes in several areas of their lives.* *Advanced* thinkers consistently analyze their thought processes with the intentions of improving both their intrapersonal skills and interpersonal skills. They are able to use the thinking of others to understand and improve their personal relationships and life outcomes (Elder & Paul, 2013b). *Advanced* thinkers are effective. Again, unlike *Practicing* thinkers, *Advanced* thinkers are successful across different areas in their lives locally. However, as with *Practicing* thinkers, *Advanced* thinkers are not seeking global influence.

Some Implications for Self-Application: In order to embrace the *Advance* thinker stage of intellectual development, you must

1. Be willing to evaluate your core beliefs more often than not. Evaluating your core beliefs will allow you to make more in-depth and more insightful intellectual self-assessments and decisions based on your values.
2. Be willing to dive deep morally and assess your integrity.
3. Be willing to allow others to have flaws in their thinking and humbly teach them to improve their thinking. By allowing others to have flaws in their thinking:
   a. You give yourself permission to have occasional flaws in your thinking. By giving yourself permission to have occasional flaws in your own thinking, your expectations (whether conscious or subconscious) for yourself and others to be perfect are relaxed.
4. Have courage!

In order to propel yourself forward to the *Accomplished* thinker stage, you must actively assess and measure your thinking from a global perspective.

The Accomplished Thinker

Accomplished thinkers encompass the forward-moving characteristics of the Practicing and Advanced stages, except these thinkers do it locally and globally. They are still constantly and consistently working at controlling their life outcomes by monitoring and revising their conscious thinking strategies for continued improvement. Elder and Paul (2013b) would disagree with me when I say that *Accomplished* thinkers are consistently successful even at the subconscious levels because their thinking about their thinking has paid off. Their diligent and consistent intellectual monitoring has created successful scripts or habits that lead to positive outcomes, and, due to their consistent self-assessment, they tend to quickly identify outdated scripts and move to change them. At this stage, any egocentrism is managed well with little room for relapse (Elder & Paul, 2013b).

Like *Advanced* thinkers, *Accomplished* thinkers are very successful. However, *Accomplished* thinkers expand their success to reach beyond thinking about and managing just local relationships: They also think about and act upon global issues and global success.

Some Implications for Self-Application: Wow! If you are an *Accomplished* thinker before this class ends, then you have accomplished a feat that takes most people a lifetime (if they ever reach this stage at all). However, your instructor and I want you to learn how to either stay here or to skillfully call on this level of thinking when you need it. Remember, we *can* regress in our intellectual abilities. So, IF you want to remain an *Accomplished* thinker—and I say "if" because being here all the time in every area of your life can be extreme at times—then you must follow the guidelines that follow. But I must say it also is an AWESOME experience to solicit this stage of thinking only when you need to. So, back to my point ... if you want to *remain* at this stage of thinking, you must do the following:

1. Continue to take authority over key forward-moving concepts expressed in each of the other stages.
2. Engage in systematic thinking and thought assessment by treating emotions and behaviors as symptoms of thinking.
3. Engage in authentic humility.
4. Engage in the strictest standards of *values-based* integrity and morality all the time. If I had to quantify what I mean by "all the time," I would arbitrarily say 95% to make a clear point.
5. Finally, at all times, exercise the courage it takes to endure.

Okay. Now that all six stages have been explained, I want you to allow your brain to absorb the key information in each stage. Remember when I told you to keep on your *Bloom's Taxonomy* glasses? Well, now I want you to use your understanding of *Bloom's Taxonomy* to help you summarize each stage within *Stage Theory*.

Exercise

First, using the chart that follows, gather information at the level of knowledge by recording the names of all six stages in *Stage Theory*. Then, go back and read each stage one at a time. As you do that, I want you to analyze first and then summarize in your own words what you are reading. (Hint: Use the action verbs from the earlier *Bloom's Taxonomy* [Figure 2.01] located at the level of analysis to help you evoke insights and also use the action verbs at the level of *comprehension* to help you summarize.)

Write your summaries next to the appropriate stage in the chart provided. Do not hesitate to revisit *Bloom's Taxonomy* if necessary.

Knowledge	Analysis & Comprehension
Stage 1: _____	Summary:
Stage 2: _____	Summary:
Stage 3: _____	Summary:
Stage 4: _____	Summary:
Stage 5: _____	Summary:
Stage 6: _____	Summary:
My overall summarized analysis of *Stage Theory* is:	

Because I am optimistic, I will say to you, "Great job engaging! Now it's time to reflect."

Let's analyze, compare, and assess

- Now that you understand each level of *Stage Theory*, which level of thinking best describes you **and** what do you need to do to achieve the next level?

_____

_____

_____

Let's analyze

- Explain the relationship between the different levels of academic thinking in *Bloom's Taxonomy* and the levels of intellectual development in *Stage Theory*. Write your analysis below.

_____

_____

_____

Now that you are ready for the last two theories of the *Super Six*, just remember this course is grounded in CRITICAL THINKING intended to empower you and energize you to action. That means that the first four of the *Super Six Theories*—the *Three Domains of Learning, Bloom's Taxonomy, Stage Theory,* and *The Elements of Thought*—and the next two—*ABCD Theory* and *Values-Based Mottos*—should be used as thinking frameworks in which to perceive additional information in this chapter, forthcoming chapters, and in your life regardless to how inspiring or uninspiring the environment or the experience might be. That way, you can take mindful actions toward your success.

If you need to take a break, now would be a great time.

The ABCD Theory: To Assess and Discover the Will to Change

Have you ever tried to lose weight or gain muscle mass to no avail? Have you ever tried to spend less time on social media but couldn't because you thought you might miss something? What about smoking? Regardless to what you are smoking, have you ever tried to stop—and then found yourself doing it again? Let's think about school for a second. How many times have you said, "I am going to do better this time"? Or to our *seasoned* students and returning veterans, does being in school after several years bring you discomfort? Finally, THE BIG question: Have you ever tried to stop yourself from saying the wrong thing or doing the wrong thing, yet you just keep talking and talking or doing and doing as if you had no control? If you said yes to any of these situations or others that I have not mentioned, I say, "kudos" to you for TRYING to change. I also say, have no despair because now there is real help. It's called the *ABCD Theory*.

ABCD THEORY: NUMBER FIVE OF THE SUPER SIX

If you will remember in Chapter I (the *Welcome Chapter*), there is a section on *Ownership & Accountability*. In that section, emphasis is placed on perceptions and a person's ability to reasonably change his or her view of things in order to bring forth greater probabilities of success.

Well, the *ABCD Theory* is a great tool all by itself, but when integrated with the *Three Domains of Learning* and *The Elements of Thought,* that combination can be just the right mix to help you not only take ownership of your actions but to help you decrease your number of failures by increasing your number of successes.

The *ABCD Theory* is a complex, therapeutic interplay between the *Three Domains of Learning*—a.k.a., a person's thoughts, feelings, and behaviors. Dr. Albert Ellis, the founder of the *ABCD Theory* or *REBT* therapy, introduced this concept and therapy to the world in the mid-1950s.

Now before I briefly explain the *ABCD Theory*, let me personally express my disclaimer. Although I have added this theory to this book (as well as other theories), I do not agree with all of the original claims and/or the personal philosophies of their founding fathers. I do, however, think each of the theories chosen for this book, when integrated with people's personal beliefs, are among the best approaches (within reason) to help people create balance and success in their lives.

Moving On...

Again, the *ABCD Theory is a complex assessment of a person's cognitions, emotions, and behaviors* (Ellis, 1973, 2001). It is also a means for self-assessment and lasting change. The validity of the *ABCD Theory* rest upon the following principle: The *A* or *Activating Event is an experience that has no meaning until the person experiencing it gives it (the Activating Event) meaning. The **B** is the meaning (or Beliefs, or thoughts) about *A* that is applied.*

According to Dr. Ellis, **B** or *Beliefs* about *A*, the *Activating Event,* come in two forms: explicit and implicit (Ellis, 1973, 2001). I use the terms *conscious thinking* and *subconscious thinking* instead.

Just what is conscious thinking and subconscious thinking? According to *Merriam Webster Dictionary* (2015), **Conscious thinking** *refers to explicit thoughts and beliefs of which a person is aware.* **Subconscious thinking** *refers to implicit thoughts and beliefs of which a person is not aware and yet is still responding to those thoughts and beliefs* (2015). For example, an English student named Vanessa always has a hard time writing her essay papers. Whenever the writing assignments are given, Vanessa tends to stress out, procrastinate, and sometimes turn in late work. So, Vanessa's writing struggles would represent her *A*, *Activating Event,* and Vanessa's negative thoughts and beliefs that she will never write well enough would be her **B**, *Beliefs.* So, if Vanessa is aware of the fact that she is responding to those thoughts and beliefs, then those thoughts and beliefs would be considered *conscious.* However, if Vanessa is unaware of those thoughts and beliefs and yet she is reacting to them, then those thoughts and beliefs would be considered *subconscious.*

Finally, there is the *C* of the *ABCD Theory*. The *C* or the *Consequences* within the *ABCD Theory* naturally follow a person's **B**, *Beliefs.* If we were to use Vanessa again as an example, then Vanessa's increased stress level and procrastination would be a direct and natural consequence to her negative thoughts about writing. Now, there are many kinds of *Consequences,* but for our purpose, we will focus on three different categories: 1) *emotions or affective symptoms*; 2) *behaviors or psychomotor symptoms*; 3) *physiological symptoms*. Technically, there is a fourth category of consequence that happens often, and that is where one line of thinking provokes additional thinking and so on. Nonetheless, I choose just these three broad categories because most, if not all, of our reactions to life can be placed in one of these three. To illustrate, feeling sad would be considered an *emotion*; the act of crying—the "doing" if you will—would be considered a *behavior*; and finally, the stress that comes with the crying and sadness would be considered a *physiological symptom*. In Vanessa's case, her *C*, *Consequence* is *emotional* because she is frustrated; *physiological*, because she tends to get stress headaches; and *behavioral* because she procrastinates. And as for your information (FYI), *Consequences* do not always result in all three categories.

Now let's look at the *D* of the *ABCD Theory*. The *D* represents the act of *Disputing* unproductive beliefs and/or outdated scripts. The *D* or *Disputing* is a critical thinking technique that serves as a way of reasonably and logically changing one's unproductive beliefs and outdated scripts to productive beliefs and more relevant scripts.

Scripts *are preconceived thoughts, emotions, and/or behavioral reactions to Activating Events*. Each of these events is susceptible to transformation; and as a result of *Disputing* these scripts and unproductive beliefs, people tend to restore a healthy balance among their thoughts, emotions, and behaviors (i.e., the *Three Domains of Learning*) (Ellis, 2001).

Now let's see what the *ABCD Theory* might look like. Here's my layman's illustration of the *ABCD Theory* (Diagram 2.01). It will be *slightly* different than that of Dr. Ellis', but beneficial nonetheless. And, thanks to one of my students, Steven Scroggins, I have further explained the *Activating Events* to include intended meaning. If you are interested in Dr. Ellis' original work, please visit www.albertellisinstitute.org.

Diagram 2.01: *ABCD Theory; Assessment, Dispute, & Change*

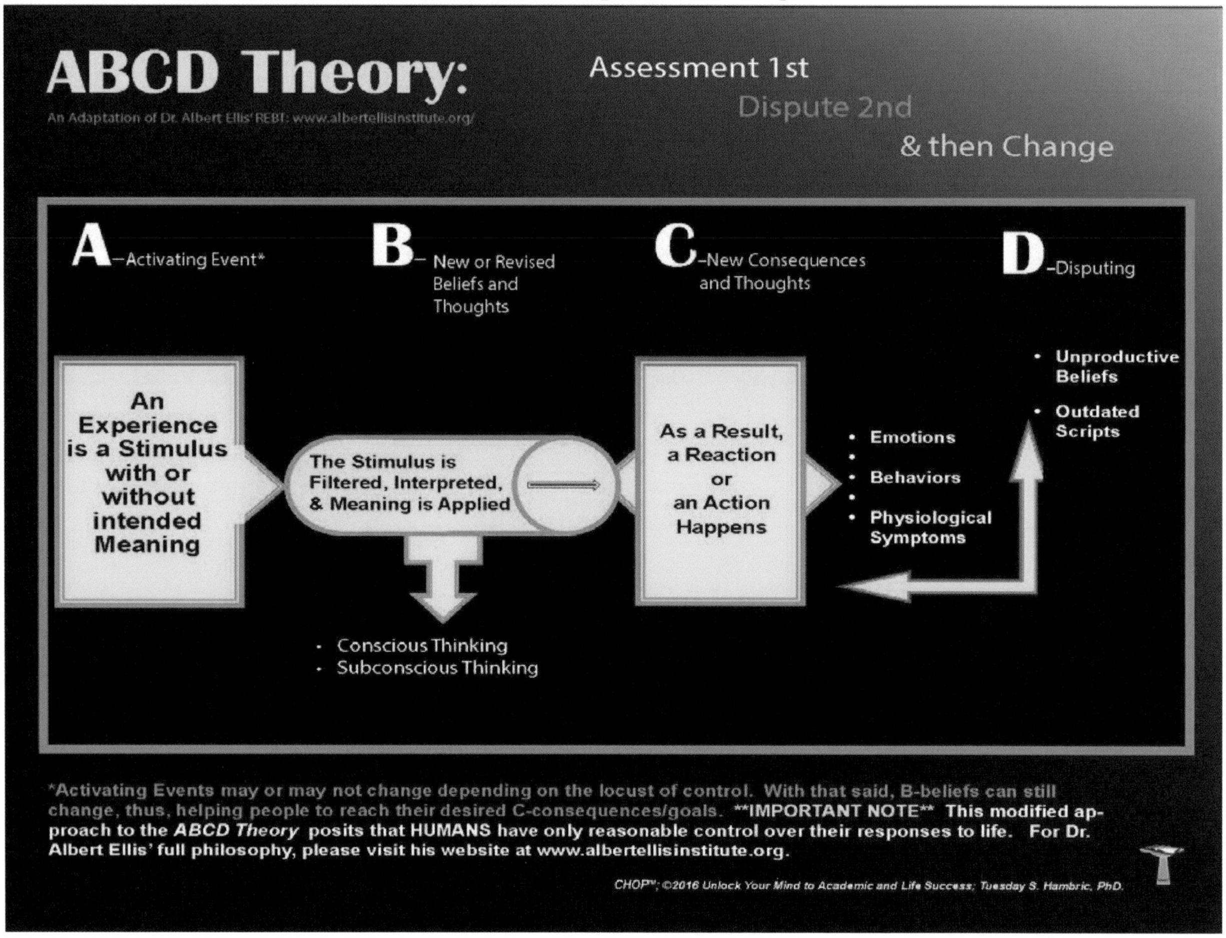

Connecting the Dots by Checking for Knowledge and Analysis

Now, using Diagram 2.01, let's examine the *ABCD Theory* and see what we can proclaim about self-management (i.e., taking ownership and holding ourselves accountable in all three of *Bloom's Domains of Learning*). We will approach this segment of learning and engagement by using a modified form of *The Socratic Method*. This is the exact same question-and-answer method you have used to learn all the other theories.

- When you see the words **Activating** and **Event** in Diagram 2.01, do you think either of those terms means a negative experience, a positive experience, or neither?

  _____

  _____

  _____

If you said, "It can mean either" then you and I are in agreement. *Activating Event* means an experience is happening or has happened and is available **for you to interpret and/or apply your thoughts and feelings** regarding that event. Keep that in mind because this is key. Let's examine further…

- According to the *ABCD Theory*, A may or may not have implied meaning. What happens to that event and its meaning according to the *ABCD Theory* and the diagram? In other words, how does the A, the *Activating Event*, become meaningful for the person receiving the experienced event? Be sure to examine the diagram as a whole as well as its individual parts closely. To gain insights, be sure to look at the illustration's flow of information and what you've read so far. Once you've finished, write down your answer:

  _____

  _____

  _____

Okay, that seemed pretty simple. Let's step it up a bit. ☺.

Still using Diagram 2.01, does the *ABCD Theory* imply that each person is responsible for his or her own consequences? For argument's sake, let's make sure we are all using the same definition of consequences. *Consequences* in this case—and for every time we refer to the *ABCD Theory*—will mean *different types of emotional, behavioral, and physiological responses or symptoms*, just as the diagram shows. Now answer the question but be sure to think it through. Try to think of different situations where *it appears people may not have control* over their emotions, behaviors, and physiological symptoms, and then think of situations where *it appears people may have control*.

- After analyzing both scenarios, write down whether or not you think the *ABCD Theory* implies that each person is responsible for his or her own consequences.

  _____

  _____

  _____

- Finally, let's examine the **D**, *Disputing*. What role does element **D**, *Disputing*, play in the *ABCD Theory*?

_____
_____
_____

- Using the *ABCD* diagram and paying careful attention to its flow, what would be a naturally successful consequence of **_D_**, *Disputing*? Hint: The answer is implied in the diagram's flow.

_____
_____
_____

- We've thought about what the theory implies. Now, I want to know your opinion. Do *you* personally believe that, *within reason*, people are responsible for their own consequences? Why or why not?

_____
_____
_____

Note that, in the last question, I added the words "within reason." That is because I believe we have control *within reason*, although you might not agree with me. For that matter, you might not agree with the author of the *ABCD Theory*, Dr. Ellis (2001), who says we are fully responsible for our own misery. Either way, your opinion is worth sharing and discussing in class. So, please be sure to bring your thoughts to class and ask any questions you might have as they relate to this material. If you are taking the class online, please post your questions in the appropriate areas for further discussions. In the meantime, we will tackle a couple more questions and some elaborations before we move on to the last of the *Super Six Theories*.

Let's Engage…

To shake things up a bit, let's think more creatively than what we've done already. Here is another *Insight: Penetrating Below the Surface*. Once you are finished reading it, I will have you engage in a purer form of Socratic reasoning. The goal of this exercise is to give you an opportunity to use your critical thinking skills to transcend or go beyond the boundaries that I have presented so far. Okay? You've got this. Here we go…

Peacefully Floating in the Wind or Sailing into a Storm

Jason Gowns had nothing but a bright future ahead of him ... well, so it seemed. Jason was a handsome 20-year-old college sophomore who was admired by all. Jason excelled in everything he did, including

sports and music. He was the starting linebacker at Kilmore State University in Yapaloo, Texas, and arguably one of the most talented guitar players of his generation. One day after a long study session with his academic tutor, Jason met a woman whom he thought was the most beautiful women he had ever seen. She was a freshman at his school.

Elka Yohahn was an intelligent and ambitious 19-year-old European, who attends Kilmore college on an academic scholarship. Jason and Elka agreed to go out, and before long they were in love.

Jason proposed to Elka on the day of his graduation in front of all of his family and their friends. Feeling the pressure of the situation and desperately wanting this relationship to be different from her last relationship, Elka quickly accepted his proposal.

Now, with the wedding date set for exactly one year from the day of their engagement, Jason and Elka nonchalantly began to plan their nuptials and future, but without considering the fact that Jason had yet to receive a job offer. Jason and Elka simply forged ahead planning their lives together. They informally discussed having kids, their finances, and possible living arrangements, but their talks never reached the levels of analysis and application, only knowledge and comprehension. In other words, they listened to each other's thoughts and feelings. They understood each other's points of view, but not one time did they create hypothetical situations to see if different circumstances might change their views. They missed the opportunity to use the "what if this..." or "what if that..." questions. Finally, sex was never discussed. Jason and Elka felt there was no need to discuss sex because they had already been intimate with each other since their fourth date with no complaints.

Situation

Jason is now a 22-year-old graduate with a degree in finance who is seeking employment. He comes from a middle-class family in a small town called Inland, Texas. Jason's parents are both labor workers, but his two older siblings are both degreed and professionals. Neither Jason nor his family has ever traveled outside of Texas, and Jason is in no rush to do so. He loves the small hometown feel and thrives in routine settings. *Jason values family, hard work, and commitment.*

Elka Yohahn is now 21 years old. She is a junior in college, with one year left until graduation. Elka was born in Europe but moved to the United States with her American father when she was age 10. Her mother and father divorced, but, because Elka was close to her mother, she often traveled back and forth between the United States and Europe.

Elka has two younger sisters who live with her mother and their father in Europe. Elka also has a stepmom due to her father's new marriage. Elka's father and stepmom are both lawyers who run their own private law practice in the United States. Elka has had only one serious relationship prior to Jason, and that relationship was with Sam, her ex-boyfriend. Elka dated Sam for a little over two years before she broke up with him due to his infidelity. Now, resulting from her Sam's infidelity and her parents' divorce, Elka has a hard time trusting the idea of relationship commitment and often shies away from lengthy obligations.

Elka enjoys traveling around the world and loves the lavish lifestyle. ***Elka values hard work, spontaneity, and freedom.***

- Are Jason and Elka peacefully floating in the wind or sailing into a storm? Pause for a moment and use the critical thinking theories to help you answer this question and those that follow.

  _____

  _____

  _____

- Use the *ABCD Theory* to assess at least one potential roadblock that you foresee with Jason and Elka's relationship. In other words, pick one likely problem that Jason and Elka might have as a couple and then appropriately label that problem and your predictions about the problem with the letters or components of the *ABCD Theory*. *Be sure to only use the **A**, **B**, and **C**, and **not** the **D** because you are ONLY assessing the situation not correcting it.* Use the upcoming section to record your assessment:

  *A*ctivating Event (write down the problem you predicted):

  _____

  _____

  _____

  ***B**eliefs* and thoughts about the *Activating Event* (use circumstantial evidence from Jason and Elka's story to support the problem you predicted).

  _____

  _____

  _____

  ***C**onsequences* (record any *consequences* that would naturally follow your written beliefs regarding the activating event).

  _____

  _____

  _____

Great work thus far, but let's mentally outline and clarify what you have done… So far, you have taken a realistic case study and analyzed it and then taken your analysis and paired it with the different parts/concepts of the *ABCD Theory*. In essence, you have practiced using the necessary skills to help you identify possible flawed thinking, emotions, and/or behaviors in a given situation. With that said, how well did you do? Let's compare your conclusions with one of my own (keep in mind that my way is just a guide).

Here, I have presented only ONE example of a hundred different ways a person could have answered the preceding three questions. So please simply use this as a guide to evaluate your own progress.

One of many possible assessments for Jason and Elka is

1. I think Jason and Elka are sailing into a storm.
2. My assessment to the *ABCD Theory* question: **_A_** = It is possible that Elka does not trust Jason. **_B_** = Elka's thoughts are, "I love him, but I can never fully trust any man." My support for this claim is in the story where it states that Elka's parents divorced and her last boyfriend cheated. As a result of this, I think Elka will have lingering trust issues and those issues may be *subconscious*."
3. **_C_** = Elka will model her learned behaviors of not "fully trusting," and she will not commit to the relationship. Without help, Elka's love could lead her to marry Jason, but her lack of commitment fueled by distrust could lead her to falsely accuse him of cheating and divorce.

All right, that was me applying the assessment phase of the *ABCD Theory*. Again, my assessment is just one of many possible examples. If you haven't already, compared your work with mine by checking to see that you've applied each concept—the **_A_**, the **_B_**, and the **_C_**—properly. The key here is to be sure that: 1) your "**_A_** or *event*" is a potential problem that you see in Elka's and Jason's story; 2) your **_B_** or *beliefs* are your thoughts about the problem, keeping in mind this will be supported by evidence used in the story (not to *replace* but to *support* your thoughts or beliefs regarding the potential problem); 3) be sure that your **_C_** or *consequence* is a consequence or reaction that would naturally follow your supported thoughts about the potential problem.

Once you are finished comparing your assessment with the one I provided, let's move on to *disputing*.

The **_D_** or ***disputing*** in Albert Ellis' theory is a critical thinking technique that Ellis uses to rationally and logically change unproductive beliefs and outdated scripts to productive beliefs and more appropriate and relevant scripts. However, because he is an expert on his own work ☺, we will leave his techniques to him and use what I call "the laymen's version" of *disputing*.

I want you to use *The Elements of Thoughts* and its *Intellectual Standards* to dispute or assist in correcting what you might think is Elka or Jason's flawed thinking. I chose this theory to assist in correcting or **_D_**, *disputing*, because 1) you are already familiar with it, and you have already examined it; and 2) it works very well as a systematic way of disputing, which also helps to propel you into the *practicing* thinker level stage of *Stage Theory*. (Look at that. Here we are back full circle integrating the *Super Six Theories* via CHOP®. Now it's time to apply this theory.)

If you need to revisit *The Elements of Thought* and its *Intellectual Standards*, then please do so. It can be found in this chapter under the *Stage Theory* subsection.

Okay, so let's attempt to *dispute*. Because you are to use *The Elements of Thought* and its *Intellectual Standards* to dispute Elka or Jason's proposed outdated scripts, then you must first look back at your proposed **_B_** or *beliefs*. The reason for this is so that you can figure out which part of our proposed **_B_** or *beliefs* correspond with what parts of *The Elements of Thoughts*.

For instance, let's revisit my B or *beliefs*. I stated that, **_B_** = Elka's thoughts are:

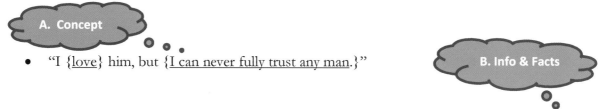

- "I {love} him, but {I can never fully trust any man.}"

    a.   My support for this claim is that in the story it is stated that {Elka's parents divorced and her last boyfriend cheated.}

    b.   As a result of this, {I think Elka will have lingering trust issues and those issues may be subconscious.}

Notice how I have underlined and labeled parts of my **_B_** or *beliefs* with aspects of *The Elements of Thought*.

Now that I have labeled my and potentially Elka's thinking, it's time for me to use the *Intellectual Standards* to logically and rationally dispute those thoughts. Let's take the second concept (b):

- "I can never fully trust any man."
  - o I would ask Elka, "Why would you see Jason as a man you cannot trust? Do you have evidence of things he has done that would cause you not to trust him?"
    - ■ By asking that question, I am also asking Elka to reflect on and justify the **depth** and **breadth** of her love for Jason. Once she explains her answer, I would follow up with another question.
  - o I would ask Elka, "Do you think it is **fair** to Jason to enter into a committed relationship with him when you don't fully trust him?"
    - ■ By asking this question, I am asking Elka to see things **from Jason's perspective**. This gives her a **clear** opportunity to appeal to **logic** and reasoning that would be **relevant** to Jason.

I could go on and on using the different *Intellectual Standards* to assess Elka's thinking—which, by the way, appears to be faulty—to help her help herself to a more successful and balanced life. But now it is *your* turn to dispute your proposed **_B_** or *beliefs*.

Just as I did, rewrite your **_B_** or *beliefs* on the lines below. Also, underline the different parts of your statement that correspond with the different parts of *The Elements of Thought*. Do what I did and use the cloud or thinking bubbles to help guide you.

_____

_____

_____

Good work so far. Now that you have written and labeled your proposed **B** or *beliefs*, it's time for you to also use the *Intellectual Standards* to logically and rationally dispute those thoughts. You will do this by posing two *disputing* questions.

The key to composing, or coming up with, disputing questions is to ensure that your questions solicit answers that reflect some or all of the *Intellectual Standards*—fairness, clarity, relevance, logic, accuracy, depth, and breadth—as they relate to the given situation. Use the below lines and prompts to guide your thinking as you record your questions and justification regarding the *Intellectual Standards*.

- Look at your **B** or *beliefs*. Take one part of it that you want to dispute and write it here.

  _____

  _____

  _____

- Next, write your first appropriate question below that disputes the above element. Keep in mind your question should be one that will help Elka or Jason think about fairness, logicalness, relevance, etc.

  Question #1: _____
  - By asking Question #1, which part of the *Intellectual Standards* are you using to give Elka or Jason an opportunity to reflect? Please write out your justification using complete sentences.

    _____

    _____

    _____

- Now, write your second appropriate question here that disputes your/Elka's beliefs.

  Question #2. _____
  - By asking Question #2, which part of the *Intellectual Standards* are you using to give Elka or Jason an opportunity to reflect? Please write out your justification using complete sentences.

    _____

    _____

    _____

How did you do? I realize that, for some of you, it may have been a bit awkward to have to think in such "matter-of-fact" ways about your thinking. But basically, you just used the *ABCD Theory* to engage once again in *meta-cognitions* (a.k.a., thinking about your thinking).

Okay, okay ... I know that was a lot. But just think, that is only ONE of many ways in which Jason and Elka could engage in self-management, self-discipline, maturity, and all the other great characteristics that come along with being RESILIENT and SUCCESSFUL *on purpose*.

Well, I hope this portion of the reading helped to strengthen your understanding as it relates to the *ABCD Theory*, and I hope all of the earlier readings helped you to construct your own critical thinking platform. Because at this point, the plan *was* and *is* for you to have learned five different theories that would equip you with a theoretical foundation and theoretical insights that would prepare you for both hypothetical and real-life applications. Remember, the formula for success is

(TP + TA)SLOs = Intentional Academic and Life Success.

(When expressed verbally, this reads, *Theory Processed plus Theory Applied, Powered by Student Learning Outcomes equals Intentional Academic and Life Success*)

At this time, I am suggesting we do a reality check—and I choose to employ *Stage Theory*. *Stage Theory* requires us to remember the fact that the quality of our thinking directly relates to the quality of our life successes or failures in life. It also requires us to intellectually humble ourselves to ensure that we seek out and find the flaws in our thinking.

So, I want you to step back from all of this and go do something enjoyable. Seriously, take about 15 to 20 minutes to relax. Then come back. If you need to take a day and can afford to take the day, then do so. But, when you return from the break, you should be able to answer the next couple of questions. If, for whatever reason, you cannot answer both questions correctly, then reread the theories that closely aligned with the questions in which you were unable to answer.

The requests are:

- Without revisiting your notes or the book, list the names of the five *Super Six Theories* covered so far.

  _____

  _____

  _____

- Also, without revisiting your notes or the book, again list the names of the five *Super Six Theories* presented so far, along with each of their major components (major parts).

  _____

  _____

  _____

If you answered correctly the aforementioned questions, then you are ready to rock and roll. I am impressed! If you did not know the names of the theories or the major parts of the theories at this point, then you will be in the exact same position you were in before you started reading this book. Do you know what that position might be? That position is one where you still do not know the names of the presented theories or how they work. Some of you may be concerned about that and are already planning to commit to memorizing and deeply learning any missed material. But others of you might be thinking "Oh well" or "That's funny."

Well, it's actually not funny, at least to me it isn't. It's not funny to me because, as a result of not knowing the basic names of the theories and their elements, you will not be able to successfully recall and use these theories when needed; thus, you would be less likely to have consistent and lasting success on purpose. And, we don't want that. One of the major goals and purposes for this class and material is for you to be *resilient, calculated, self-directed, and intentionally successful*. It is for you to take what you have learned so far and use it in your other classes and in your life to be successful. So, again, if you can't answer both of the aforementioned questions *completely*, then please humble yourself and make time to go back and re-engage. Be sure to 1) read analytically and 2) do all the thought-provoking work.

Welcome Back!

Values-Based Mottos: Approaching Success Holistically

So far, we have learned a lot about five different theories that were primarily designed to address academic and intellectual success through critical thinking. Nevertheless, we have yet to discuss or apply those theories to what some people might call *Personal Success* and others might call *Spiritual Success*.

But, no matter what you, other people, or I call it, this kind of success is arguably THE most important type of success. It is the most import type of success because it is success that's driven *by what a person believes*. So, throughout the remainder of this section, I will mainly use the term *Personal Success* to represent *Spiritual Success* because *Spiritual Success* is *personal*.

Let me explain. You see, when I use the term **Academic Success**, I am referring to *the act of using relevant critical thinking skills to meet all the requirements to graduate or all the requirements to attain an artifact that illustrates all educational goals were met*. For example, a certificate of completion in plumbing or welding, or a core complete certificate that guarantees transfer to a university and so on, serves as an artifact that represents academic success. Now, when I refer to the terms **Intellectual or Social Success**, I am referring to *the act of intentionally using critical thinking skills that create social advantages over others in the humblest of ways*—and please take seriously, what it means to be humble, because having advantages in life also brings about great responsibilities and moral expectations.

When I refer to **Personal Success**, I am referring to *the act of intentionally using one's values and critical thinking skills to make decisions that reflect his or her personal identity—desired thoughts, feelings, and behaviors*.

If you and I are of similar minds right now, then you might agree with me that *Personal Success* should be used as a person's personal life map. In other words, it should serve as *a moral compass or navigation system*, which is the very *light* that guides all of their other successes. Yes? No? Follow me here…

Again, **Personal Success** is the act of intentionally using one's values and critical thinking skills to make decisions that reflect his or her desired thoughts, feelings, and behaviors (i.e. the *Three Domains of Learning*). So, if a person pursues any kind of success without aligning it with his or her Personal Success, then that person could very well be in opposition of his or her own beliefs, therefore creating internal conflict and misery.

Moreover, if a person is intentionally or *un*intentionally pursuing things that make him or her miserable, then that person just might be living a life without true purpose, the same as a life without reflection as an *Unreflective* thinker or perhaps a life with challenged reflections as a *Challenged* thinker. If a person is living a life without ever correcting his or her thoughts, then that person is in need of *hope* and *alignment*. For if we lack both hope and alignment, we have no resiliency.

Yes, we have gone right back to resiliency. Remember, I said in Chapter I that the key to intentional academic and life success is resiliency, and that the door to resiliency is *Customized Higher Order Processing—CHOP*®? Well, **Resiliency** *is the ability to seek out and understand knowledge and then through analysis, apply its wisdom. It is the ability to think critically by perceiving experiences in ways that will bring true success* (Hambric, 2011).

No matter the problems or how the problems may present themselves, resiliency creates alternatives and opportunities to take charge, to overcome, and to succeed. Resiliency creates hope. *Personal Success* establishes the foundation that promotes balance, self-reflection, and resiliency; thus, *Personal Success* should be the very foundation on which all other successes are built. So, because core values prove so important, let's discover your core values together. Let's establish the road to *Personal Success*.

VALUES-BASED MOTTOS: NUMBER SIX OF THE SUPER SIX

Values-Based Mottos *are acronyms or sentences made up of a person's chosen values and beliefs, used as guidelines to maintain a state of homeostasis or balanced living.* Do you have a motto? What do you currently use as a way of maintaining Personal Success and balance in your life?

We are going to do an experiment together that can be loosely referred to as *grounded theory*. In other words, I will ask you a series of questions that you will answer, and, based on your analysis of your answers, you will discover or unveil your core beliefs. Finally, you will create a motto and an explanation of that motto, which should closely represent your core beliefs. Now, the reason for the experiment is for you to create a motto that you will use from this day forward as a guide to help you make insightful, values-based decisions daily.

Now before we start, stop and process the proceeding questions; if you don't, you will be doing what I call "punching the ticket." In other words, you will do the assignment and not care. That's a waste of your time. Think it through and find a real and meaningful reason as to why it's important to know what you truly value and why it is important to capture it in a motto. **STOP, THINK, and DRAW A CONCLUSION**.

Tell me in your own words why it is important to have at least one motto that represents who you are, your ideals, or the causes for which you would stand.

_____

_____

_____

Now, think about how you currently make decisions and tell me if having a motto grounded in your core beliefs really help you make insightful decisions. Explain your answer.

Let's Engage…

Okay, now that you have seriously connected, let's get started discovering your values. Answer the following set of values exploration questions. React honestly to the following questions with whatever comes into your mind. However, also bear in mind you are trying to capture: **1)** verbiage that is near to your heart and describes your convictions; **2)** verbiage that comes up often; **3)** verbiage that describes you whether you like it or not; and **4)** verbiage that describes your duties as well as your aspirations.

- Who are you?

- Where do you spend your money?

- On whom do you spend your money? Yourself or other people? Be specific.

- Where do you spend your time?

- With whom do you spend your time?

- What discussion topics make you excited?

- What discussion topics make you angry or frustrated?

  _____

  _____

  _____

- What personal or social causes do you make time to fight for?

  _____

  _____

  _____

- What are your positive characteristics?

  _____

  _____

  _____

- What negative characteristics do you have but would like to change?

  _____

  _____

  _____

- What characteristics or convictions would you like to have that you currently do _not_ have?

  _____

  _____

  _____

- For whom do you feel or think you are responsible?

  _____

  _____

  _____

- Finally, when it is all said and done and your final days have drawn near, what will people say you proudly represented?

  _____

  _____

  _____

Now it is time to analyze your own answers. This can be a bit tricky because only _you_ can declare _your_ true values. So, I will really try to make this simple by giving you an example of my answers as well as my analysis of my answers. From there, you can use it as a guide to analyze your own answers. If you struggle, ask your instructor for assistance. But for now, see Figure 2.04.

Figure 2.04: *Values Exploration; Answers Revealed*

Dr. Hambric's Values Exploration—Answers Revealed

1. Who are you? Christian, Wife, Mother, Teacher, Daughter, African American, Woman, and Veteran
2. Where do you spend your money? Vacations, Educational Summer Camps, Bills, and Savings
3. Where do you spend your time? At Work, At Home, and On Vacation
4. On whom do you spend your money? My Family
5. With whom do you spend your time? My Family and Students
6. What discussion topics make you excited? God, Critical Thinking, Learning, Society, Science, and Culture
7. What discussion topics make you angry or frustrated? Things Without Balance, and Ill-Advised Statements
8. What personal or social causes will you make time to fight? Religious Rights and Teaching and Learning
9. What are your positive characteristics? I am Optimistic, a Life-Long Learner, Intra-personal, Interpersonal, and Task-Oriented
10. What are your negative characteristics? Control Nut
11. What characteristics or convictions would you like to have that you currently do not? More Patience
12. For whom do you feel or think you are responsible? Self and Family
13. Finally, when it is all said and done and your final days have drawn near, who or what will the people say you proudly represent? God, Helping, Loving Relationships, Teaching and Learning

CHOP™; ©2016 Unlock Your Mind to Academic and Life Success; Tuesday S. Hambric, PhD.

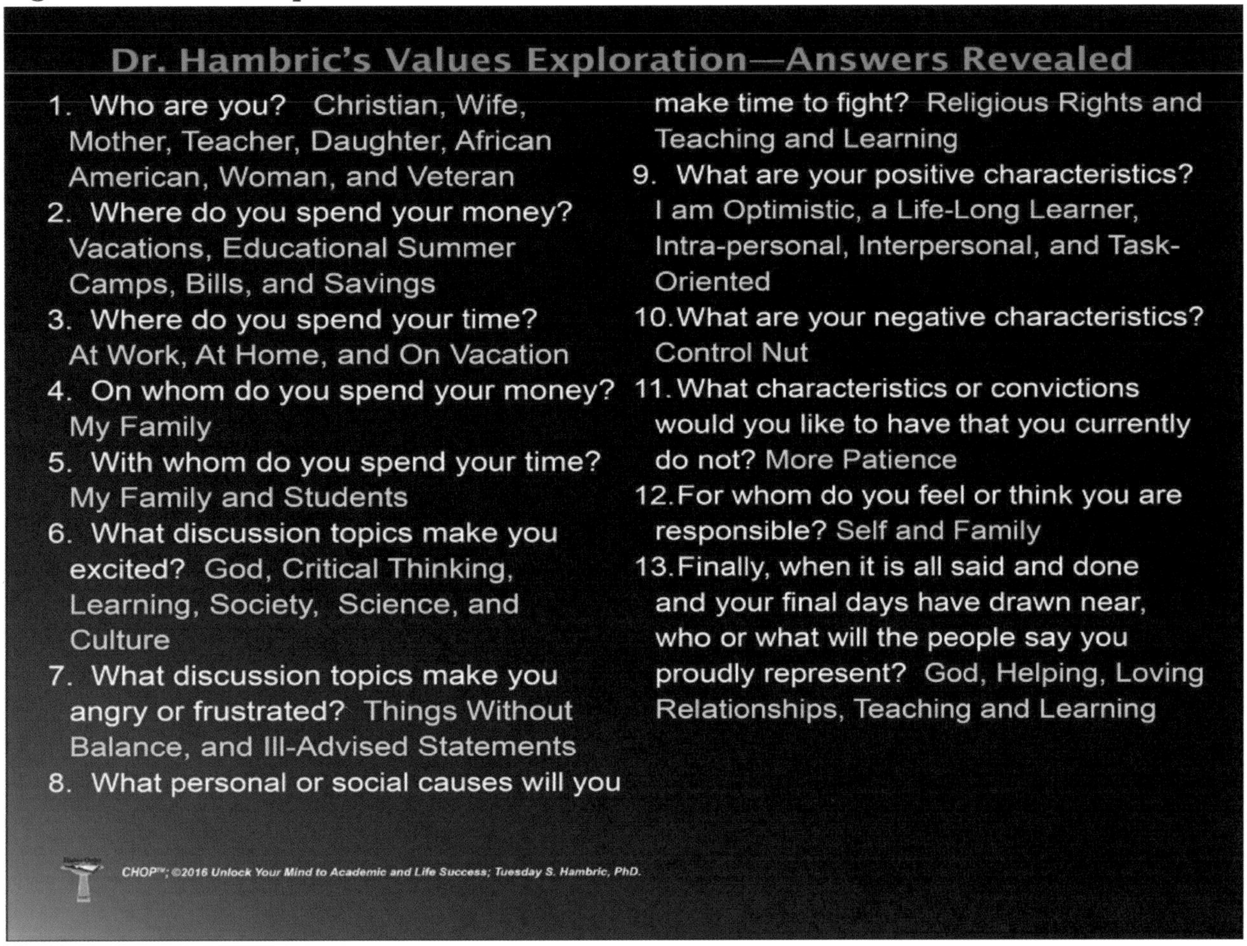

Notice in the illustration how I have highlighted my personal answers in orange. Now, look at the next figure (Figure 2.05). Notice how my answers have been replaced with "values," which more broadly or narrowly describe the values I'm attempting to communicate. These values are words that more closely represent who I am or who I am striving to be while still remaining true or aligned with how I originally answered the questions.

Figure 2.05: *Values Exploration; Answers Labeled with Values*

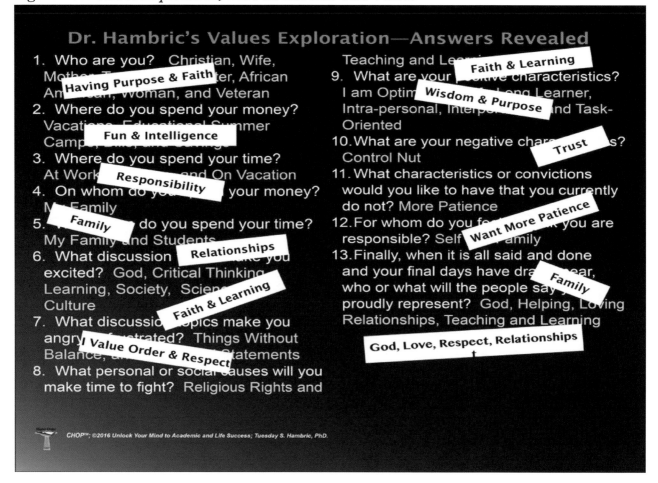

Now it's your turn. Look closely at your answers to the *Values Exploration* questions:

1. Highlight or make note of the key words in each of your answers.
2. Analyze the key terms by broadening their definitions to be more encompassing or narrowing them down to be more specific.

Now choose from the "Values: Example Vocabulary List" provided in Figure 2.06 or from your own vocabulary. Choose whatever values best describe you now and/or who you would like to be in the future (Brown, 2005). Again, use your answers to the *Values Exploration* questions to guide your thinking. Remember, if desired words from the list in Figure 2.06 are missing, add your own.

Figure 2.06: *Values; Example Vocabulary List*

"Values"—Example Vocabulary List...

Beauty	Individualism	Equality
Convenience	Team Work	Justice
Friendships	Family	Learning
Intelligence	Loyalty	Faith
Honesty	Kindness	Choices
Having Purpose	Integrity	Order
People	Creativity	Freedom
Safety	Money	Power
Relationships	Happiness	Love
Nature	Materialism	Integrity
Fitness	Fun	Life
Self-expression	Discipline	Respect
Accomplishments	Diversity	Recognition
Spontaneity	Selfless Acts	Wisdom
Knowledge	Responsibility	Technology

CHOP™; ©2016 Unlock Your Mind to Academic and Life Success; Tuesday S. Hambric, PhD.

Finally, we move on to the last phase of this exercise, i.e., the most important phase. Now that you have a list of your values, you are to create a *Values-Based Motto* that you love and anticipate using daily. Here's how it works.

Use your personal list of values to create a *Values-Based Motto*. Your motto can be for, example, one word, e.g., LOVE. If you choose this route, then each letter in that word could represent one or more of the values most meaningful to you. Let's again use the acronym LOVE. The L could stand for *life*, the O could stand for *order*, the V for *victorious*, and E for *equality*. Or your motto can be a phrase like, "To Truly Love Everyone is to Show Thy Self Approved." Here, each word or essence of the phrase can represent each or some of your most meaningful values. Either way, no matter how you create your motto, it needs to be something by which you strive to live.

In Figure 2.07, you will find a display of my daily motto. Let's examine it closely and evaluate it to be sure you have clear instructions regarding the task of creating a motto. So, let us use my motto to check for clarity and accuracy: 1) Are all my values present, and if not, is that okay? 2) Did I use a phrase and/or an acronym? (You don't have to use both. It's up to you.) 3) Did I explain the values? 4) Are the values explained in a way in which I can use them daily?

Figure 2.07: *Hambric Family's Values-Based Motto*

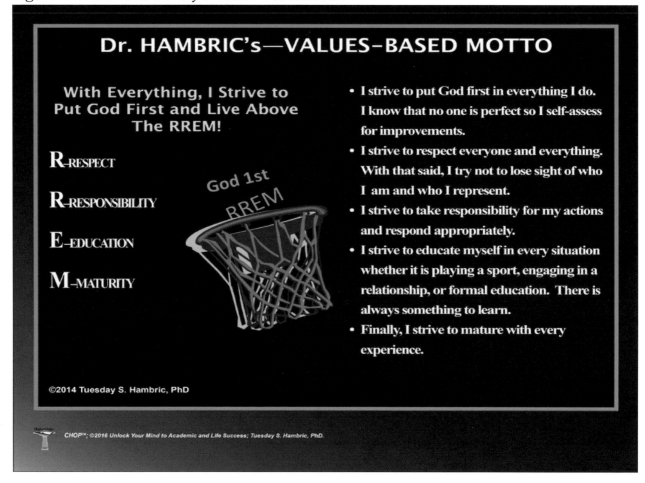

Notice how my values—purpose, family, respect, faith, responsibility, maturity, and intelligence—are all directly represented. Did you also see how love, trust, and patience are *indirectly* represented or represented by default? You see, in order to truly carry out my motto, I have to genuinely love, trust, and have patience with myself and for others. Otherwise, everything I strive for would be in vain the majority of the time.

Now there is still one of my major values missing. That value is fun. **Fun** is one of my key values that did not make the motto. Well, what that tells me is that I really need to relax and vacation more—or it is telling me that *fun* is something I am going to naturally do, and so I don't need a motto for that. ☺

Okay, now it's your turn. If you haven't done so already, go back and engage by answering the motto's exploration questions. When you are finished, create a motto that represent your values and record your values and motto here.

_____

_____

_____

So, what did you think about the *Values-Based Motto* exercise? I hope it was revealing to you, and I hope it helped to bring a little more clarity and purpose to your life. With that said, I know sometimes this exercise can bring a bit of anxiety to some students, some of whom have no idea who they are or who or what they represent. In that case, I say *no* problem. You can do what I did more than 30 years ago (and yes, it still works! ☺).

And that is, drum roll please ... *Write down a list of values and characteristics that you admire* **in others.** Then merge those values and characteristics in such a way that it creates the person you would *like to* become— sort of like, a collage of *art*—living *art,* which you created and molded *just for yourself.*

I did exactly this way back when. At 12 years old, I decided who I was going to be by watching the lives of others: my mom, my dad, my sister, my brothers, my friends—and even strangers. I decided which parts of their character I was going to embrace and which parts I was going to avoid like the plague. ☺ Thus, I created the ideal "me"—and some of you may find yourselves doing the same thing now. Finally, there is no shame in discovering *you*. Besides, I think I turned out pretty good. ☺

Moving On...

It is now time to practice all of these theories with real-life activities and practical exercises. Please revisit whatever theories you need to revisit. The more familiar you are with the names of the theories, their major components or elements, and how those elements work alone and then together, the better off you will be when it's time to use *CHOP*ᴿ and apply the concepts. When it is all said and done, you will have purposefully *Unlocked Your Mind to Academic and Life Success!*

Chapter III

CHOP® Academically

Customized Higher-Order Processing©

An Applied Integration of Cognitive-behavioral Frameworks, Self-Tailored to Develop Your Academic, Social, and Personal Skills for Success

Chapter III gives you plenty of opportunities to use *CHOP*[R] academically Chapter III helps you strengthen your academic skills using the *Super Six Theories*, but, more specifically, you will further develop and master your critical thinking and doing profile, thus becoming a *Healthy Autonomous Learner.*

MENTAL NOTE

Please keep the following in mind as you turn the page to continue your reading:

- Remember you are to use *CHOP*[R], *Customized Higher Order Processing.*
- Practice using the ***critical thinking and doing profile*** you developed in Chapter II. This is simply you deciding which of the *Super Six Theories* are your favorites and master them.
- Focus on both your critical thinking and doing profile and the PROCESS of teaching and learning. Remember the goal is to become a *Health Autonomous learner.*

Customized Higher Order Processing (CHOP®)

As stated at the end of Chapter II, it's now time to practice, practice, practice, and practice some more using all of the *Super Six Theories* with real-life situations and practical exercises. Again, please revisit the *Super Six Theories* as often as necessary. The more familiar you are with the names of the theories, their major concepts or elements, and how those elements work alone and then together, the easier it will be for you to apply these concepts using *Customized Higher Order Processing (CHOP®).*

Checking In...

As you read and engaged in previous chapters, did you notice one or more of the *Teaching and Learning* techniques I used? Yes, I incorporated several techniques like *The Socratic Method* and *Opposing View*, but there also were three others I want to bring to your attention. They are *Accommodation, Repetition,* and *Assimilation.*

Accommodation *is when I introduce new material to you, and then your brain and mind processes that material in ways that help you to understand it, make room for it, and then store it* (Siegel, 2015; Shaffer & Kipp, 2013). Now, because such information might be new or simply super-significant, I tend to repeat that information or restate it in many ways for a couple of reasons: **1)** so that your brain deems that information important and makes it easy to recall; **2)** so that you experience learned information in more than one context or domain—and that is called **Repetition**. Finally, there is **Assimilation**, which is when I bridge a connection between previously learned information and newly introduced material (Shaffer & Kipp, 2013).

Now, why do you think I took a bit of time to explain these techniques? Firstly, because I have no secrets when it comes to teaching and learning! I want you to become *information literacy gurus.* I want you to know *what* you are doing and *why* you are doing it. Otherwise, you may miss being able to discern the things that are important and relevant, and, without this discernment, you may miss the learning altogether. This is critical because, by knowing your purpose, you can better prepare for and successfully carry out the different tasks that are placed before you. By the way, these statements speak to the element called *Purpose* within the eight *Elements of Thought*.

Secondly, I shared the learning techniques with you because the more you know about my approach to teaching and learning and that of other instructors, the better equipped you will be to becoming a ***Healthy Autonomous learner***, i.e., *a learner who is self-directed and yet interdependent* (mentioned in Chapter I).
Finally, by knowing these simple techniques, *you will best be able to learn, store, and recall information when needed*. Whether it is in this class now, in future classes, or in your personal life, making room for new information by linking it to well-known information and repeating it often is only a few of *the best practices that lead to Academic Success*.

Now, toward the end of Chapter I (*Welcome to College*) I stated, "Throughout this course, you will learn practical cognitive skills that lead to behavioral skills." Well, you have done a great job of engaging so far, but now we are at the point of *adaptation* and *incorporation*. We are now at the point of *taking action that is situation-specific or context-specific*. Again, if you will recall from Chapter I, the program's formula (*Unlock Your Mind*) for success is **TP + TA^{SLOs} = Intentional Academic and Life Success.**

Well, we have achieved the TP (theories processed) part by understanding and further examining the *Super Six Theories*, but now it is time to address the TA^{SLOs}. In this chapter, we will focus on TA^{SLOs} (theories applied powered by *Student Learning Outcomes*), mainly within the context of *Academic Success*. However, I want you to think about how you would use this information both socially and personally as well.

I will continue to use a modified version of *The Socratic Method* as a means of teaching, while you purposefully attempt and then master performing your *Student Learning Outcomes (SLOs)*. Try to continue to work in this manner until you've achieved your desired academic advantage. Let's get started.

Study Skill: Information Literacy Turned Information Savvy

Workforce Skill Acquisition: Information Discernment

First things first. It is common knowledge that information is no longer bound by libraries or by the books we own and cherish. Nor is information bound by the newspapers or magazines we once piled high after reading them. As of today, information access is ever increasing; it is broad, immense, and static—and yet fluid. It is easily accessible and yet hard to find. Information is in high demand and yet always in our possession. So, whatever multimedia devices we own, or whatever family or friends we engage with, or people and businesses we encounter, we have access to all kinds of resources and all kinds of information everywhere. Thus, the library is no longer information's main hub. With that being said, the library is still a valuable resource that should remain relevant, well used, and respected. The library's unique collection of information and the expertise of the librarians are now proving to be the library's very own Bixby, Alexis, and Siri. So, when you can't find what you are looking for and you've exhausted your own abilities, seek out a librarian. They are priceless.
Moving On…

When it comes to information literacy, it was and still is imperative that we fully understand its function and its flow. We *must be* literate or *have the ability to quickly become* literate, with every experience we encounter. In other words, to improve we must be able to process the *As* or *Activating Events* of life, as explained by the *ABCD Theory*. We must be able to *process information within different contexts and within different levels of thinking*. So, I say, let's move on from being information literate—or from only being able to read and write, to being information savvy.

Okay, so what is *information savvy*? To be **Information Savvy** *is the ability to discern whether or not information or resources are relevant to the task or inquiry; whether information or resources are usable to make or support a logical premise, claim, or argument; and, whether information or resources are creditable among an audience, and/or timely, significant, or noteworthy.* In other words, whether we are reading, taking notes, dissecting instructions, interpreting various communications, writing, understanding and manipulating numbers, or simply self-managing, we will still need to be able to accurately process information not only for ourselves or our intended need but for our intended audience as well.

As we move on from just being information literate, to applying information's concepts in a variety of ways via *Student Learning Outcomes* (*SLOs*) and various skills learned, you will quickly see how you are progressing from being information literate to being information savvy. Each *SLO* and skill presented has been carefully researched to help you develop resiliency and to ensure you are acquiring marketable skills that can be added to your résumé and demonstrated as needed. At the end of this chapter and all of its tasks, you will be able to research and assess a variety of resources (information, people, places, and things) for their credibility, utility, and appropriate applications.

Study Skill: Analytical Reading

Workforce Skill Acquisition: Analysis

Earlier in Chapter I, I briefly shared with you what it means to read analytically. Well, here is a more hands-on version of that. By the end of this section, you should be able to create your own *analytical reading* strategy that works best for you.

When reading gets difficult, do you find yourself reading information over and over again? If yes, I call that *fruitless reading*. It's now time to change that. Let's use *CHOP*® along with *Stage Theory's Practicing* thinker level to help you break that habit. Now don't get me wrong. I am well aware that there are several reasons why a person would want to read material more than once; however, those efforts are *on purpose and fruitful*—not fruitless. For example, a person might read something for the first time at the level of knowledge and comprehension and then a second time simply because they want to use the information to create something or discover new ideas.

Let me ask you this: How well do you read? Do you tend to read information two or more times because you have trouble understanding the material the first time? Or do you generally understand the words but have a hard time connecting your purpose for reading to your learning goal? Finally, are you a more advanced reader, but yet you still find yourself confused when you're trying to interpret the more intense sections of your reading? Well, believe it or not, all of that may have something to do with your life filters, background noise, or lack of academic tools. Either way, what do you *do* about fruitless reading? The answer is—**you use** *CHOP®*

So, let's do that. Let's use *Customized Higher Order Processing* to chop up one or more of the *Super Six Theories* and use them purposefully to devise a comprehensive reading plan. I want you to devise a comprehensive reading plan that will aid you in becoming a fruitful reader.

Once you get started, I am going to request that you *choose <u>one</u> or more of the Super Six Theories as a guide to help you devise a comprehensive approach to reading.* But you are to be smart about this: Don't "punch the ticket" and just write down some stuff that you know does not make sense. Use this time to devise a reading strategy that will assist you in all your classes and in your personal life. Now don't sweat it; I am here to help. Before I ask you to do this yourself or with your study group, I will first show you my example. ☺ Hey, we're in this together—at least for now, anyway. ☺ The reason I express that is because at some point every pupil needs to become his or her own teacher.

I want you to keep in mind that you can choose any theory you want that best fits your unique learning style. However, I recommend you choose *Bloom's Taxonomy* and master it. *Bloom's Taxonomy* is used throughout all levels of higher education. Some instructors are using it on purpose, whereas others are unaware; either way, by mastering its use, you practically guarantee your own success.

So, the next thing you will see is a written explanation of my thoughts as I think through the task of creating a comprehensive reading plan. I want you to see how the preparation for a task is just as important as actually doing the task itself. Therefore, PLEASE take your time and examine what I have done because, by the end of this academic section, you will be doing this on your own.

So here it is. Below is an integration of three theories that I used while employing *CHOP®*. I did this to demonstrate the first *Student Learning Outcome*.

- *Task*
  - ○ To use *CHOP®* to construct a synthesized theoretical approach to reading. In other words, use two or more theories to create a reading plan.

- *Student Learning Outcome*
  - ○ *The SLO* is to use *CHOP®*—
    At the end of this task, you should be able to construct a synthesized theoretical approach to learning that leads to mindful developments and deductions in academia via ***reading***, notetaking, dissecting instructions, communication, and empirical and quantitative reasoning.

- *The Super Six Theories Used for CHOP®*
  - ○ *Stage Theory*
  - ○ *The Elements of Thoughts*
  - ○ *Bloom's Taxonomy*

The written explanation of my thoughts: I am thinking … "Okay, what am I doing again?" I then look back at the task to remind myself. I think, "Okay, I need to create a reading strategy using two or more theories. Okay, okay, I got this. *Hmm …* The *Practicing* thinker stage of *Stage Theory* is a great place to start." It is a great start because systematic intellectual self-assessment is needed, and *The Elements of Thought* have been identified as a tool for intellectual self-assessment starting with the *Practicing* thinker stage. In other words, I have to think about my thinking as it relates to reading, and so right away, I am engaging in meta-cognitions—I am thinking about my thinking. Then, I recall that *Stage Theory* tells us that the quality of our thinking directly relates to the quality of our life outcomes; at the moment, my life outcomes is to accomplish the task at hand, which is devising a comprehensive reading strategy. (If you need to revisit Chapter II's information on the *Practicing* level thinker within *Stage Theory*, please do.)

Next I think, "Let me recall the task and its <u>purpose</u> because if I misunderstand the task itself or its purpose, then my <u>concepts</u> and <u>conclusions,</u> along with all the other elements within *The Elements of Thought*, just might be faulty or incorrect altogether." So, to review the task, what I am really doing is simply checking for clear understanding, checking for clarity. I look to <u>clarify</u> the instructions, to "Design a Comprehensive Reading Strategy." I think, "*Hmm*, well as far as I can tell, the instructions are straightforward, except for this one glitch. The word, "comprehensive" … h*mm* … I'm not sure what that means" (*play along!*). So now, I am going to use *Bloom's Taxonomy* to assist me. (If you need to revisit Chapter II's information on *The Elements of Thoughts*, *Bloom's Taxonomy*, and the *Intellectual Standards*, please do so at this time and then return here.)

Bloom's Taxonomy implies that we cannot process or use any of its levels of thinking without starting at the first level, and then POSSIBLY moving through each level consecutively to gain greater insights. Well, since I don't know the definition of the term *comprehensive*, I will start at the level of <u>knowledge</u> in *Bloom's Taxonomy* and research to see what that word means. Once I do that, I will then restate the definition in my own words, using previously learned information to assimilate the new information. That way I can truly <u>comprehend</u> the new term, and I will be better able to recall and <u>apply</u> it later when needed. So, I looked up the word *comprehensive*: it means *complete*. Thus, I simply replace the word *comprehensive* with the word *complete* (Design a ~~Comprehensive~~ Complete Reading Strategy). Now I am safe to move forward because I better understand the assignment. (Again, if needed, revisit Chapter II's information on *Bloom's Taxonomy*.)

Now so far, I have explained to you in writing how I would use *CHOP®* to think through the given task. I chopped up three different theories and used them in a way that best fits me and how I would ***prepare*** to do the task—the task being *CHOP®*—to construct a synthesized theoretical approach to reading or a comprehensive reading strategy. Now I am going to show you, in an illustration, the results of my mental preparation using systematic thinking.

The results of my mental preparation: Here is my comprehensive reading plan. Even though I used three of the other *Super Six Theories* to help me think through and prepare, I will only use *Bloom's Taxonomy* to create and illustrate the final product.

Figure 3.01: *Hambric's Comprehensive Reading System*

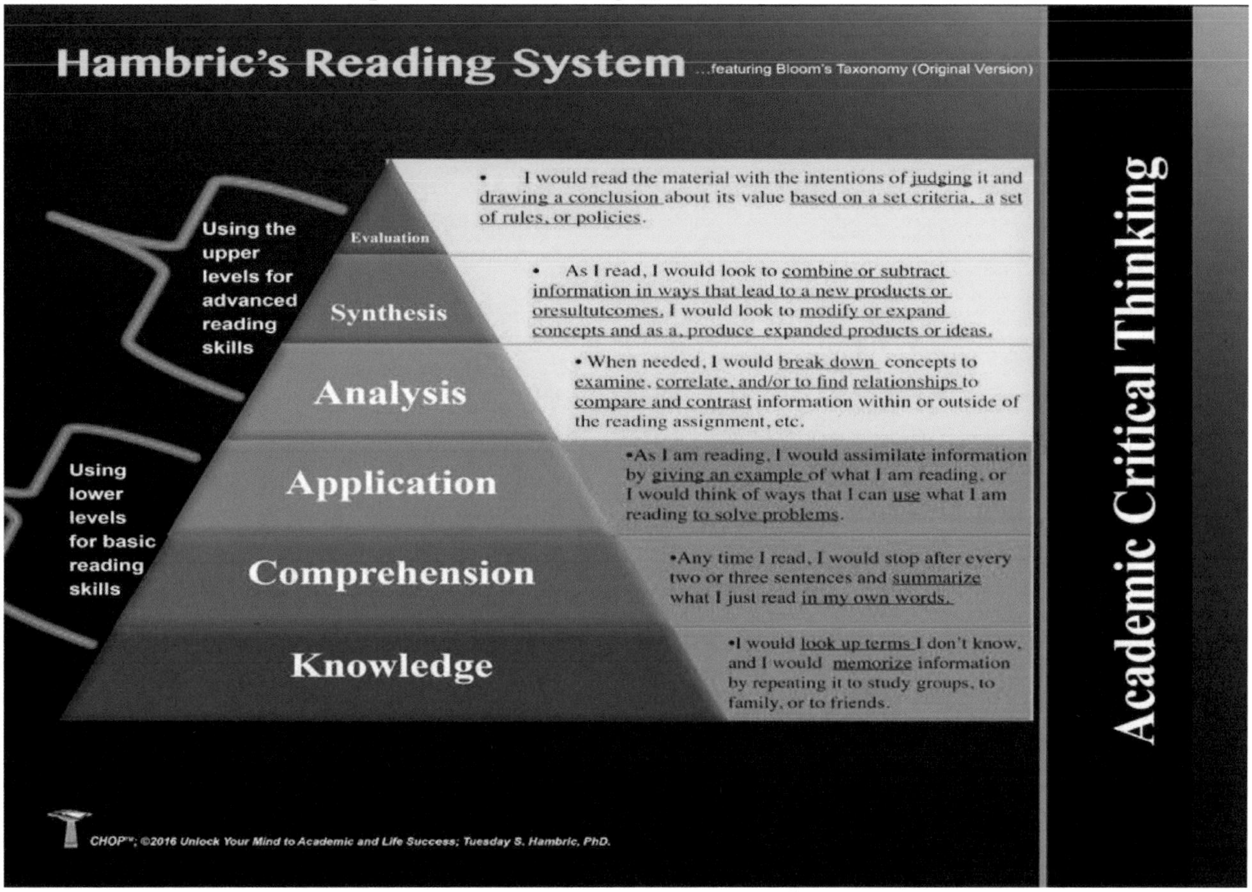

Hambric's Reading System ...featuring Bloom's Taxonomy (Original Version)

Using the upper levels for advanced reading skills

Evaluation
- I would read the material with the intentions of judging it and drawing a conclusion about its value based on a set criteria, a set of rules, or policies.

Synthesis
- As I read, I would look to combine or subtract information in ways that lead to a new products or oresultutcomes. I would look to modify or expand concepts and as a, produce expanded products or ideas.

Analysis
- When needed, I would break down concepts to examine, correlate, and/or to find relationships to compare and contrast information within or outside of the reading assignment, etc.

Using lower levels for basic reading skills

Application
- As I am reading, I would assimilate information by giving an example of what I am reading, or I would think of ways that I can use what I am reading to solve problems.

Comprehension
- Any time I read, I would stop after every two or three sentences and summarize what I just read in my own words.

Knowledge
- I would look up terms I don't know, and I would memorize information by repeating it to study groups, to family, or to friends.

Academic Critical Thinking

CHOP™; ©2016 Unlock Your Mind to Academic and Life Success; Tuesday S. Hambric, PhD.

First, it is important that you recognize how I use *Bloom's Taxonomy* in Figure 3.01 to accomplish the task at hand. So, if you haven't already done so, study first Figure 3.01 and then return here for guidance.

Welcome back. Here is an explanation of what I did. I took the overall meaning of *Bloom's Taxonomy* and understood it as a complete tool. Then, I dissected it. I took each level of thinking and understood it as its own function. Once I gained insights from that, I used the different components to create a reading system that works on all levels.

To further understand what I just stated, refer again to Figure 3.01.

Checking In...

Now, before you create your own comprehensive reading strategy, I want you to react honestly to my given example. Think about how the first step was *cognitive preparation* and then how that led to the actual illustration and its explanation:

- What were your initial thoughts when you first started reading my approach to creating a reading strategy?

_____

_____

_____

- What are your final thoughts now that you have seen the results?

_____

_____

_____

Okay, now that you have had time to study and reflect upon my example, please choose <u>ONE</u> or more of the *Super Six Theories* as a guide to help you devise your own comprehensive approach to reading. Again, be smart about this. Don't "punch the ticket." Use this time to devise a reading strategy that will assist you in all your classes and in your personal life. Submit the answers to the following requests:

- State the given *task*.

_____

_____

_____

- State the given *Student Learning Outcome*.

_____

_____

_____

- State the *Super Six Theories* **you will use to employ** *CHOP®* and to accomplish the given task.

_____

_____

_____

- ***Insert your finished product below***. It should be an <u>*illustration*</u> with a <u>*summary*</u> of how your comprehensive reading strategy works. However, you do not have to explain your cognitive preparation. Finally, you can submit your work using preferably one (but not more than two) PowerPoint slides.

_____

_____

_____

Let's keep moving forward. Notetaking is next, and we are not going to use your usual process, so I hope you'll appreciate the differences. ☺

Chapter III: *CHOP® Academically*

Workforce Skill Acquisition: Information Processing and Refinement

Let me start by saying *no*. No, I am not going to teach you how to take notes using the Cornell system, outlining, or concept maps. Besides, most of you learned basic notetaking back in high school or in some other system of formal education. And *no*, I am not going to teach you how to take notes according to your learning style. Again, it is more likely than not that you have been previously exposed to your own personal learning style.

With that expressed, if you are not already familiar with your learning style or your preferred way of taking basic notes at the level of knowledge where you repeat exactly what's being said, then you will need to find a free learning-style inventory in the library or online. Further, you will need to research the different methods of jotting down notes. Once found, you will need to pick one that best suits you. Again, you can find all of this information in a library or by conducting a simple online search. Once engaged, you will get a ton of visual examples as well as explanations. When you have finished, turn back to this page to learn more about the *Hambric's Notetaking* <u>*Refinement*</u> *System*. It is designed to greatly improve your basic notetaking and study experience (Hambric, 2013).

If you stopped for needed research, kudos to you, and welcome back. If you are already set, then that's great. *Moving Forward…*

Hambric's Notetaking Refinement System

Hambric's Notetaking Refinement System (HNRS) *is a four-level in-depth conversion of lecture notes (e.g., terms, concepts, theories, ideologies, formulas, etc.) using Bloom's Taxonomy.* It is the act of taking the definition of a word, concept, formula, etc., and progressing that word, concept, or formula from the level of knowledge to the levels of comprehension, then application, and then analysis. The key to the *HNRS* is to ensure that you have the basic information—information at the level of knowledge—accurately written and as true as possible. This will help to stabilize or to ground your understanding of the original information as you develop it into higher forms or a more evolved form of thinking.

Again, however, you choose to capture or write down the information from any given setting is up to you. Nonetheless, I do encourage you to choose a method that best fits your preferred way of learning. For example, if you are a ***visual learner,*** *that means you learn best by seeing concepts, charts, and illustrations.* So, you may want to try mind mapping or the outline method. Regardless of which method you choose, however, be sure to use *two or more colors as well as charts and graphs in your notes* (Brown, 2005). (I recommend the same thing when such learners are using the *HNRS*. I recommend that *visual learners color code their notes whenever possible to give yourself quick visual references or cues during the test.*) It also helps a lot to <u>***picture***</u> what you are studying so you can have the information grouped by color and coded by color. This helps with organization and recall.

If you prefer to hear things explained, then you are an ***auditory learner*** (Brown, 2005). In this case, I suggest you *record every lecture and then play it back for transcription.* While transcribing, you would capture your notes as is, and then move on to using *Hambric's Notetaking Refinement System*. Then, after you have transcribed your notes at several levels of thinking within *Bloom's Taxonomy*, your next step would be to *read aloud your notes for memory reinforcement and storage*. This will help commit the information to your memory in a variety of ways accompanied by a variety of meanings.

Now, on to the group that tends to be today's largest group of learners: the hands-on learners or *kinesthetic learners*. **Kinesthetic learners** *gain insights from doing or performing a task* (Brown, 2005). So, here I would suggest employing the outline or the Cornell method, so that you are capturing as many notes as possible in written form. Also, you must add plenty of examples that capture the essence of what is being communicated, and, wherever possible, *act out what you are studying*. When acting is not possible, pair up studying with a physical motion.

For example, if you are a basketball player, try putting your notes on large poster boards, which you then tape to the wall in the garage or in your dorm room. Now, while you are studying from the notes on the wall, you can also work on your dribbling skills. Also, you can increase your conditioning by performing a quick burst of exercises like sit-ups and push-ups between poster boards. It's like doing circuit training with study stations. ☺ When it is time to recall the information, your brain will link either the movement with the information or the information with the movement. As you are testing, quietly imagine both your notes and the movements for information recall.

At this point, I think you are ready to move on to a more advanced stage of notetaking: the *refinement stage*. We will use the story of *The Chattering Teacher* to help us to understand, gain deeper insights into, and apply *Hambric's Notetaking Refinement System*.

Insights: Penetrating Below the Surface; Application of Theories...

Lost in the Professor's Chatter

Ms. Rodwhite entered class as she always did: cheerful and with a smile. "Good morning," she said. "I take it you guys had a wonderful weekend?" Now the students LOVED Ms. Rodwhite because it was easy for them to get her off topic by bringing up current events. "I had a great weekend!" one student answered. Another named CJ said, "I worked all weekend." To CJ's surprise, Ms. Rodwhite did not ask for elaboration. As a matter of fact, she quickly jumped right into the lecture. "Wow!" CJ thought. "Ms. Rodwhite actually seems focused today."

Today's lecture was on the integumentary system—as this was an *anatomy and physiology* class—and Ms. Rodwhite introduced several terms in class. One term was *epidermis*. She stated, "*Epidermis* is a keratinized stratified squamous epithelium consisting of four distinct cell types and four or five distinct layers (Marieb & Hoehn, 2013, p. 151)." She then paused to give her students time to take notes.

Regrettably, for CJ, the pause was just the amount of time Ms. Rodwhite needed to get off-topic herself. She'd had a rough weekend and needed to share. "My car stalled on the Interstate, and no one stopped to help me. To add insult to injury, the bill to fix my car exceeded the money I had saved in my emergency fund."

Ms. Rodwhite went on and on about how the car had given her trouble that weekend, and the students took full advantage. The conversation went from her troubled weekend to the troubled weekend of everyone else who shared. CJ became frustrated and then simply stared off into daydream land … "I wonder if the guys are going to the game tonight," he thought.

Noticing the time was passing, Ms. Rodwhite refocused the class and gave a final transition as she quickly brought the class to an end. "Okay guys, we have a pop quiz on Wednesday, so be prepared." Unfortunately, for CJ and his peers, the teacher had only covered key definitions swiftly, without examples or elaborations. "Wait, what?" CJ thought with concern. "I am a science major, and I cannot afford to fail this class." So, CJ went up to Ms. Rodwhite after class and asked her what would be on the pop quiz. She told him to just study the definition that she gave in class and the others located in the PowerPoint online.

Situation

Ms. Rodwhite taught her class at the level of *knowledge*. This is evident because she only read from slides and stated the definitions of key chemistry terms without examination or giving any examples. CJ's past experience has taught him that, whenever a teacher tells the class to study the basics, it means they will give the class the basics … and a whole lot more.

CJ recognized that his work outside of class just became harder than it had to be: *Oh, if only Ms. Rodwhite had stayed focused and given more in-depth information in class.*

That all happened on a Monday, and now CJ had to (by himself or possibly in a study group) learn to examine the different terms in anatomy and physiology and give examples of them to be his most prepared for Wednesday's pop quiz.

To help CJ, let's practice *Hambric's Notetaking Refinement System*. First, I will give you an example. Then, you will demonstrate your understanding by developing your own illustrated example and submitting it.

- *Task*
    - To choose a word from Mrs. Rodwhite's anatomy and physiology class and then use it to demonstrate *Hambric's Notetaking Refinement System*.

- *Student Learning Outcome*
    - *The SLO is to use CHOP®:*
        At the end of this task, you should be able to construct a synthesized theoretical approach to learning that leads to mindful developments and deductions in academia via reading, ***notetaking***, dissecting instructions, communication, and empirical and quantitative reasoning.

- *The Super Six Theories Used for CHOP®*
    - *Bloom's Taxonomy*

I will use the word *epidermis* from the science class in the story to demonstrate *Hambric's Notetaking Refinement System*. But first, let's look again at Ms. Rodwhite's lecture information. In class, Ms. Rodwhite stated,

"*Epidermis* is a keratinized stratified squamous epithelium consisting of four distinct cell types and four or five distinct layers" (Marieb & Hoehn, 2013, p. 151).

So, let's look at Table 3.01. This table represents four different notecards. I used Ms. Rodwhite's words regarding *epidermis* to create the first level of notecard: Knowledge. I did that because those words originated directly from the class lecture and textbook, making it the primary resource. Further, in Table 3.01, you will find examples of the word *epidermis* refined and/or progressed into the levels of comprehension, application, and analysis, each one representing another level and notecard. Please stop now and review the table. In your review of the table, be sure to carefully orient yourself. Start in the top left corner and take your time reading from left to right.

Table 3.01: *Hambric's Notetaking Refinement System*

HAMBRIC's Notetaking Refinement System—Complex

Level of Notecard and Action Word	Front Side of Notecard Information being Studied	Back Side of Notecard Information at different levels
Knowledge To *record verbatim* the facts	**Epidermis**	"**Epidermis** is a keratinized stratified squamous epithelium consisting of four distinct cell types and four or five distinct layers" (Marieb & Hoehn, 2013, p. 151).
Comprehension To *paraphrase* or explain in my own words	**Epidermis**	Basically, *epidermis* is groups of **simple proteins** formed as **scales** to create protective **layers** of **skin that secretes, transports, and regulates cell functions**.
Application To *use* the concept to provide an example	**Epidermis**	An example of **epidermis** and its function is when the moisture in my **skin** has **secreted** and my skin gets so dry that the **scales** appear and I have to rehydrate.
Analysis To reveal and *examine/analyze* using hypothetical thinking (if this, then what?)	**Epidermis**	If the functions of the **simple proteins** do not **function properly**, then I would retain water in my skin, thus having water weight.

Now, there are a couple of facts I want you to notice in Table 3.01.

- First, I want you to identify each level of thinking in the first column of Table 3.01.
- Next, I want you to identify the *action verb* I used to refine each set of notecards to correctly align my note conversions to their corresponding level of thinking.

The action verbs are easy to find: They are located in the left column, immediately underneath the levels of thinking, and used within a short sentence. If you need more help, double-check your answer/thinking by using *Hambric's GO-TO Table of Bloom's Taxonomy Verbs* in Table 3.02. It will show you the specific verbs that are assigned to specific levels of thinking and help you sort through the notecards in Table 3.01.

Table 3.02: *Hambric's GO-TO Bloom's Taxonomy Verbs*

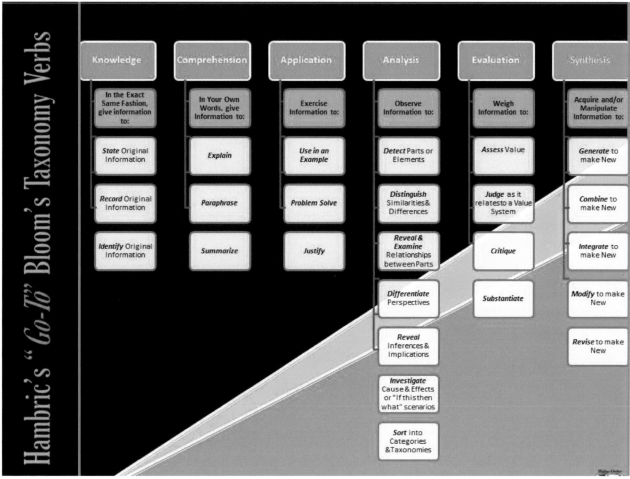

Table 3.03: *Hambric's Notetaking Refinement System: Explained*

HAMBRIC's Notetaking Refinement System—explained

Level of Notecard and Action Word	Front Side of Notecard Information being Studied	Back Side of Notecard Information at different levels
Knowledge To *record verbatim* the facts	**Epidermis**	"**Epidermis** is a keratinized stratified squamous epithelium consisting of four distinct cell types and four or five distinct layers" (Marieb & Hoehn, 2013, p. 151).
Comprehension To *paraphrase* or explain in my own words	**Epidermis**	Basically, **epidermis** is groups of **simple proteins** formed as **scales** to create protective **layers** of **skin that secretes, transports, and regulates cell functions**.
Application To *use* the concept to provide an example	**Epidermis**	An example of **epidermis** and its function is when the moisture in my **skin** has **secreted** and my skin gets so dry that the **scales** appear and I have to rehydrate.
Analysis To reveal and *examine/analyze* using hypothetical thinking (if this, then what?)	**Epidermis**	If the functions of the **simple proteins** do not **function properly**, then I would retain water in my **skin or membranes of protection**, thus having water weight.

CHOP™: ©2016 Unlock Your Mind to Academic and Life Success; Tuesday S. Hambric, PhD.

Now, a couple of concepts I want you to notice and address through examination are

- How is one level of note different than the next level of note?

  _____

  _____

  _____

- How is each notecard conversion still true to the original/primary source, i.e., the level of knowledge?

  _____

  _____

  _____

Now, as with everything that I do in my own class and within this resource, the presented material leads to some form of action, and, since I love the question, reflection, and answer process— *The Socratic Method*—let's continue with that.

By the way, great work actively engaging through examination. Now, this time around, instead of me immediately telling you what I did, let's have ***you explain to me what I actually did*** to refine my notes on *epidermis*.

Please answer the following questions:

- First, what was my ***task***? I ask this question because I want you to always stay focused on what you are doing and why you are doing it. So, again, what was my ***task***?

  _____

  _____

  _____

- What ***Student Learning Outcome*** did I attempt to accomplish?

  _____

  _____

  _____

- State the ***Super Six Theory*(ies)** I used to <u>accomplish</u> the given task, i.e., not to think through the task but to *accomplish* the task.

  _____

  _____

  _____

- Within each level of *Bloom's Taxonomy*, remember that there are specific action words that guide my thinking. With that said, state or explain the verb(s) I used to convert the teacher's definition of *epidermis* from the level of knowledge to the levels of comprehension, then the level of application and finally the level of analysis. In other words, tell me how I used *Hambric's Notetaking Refinement System* and *Hambric's GO-TO Bloom's Taxonomy Verbs* to construct a refined notetaking system.

  _____

  _____

  _____

What did you come up with? Did you discover that I used the *action* word or verb <u>paraphrase</u> to refine the definition of the term *epidermis* to the level of comprehension? And did you notice that I used the action word <u>use</u> and <u>provide</u> at the level of application to refine my notes? Did you realize that I used the verbs <u>reveal</u> and <u>examine</u> to refine my notes to the level of analysis?

So, now just think: If <u>you</u> use the *HNRS* in other classes as well, you will be prepared for success in each of those classes. You will be able to conquer most, if not all levels of quizzes and test questions. Just think, this can be done in history, science, math, psychology, government, etc. Whether you are asked to memorize information for a test or to analyze formulas and apply them to math problems, *Hambric's Notetaking Refinement System* has been a proven success. Let's look further.

History & Government. You might be saying, "Wait history, government, and math? No way!" Further, you might be thinking, "That's way too much work; besides, there are few definitions and way more policy, concepts, ideas, and movements within such readings." Well, I say to you, "*Yes* way!" Take history and government, for example: When you are given a large amount of information about an idea, theory, policy, or some historical movement, simply deduce from the given information what you think is the cornerstone concepts that define that theory, idea, policy, or movement. In doing so, you will have acquired the basic information that you need to create your note cards at the level of knowledge and comprehension.

Now, to refine that information, you simply take the information that you have at the levels of knowledge and comprehension and then either *compare and contrast it* with other theories, policies, or historical movements of that time or of some other time. Or, you can take your recorded information and look for cause-and-effect relationships within that body of information. In other words, convert your information to the level of analysis. By comparing and contrasting or identifying cause-and-effect relationships, you will have in essence dissected the material into smaller parts or meanings, thus giving you a deeper understanding of the said material. And just like that, you will have engaged at the level of analysis in *Bloom's Taxonomy* in both history and government.

Oh, wait! For history and government, we seem to have left out thinking and processing information at the level of application. Well, that was on purpose—because I find it easier to analyze first and then apply. ☺ If you want to apply government policies and/or historical concepts, simply use *assimilation.* (Do you remember that earlier term from the first page of this chapter? Good. Apply it.)

Now take different parts of the theory, the policy, or historical movement that you've analyzed and now deeply understand, and then use it to resolve problems involving current events or problems within your own personal life. At this point, you might be saying, "That's great but … uhm, how do I know what to write down in the first place? It *all* seems important to me!"

Well, I say that is a fair question, and here's my answer. Remember the word *integration?* I shared that with you earlier to prepare you for this moment and future moments like this. You are now using this book's material (*Unlock Your Mind's* material) to help you learn information in other classes, and, hopefully, you will use their material to help you learn further in this class. In other words, you will use science to learn in math and math to learn about art, etc.

Please allow me now to share with you how information from English class can be used to capture most of the key components in history and government and prepare for *HNRS.*

Now, besides memorizing dates, times, and places, there are some other things you may want to remember when taking advanced classes. So, to be clear … *Yes, I want you to incorporate dates, times, and places into your notes. But I want you to do that by capturing* the essence *of the entire story.* I mean, wouldn't you agree that an engaging story is far easier to recall than just mere facts?

Again, your question may be, "How do I know what to write down? It all seems important to me." Well, in English literature you are taught to capture six key components of a story. And, isn't the material in government simply a historical reading about policies and movements in the form of a story? And, isn't history class simply "HIS-story" of past events? ☺ Well, by using the rules from English literature, the hope is that you will find it quite easy to capture the most important parts of history and government to prepare your notes for future tests.

The six key components of a great story are the <u>resolution</u> (setting, characters, and plot), <u>rising actions</u>, <u>climax</u>, <u>falling actions</u>, <u>denouement</u>, and theme (courtesy of my son's sixth-grade English lesson taught by Mrs. Donna Blakely). As with all other primary resources, you want to first capture these elements just as they are written in the book. In doing so, you would be writing at the level of knowledge. Then, you would seek to understand this information at refined levels. For example, you might compare and contrast the rising actions to the falling actions to see if there is a direct or indirect relationship between the two. By doing this, you will be thinking and processing information at the level of analysis in *Bloom's Taxonomy*. Also, you would be searching for correlations and the different "cause and effect" elements. Now, just think about that for a second … Isn't that simply *THE* mandatory question that all history and government teachers ask … the old, "What is the cause of _____, and what were the effects of_____?"

To get in-depth answers to such questions and so much more, you simply use the six key English literature components to help you capture the most important part of your history and government lectures and/or readings as an effective way to prepare for the test. Take note, though: Advanced classes would require you to examine the personalities of characters, and to infer how the moods were set by the resolution, props, etc. By using the explained techniques, you should have a great set of notes AND great leverage when trying to collaborate with your instructor for their personal insights.

At this point, you might be thinking, "That's great, but not all instructors are friendly and approachable. As a matter of fact, some instructors will simply tell me to listen well while I'm in class or just read the book for further information." Well, if you thought that, then you make a good point. Here is my response.

Try to approach school and life in two ways: *independently* and *interdependently*. As an independent, exhaust all your own efforts to succeed, and, when success is still not quite achieved, think—*inter*dependence! Try then to collaborate with your instructor or, for that matter, a supervisor, parent, and so on, as much as you can until you get the hang of what's required. If that does not work (and even if it does), you still want to be in collaboration with other resources. Now when I write *resources*, I am talking about classmates, tutoring centers, family, co-workers, etc. By collaborating with your instructor and other resources to meet your needs, you increase your chances of success in school and in life by leaps and bounds.

Let me make two final points about notetaking:

- *Stay true to the level of knowledge.* It is important that you pay *attention* when refining your notes. You must always remain true to the original definition or concepts being communicated. You must be able to see evidence of the primary information (i.e., information from textbook and/or teacher's lecture notes) as you progress to higher levels of thinking.

- Be aware that *there can be more than one set of correct notes.* I want you to keep in mind that there is more than one way of thinking within each level of *Bloom's Taxonomy*. Therefore, when you use the action verbs in *Bloom's Taxonomy* to guide your thinking during the refinement stage, you may come up with a set of ideas that is slightly different than that of your peers. This idea is implied when you recognize that there is more than one *action* word within each level of *Bloom's Taxonomy* in Table 3.02. Nonetheless, I want to assure you that each of you should be well prepared if HNRS is utilized properly.

Checking In…

Please look at Table 3.04 … but before you do, take a deep breath. That way you are not confused by all the arrows. By the way, I grouped the arrows by color to help with clarity and understanding. Okay, let's analyze by examination.

Table 3.04: *Hambric's Notetaking Refinement System: Explained*

HAMBRIC's Notetaking Refinement System—Complex

| Level of Notecard and Action Word | Front Side of Notecard
Information being Studied | Back Side of Notecard
Information at different levels |
|---|---|---|
| **Knowledge**
To *record verbatim* the facts | Epidermis | *"Epidermis* is a keratinized stratified squamous epithelium consisting of four distinct cell types and four or five distinct layers" (Marieb & Hoehn, 2013, p. 151). |
| **Comprehension**
To *paraphrase* or explain in my own words | Epidermis | Basically, *epidermis* is groups of **simple proteins** formed as **scales** to create protective **layers** of **skin that secretes, transports, and regulates cell functions**. |
| **Application**
To *use* the concept to provide an example | Epidermis | An example of **epidermis** and its function is when the moisture in my **skin** has **secreted** and my skin gets so dry that the **scales** appear and I have to rehydrate. |
| **Analysis**
To reveal and *examine/analyze* using hypothetical thinking (if this, then what?) | Epidermis | If the functions of the **simple proteins** do not **function properly**, then I would retain water in my **skin or membranes of protection**, thus having water weight. |

Notice that Table 3.04 features the same set of notes shown in Table 3.01 and Table 3.03. However, the notes in Table 3.03 demonstrate how the second level of refined notes remain true to, or give evidence of, the *primary resource written at the level of knowledge* and that Table 3.04 demonstrates that same notion, but this time including the levels of *application and analysis*.

Now let's look further than what we did earlier … let's start with what we are familiar with and progress from there. For example, identify the levels of knowledge and comprehension, as shown in Table 3.04. Now, look at the word *epidermis*. Notice that the word *epidermis* has a red arrow that points to a particular phrase. What is that phrase? Place your answer here: _____. The phrase that you are looking for demonstrates me explaining *epidermis* in my own words at the level of comprehension.

Following that same word, you will notice that *epidermis* at the level of comprehension has a blue arrow that points to the word skin at the level of application. At the level of application, this demonstrates the word *epidermis* being used as a concept to provide a what? An _____. Finally, the word *epidermis* at the level of comprehension also has an orange arrow pointing to the phrase _____ at the level of analysis. At the level of analysis, this demonstrates what type of analytical thinking? Here is a clue, (If this, then what?) _____. If you find that you are unsure about your answers, revisit *Hambric's GO-TO Table of Bloom's Taxonomy Verbs* in Table 3.02 for the different types of analytical thinking available to help you understand. Please finish examining the entire set of notes to discover and draw your own conclusions. Take your time and follow *all* the arrows, making sure that you understand that each colored arrow will lead you to a higher level of understanding within a higher level of thinking.

- Now that you have examined the notes, what do you think? Do you think this will help you remember and learn information at much deeper levels? Yes or no and why? Submit your here.

  _____

  _____

  _____

Now, remember that critical thinking is just one of many tools you can use now or in the future, in school, at work, or at home. The more you become comfortable with purposeful thinking and converting information from one level to the other, the easier and faster critical thinking gets. If you decide to use *Hambric's Notetaking Refinement System*, give yourself plenty of time to get used to it. It really does work. If you decide not to use the *HNRS*, no problem, but be sure to add it to your intellectual toolbox for whenever you may need it in more advanced classes. Whichever you choose, you are potentially improving your chances of both academic and life success. Don't forget to add the skill of *information processing* to your résumé. Also, we will cover quantitative (to include math) and empirical reasoning shortly.

Study Skill: Dissecting, Understanding, and Prepping Instructions

Workforce Skills Acquisition: Planning, Development, and Implementation

Have you ever been handed a confusing homework assignment? Or had a professor give verbal instructions for classwork that left you confused and not knowing what to turn in? You're not alone.

Directions, guidelines, and instructions are all standard operating structures that you will encounter throughout your time in college. For some people, they are helpful tools; for others, they are potential roadblocks. Some of you will love these structures and come to depend on them as reassurance for your academic success, while others of you may dislike such structures and see them as hindrances to your creativity.

If you think in a step-by-step or linear fashion, then you may tend to use directions, guidelines, and instructions very well. But if you think more creatively, then directions and such things may cause you some stress. Nonetheless, one or more pages of compound-complex instructions can be overwhelming even to the best of us and can prove to be a real problem that escalates into an incomplete or missed assignment altogether.

Well, to avoid such problems regarding assignments and homework, you have to learn to dissect, deeply understand, and prep your assignment's instructions. All of this needs to be done *before* you attempt to complete the assignment. Learning to systematically understand *any* set of instructions not only helps you become a *practicing* level thinker, but it also adds one more intellectual tool to your toolbox for when you need it.

Let's practice…

First, I will explain my thinking as I did with the note-taking task. I will explain how I am using *CHOP®* with *Bloom's Taxonomy* and *The Elements of Thought* to dissect, deeply understand, and prep for the given assignment. Then, I will display the results of my thinking as an illustrated example. Finally, I will give you a second assignment, and you will have to do the same. So, here is my assignment: See **Figure 3.02:** *Instructions A-Information Literacy*.

Figure 3.02: *Instructions A-Information Literacy*

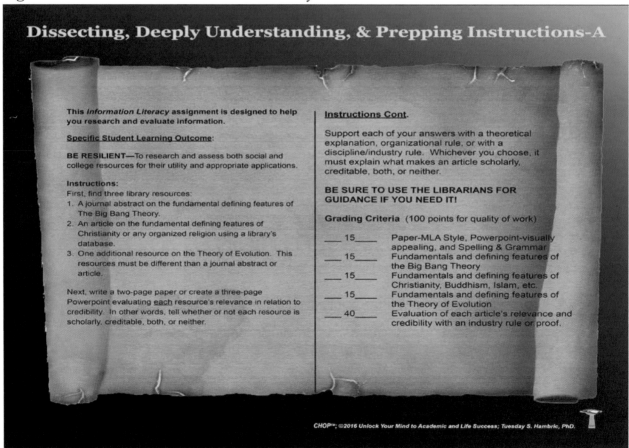

Here is the task.

- *Task*
  - o To use *CHOP®* to create a product that demonstrates you have dissected, deeply understood (analyze), and have ***prepared* to carry out** a specific set of instructions.

- *Student Learning Outcome*
  - o *The SLO is to use CHOP®*

    At the end of this task, you should be able to construct a synthesized theoretical approach to learning that leads to mindful developments and deductions in academia via reading, notetaking, *dissecting instructions*, communication, and empirical and quantitative reasoning.

- *The Super Six Theories Used for CHOP®*
  - o *Bloom's Taxonomy*
  - o *Elements of Thought*

Now that I have reviewed the task, the first thing I note is that this is a bit overwhelming—and what can I do to change that? I then think, rely on *CHOP®* and quickly identify my favorite theories to use when faced with this kind of task. Those theories are *Bloom's Taxonomy* and parts of *The Elements of Thought*. Both will help me break down the instructions and act from there.

I now have my two theories identified and fully recalled in my mind. I then create a step-by-step assessment system that I will pretty much use anytime I get a task of this nature or something similar. (As I explain the steps I created, *be sure to look back and forth between my steps and the assignment's instructions, ensuring that you clearly understand what I'm doing and to ensure I have met all the assignment's requirements*).

1. *Orienting Myself to the Instructions*. Using *Bloom's* as the source, I start at the level of *knowledge* by looking at the task *as a set of instructions*. This also serves as information and facts in *The Elements of Thought*. So, I slowly begin to use one of my many intellectual skills: I begin to read *analytically*, carefully reading from left to right and making sure to include the title in my reading. Now, because I read analytically, I am able to find good clues that reveal implied meaning and useful insights. You can do this as well. Before you move on to number two, read the task and make sure you fully understand it and what I present next.

2. *Becoming More Acquainted*. Again, using *Bloom's* as a reference point, *comprehension* for me comes when I see familiar words and/or when I redefine unfamiliar words. So, I do just that … *I read the instructions, and I literally line through some words and then replace them with familiar words*. This helps to give me clarity. Again, try this yourself.

3. *Dissecting and Deeply Understanding*. At this point, I am clear about the basic meaning of the instructions on the page, but I am not quite clear on how the final product might look. So, I *reread the instructions and begin to brainstorm concepts* as to how the final product might look. I do this by using *The Elements of Thought* and *Bloom's* level of analysis to guide my thinking. I look for *implications*, *concepts*, and *relationships* among the instructions, the grading criteria, and the *Student*

Learning Outcome. I do this because the grading criteria are going to help me know how to earn my desired grade, and the instructions will help me learn how to approach and how to accomplish the student learning outcome. Does that make sense? Good. It's time for a bit of engagement.

Checking In...

Let's do what I just said in number three: Let's look at Figure 3.02 and explore the relationship among the instructions, the grading criteria, and the *Student Learning Outcome.*

- Did you look at Figure 3.02 and come up with some thoughts on the relationship among the instructions, the grading criteria, and the *SLO*? If you haven't, do so and explain here. If you did, good! ☺ Explain here the relationship among the *Student Learning Outcome*, the grading criteria, and the instructions.

  _____

  _____

  _____

As with all of the exercises in this text, there is more than one correct conclusion. So here is ONE of many examples that can be concluded from examining the related parts within the assigned instructions.

I conclude that the instructions acted as a guide or a map that led you to, or walked you through, the act of accomplishing the *Student Learning Outcome.* The grading rubric helped you decide how well you want to do on the assignment, or you could have chosen to earn maximum points or partial points. Either way, it was there to guide your success.

Good work, and thanks for engaging in the teaching and learning process. (This is where we as instructors see the difference between our A students and our B students ... and an even greater difference between our A students and our students who make no effort at all. But I digress. Back to dissecting and deeply understanding instructions....)

So, yeah, I would venture to say that dissecting and deeply understanding your instructions are <u>**very**</u> <u>**important**</u>. As I recall from Chapter I, it is not enough to simply do the assignment or just punch the ticket. You want to learn marketable skills that you can take out into the world that will help you succeed in your career and within your family as well.

4. *Prepping the Instructions.* Here's where I rely on the work I just completed in number three: the analysis found and visual concepts formed. I use the analysis and concepts formed to brainstorm *how that might look in a finished product.* I decide if the final product will be in a PowerPoint to demonstrate a strong visual impression or if it will be a written paper, where logic, flow, and descriptive terms become extremely important to give a powerful effect.

5. *Planning the Work.* Finally, I plan out the steps and the time/deadlines it will take me to accomplish such a task. Then I am done until such deadlines approach. Here's what my prep

work might look like given the *information literacy* assignment from *Instructions A* in Figure 3.02. See Figures 3.03–3.06 for illustrated reflections that resulted from my thinking.

Figure 3.03: *The Checklist, Illustrated Results for Instructions A: Information Literacy*

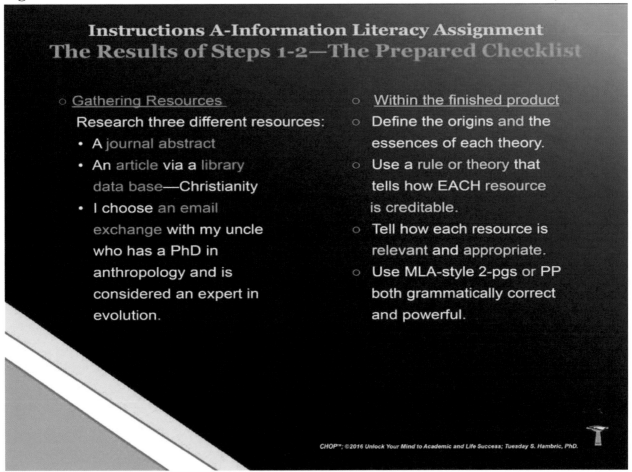

This slide demonstrates how I took the professor's instructions and made them easy for me to read and understand. I am one of those linear thinkers and visual learners that I spoke of earlier in this chapter. So, because I am a visual learner and because I think linearly, I use colors to keep me engaged and place all of the assignment's "must-haves" in order one after the other. You may do things a bit differently due to your preferred ways of learning.

Because you will have to do the same thing in the next segment, let's *engage*. So please, appease me by engaging and answering the following question:

- Carefully look at Figure 3.02: *Assignment/Instructions A* and tell me at least one major instruction that I missed placing on my *Prepared Checklist* in Figure 3.03.

_____

_____

_____

Now, I want you to study the next set of figures. These figures serve as an actual outline to my hypothetical paper, and they show how each item listed in my *Prepared Checklist* is also written in one or more of the PowerPoint figures. The rationale behind this visual outline is to ensure each graded requirement is included in my final paper or PowerPoint (see Figure 3.06–Figure 3.06).

Figure 3.04: *The Outline-Illustrated Title Page, Introduction, and Thesis*

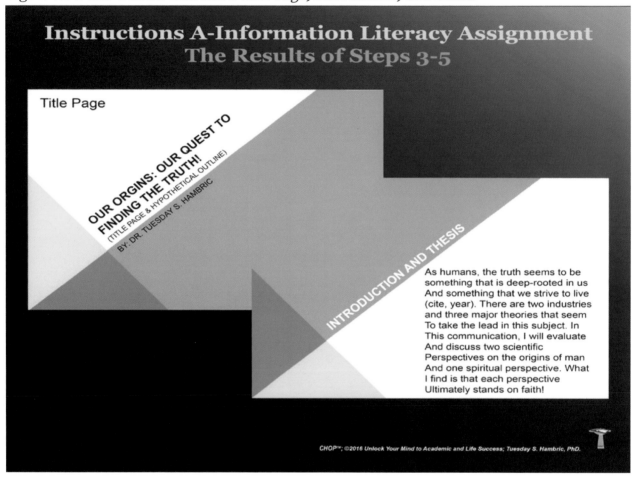

Figure 3.05: *The Outline-Demonstrated Defining Features and Credibility Statements*

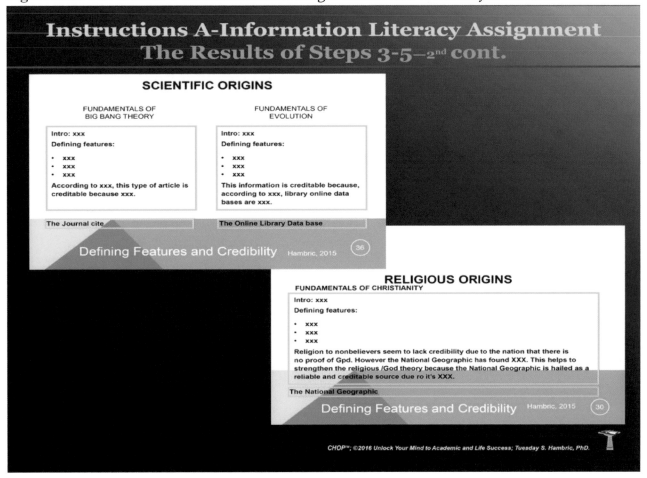

Figure 3.06: *The Outline-Demonstrated Relevance and Usefulness*

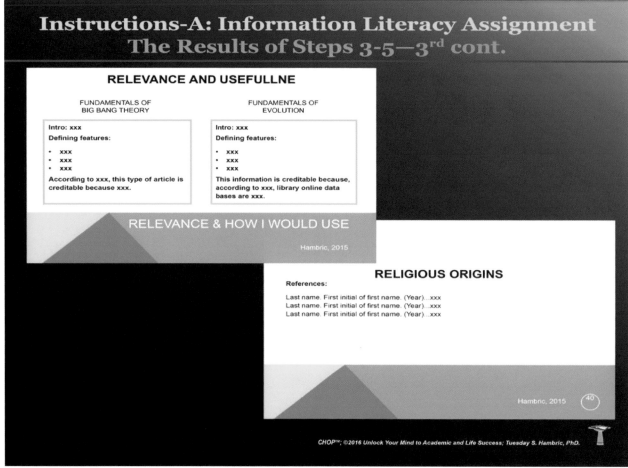

What do you think so far? Can you see <u>how</u> what I dissected and understood ended up in the *Prepared Checklist* or *Task To-Do List* and, ultimately in the PowerPoint outline? I am optimistic. Hey, good job exploring! ☺ Now, it is your turn.

Let's Engage. Here are that second assignment and set of instructions I promised you. Now it's time to get *information savvy.*

Figure 3.07: *Full STEAM Ahead: Instructions B*

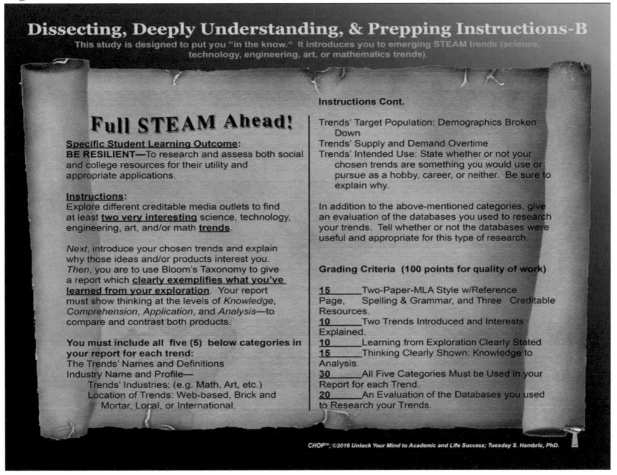

Here is your task:

- *Task*
  - To use *CHOP®* to create a product that demonstrates you dissected, understood (analyzed), and prepared to carry out a specific set of instructions.

- *Student Learning Outcome*
  - *The SLO is to use CHOP®*
    At the end of this task, you should be able to construct a synthesized theoretical approach to learning that leads to mindful developments and deductions in academia via reading, notetaking, *dissecting instructions*, communication, and empirical and quantitative reasoning.

- *The Super Six Theories Used for CHOP®*
  - *Bloom's Taxonomy*
  - *The Elements of Thought*

First, use the same headings that I used to help you *dissect, understand, and prep instructions.* For each section, you are to explain your thinking. If you need help, go back and review what I did and follow along accordingly. Be sure to use *CHOP®* with *Bloom's Taxonomy* and *The Elements of Thought* to help guide your thinking. Once you are finished with the last section, ***Planning the Work***, then create visual evidence of your ability to dissect, understand, and prep instructions.

Using Figure 3.07, explain how you would use the given assignment to:

- *Orient Yourself*

  _____
  _____
  _____

- *Become More Acquainted and Able to Explain the Assignment's Requirements to Someone Else*

  _____
  _____
  _____

- *Dissect and Understand the Implications, Concepts, and Relationships Among the Instructions, the Grading Criteria, and the Student Learning Outcome*

  _____
  _____
  _____

- *Now Prep the Instructions and Visualize the Assignment's Finished Product*

  _____
  _____
  _____

- *Plan the Work*

  _____
  _____
  _____

How did you do? There was a minimum of six things that you should have focused on as "must-haves" to complete the task of dissecting, understanding (analyzing), preparing, and fully illustrating the assignment in Figure 3.07, *Full STEAM Ahead: Instructions B.* Those six things are located in the grading criteria. If you were to include the minimum criteria in your finished product, you would at least ensure yourself a passing grade. But if you are anything like me, you are looking to excel beyond the passing grade. You are looking forward to *learning* and *earning* a maximum grade—and that is when you rely heavily on your analysis of the instructions to produce your best work. Either way, you are now ready to move forward and to succeed on future assignments. Add this—another intellectual tool—to your study skills toolbox.

Really quickly before we move to the next skill ... This is what it means to *dissect, understand, and prep for instructions*. Please don't let this be the last time you use this method. Remember, the point of the class is for you to be successful in *all* your other classes. Not only that, are you able to confidently add the skills *analyzing, planning,* and *following directions* to your résumé? I hope so. This is what great family leaders, as well as great employees, can do and what employers are looking for in graduate students. So, I just thought I'd plant the seed.

So, be sure to analytically read through all future assignments, making sure to understand and dissect them, to create a grading criterion (if one is not given) and create a *prepared checklist* or *task to-do list*.

Before the Next Academic Task, Let's Gauge Our Academic Progress...

Break: Monitoring Your Academic Progress

First things first, **please *do not ignore* this next bit of information.** So many students are afraid to check their progress at this point in their studies. It's important that you do this because, if you don't, you will have robbed yourself of the opportunity *to be resilient and to modify your efforts according to the need.*

Monitoring Your Academic Progress

It's now time to stop and check how well you are doing at this point in your studies. We will do this by measuring your **micro-grade average** and your **macro-grade average.**

So, I am going to give you a set of calculation and instructions, and I want you to use them for each of your classes. Keep in mind that some instructors will have all of your work calculated and posted for you in Blackboard, Moodle, or whatever ePlatform your school is currently using. If your work is already calculated and available to you, I suggest you still follow these instructions for each of your classes, one class at a time, to confirm your understanding of the calculations and to ensure that you don't miss your chance to make changes where they are needed.

Instructions for Calculating Your Current and Overall Grades

- First, gather your syllabi for each of your classes and then group them according to how the class grade is calculated. One pile should represent the weighted point system, and the second pile should represent a straight point system. The **weighted point system** *is when your work/assignments are categorized, and each category is worth a certain percentage of your final grade, thus having to calculate averages, then the percent of that average, and then finally adding each category's percent to assign a final grade.* The **straight point system** *is when there are no categories and your points earned are simply divided by your total possible points.* Now that you have them grouped, set them aside for now and first follow my *psychology* example. After you understand how to calculate grades using the weighted point system (for those who do not already know how to do this), then choose one or more of your weighted syllabi and calculate your own grade(s).

- Now, let's work together using this hypothetical psychology class. It is calculated *using a weighted point system*. See later in *Chapter V's "Monitoring Your Academic Progress,"* an example of *a straight points system.*

- Using the psychology syllabus here, first, look for the grading criteria and how the class is broken down into categories. Once you find it, notice how I have separated/written down all of the graded work according to the syllabuses' grading criteria.
  - In other words, when you are doing this for your own classes, if the grading criteria are broken down into categories such as homework, test, and discussions, then collect or write down each of your grades accordingly. Here is an example:

Psychology Grade Breakdown…	
Tests: 40% of the grade Notice how this class is a weighted point system.	Test One: 88/100 Test Two: 85/100 Test Three: N/A Final Exam: N/A
Homework: 20% of the grade	HW1: 40/50 HW2: 50/50 HW3: 50/50 HW4: N/A/50
Attendance: 10% of the grade	1 Absence: 90
Discussions: 10% of the grade	Dis1: 10/10 Dis2: 0/10 Dis3: N/A/10 Dis4: N/A/10
Group Presentations: 20% of the grade	95/100

- Now if this were your class, you would calculate your grades in *psychology* according to the percentage breakdown. Keep in mind that there are two overall grades in which you want to be concerned. They are
  - *Micro-grade:* A report of your grade progress, using <u>only</u> your earned attempted points and <u>only</u> your total, possible attempted points to calculate your final numbers as a weighted point system or straight point system.
  - *Macro-grade:* A report of your final class grade; the grade you would earn if you turned in all of your assignments <u>or</u> if you stopped turning in assignments without officially withdrawing from the class. The macro-grade is calculated by using <u>all</u> of your earned attempted points as well as <u>all</u> of your nonattempted points (replaced by and calculated as zeros if applicable) to calculate your final numbers as a weighted point system or as a straight point system.

Psychology Grade Breakdown…	
Tests: 40% of the grade Notice how this class uses a weighted point system. This class is broken down by categories *and* the percent of the category's average. As a result, you have to calculate each category's averages and then its corresponding percent for that section. Once finished, you add up each section's percent for a final grade percentage. Your final grade will be based on 100%. If your grade is more than 100%, it is either incorrect, or you have earned enough bonus points to place you over 100%.	Test One: 88/100 Test Two: 85/100 Test Three: N/A Final Exam: N/A
Homework: 20% of the grade	HW1: 40/50 HW2: 50/50 HW3: 50/50 HW4: N/A/50
Attendance: 10% of the grade	1 Absence: 90
Discussions: 10% of the grade	Dis1: 10/10 Dis2: 0/10 Dis3: N/A/10 Dis4: N/A/10
Group Presentation: 20% of the grade	95/100

- Your *micro-grade* would equal 72% out of 100% or a grade of C. See below what I did to compute the grade of C:
  - Tests equals 88 + 85 = 173 then (173/2) = 86.5 then 86.5 x .40 = **34.6**
  - Homework equals 40 + 50 + 50 = 140 then (140/3) = 46.66 then 46.66 x .20 = **9.33**
  - Attendance equals 90 then (90/1) = 90 then 90 x .10 = **9**
  - Discussion equals 10 + 0 = 10 then (10/2) = 5 then 5 x .10 = **.5**
  - Group Presentation equals 95 then (95/1) = 95 then 95 x .20 = **19**
  - Grade, as you go, would equal 34.6 + 9.33 + 9 +.5 + 19 = **72.43**

Let's Engage. First, orient yourself to the chart and the bullets following the chart.

- What do the numbers 88 + 85 = 173 represent? Why divide them by 2? What does the number 86.5 represent? Why multiply that by .40?

Okay great. Now that you are oriented, let's calculate your *macro-grade* in *psychology.* Using these same numbers, let's see what your grade would be if you decided to stop turning in your work without officially withdrawing from class.

Psychology Grade Breakdown…	
Tests: 40% of the grade Notice how the grade zero is assigned for all assignments not attempted. This is because you are still responsible for all of them.	Test One: 88/100 Test Two: 85/100 Test Three: 0/100 Final Exam: 0/100
Homework: 20% of the grade	HW1: 40/50 HW2: 50/50 HW3: 50/50 HW4: 0/50
Attendance: 10% of the grade	1 Absence: 90
Discussions: 10% of the grade	Dis1: 10/10 Dis2: 0/10 Dis3: 0/10 Dis4: 0/10
Group Presentation: 20% of the grade	95/100

- Your *macro-grade* would equal <u>**52% out of 100% or a grade of F**</u>

    - Tests equals 88 + 85 + 0 + 0 = 173 then (173/4) = 43.25 then 43.25 x .40 = **17.3**
    - Homework equals 40 + 50 + 50 + 0 = 140 then (140/4) = 35 then 35 x .20 = **7**
    - Attendance equals 90 then (90/1) = 90 then 90 x .10 = **9**
    - Discussion equals 10 + 0 + 0 + 0 = 10 then (10/4) = .25 then .25 x .10 = **.025**
    - Group presentation equals 95 then (95/1) = 95 then 95 x .20 = **19**
    - Grade if you decided to stop attending class without officially withdrawing would equal 17.3 + 7 + 9 + .025 + 19 = **52.32**

Your Turn. First, orient yourself to the chart and the bullets following the chart.

- What do the numbers 88 + 85 + 0 + 0 = 173 represent? Why divide them by 4 instead of 2?

- If these were your grades in the middle of the semester and your ***micro-grade*** was a 72%/C, and you stopped attending class at that time, why would your grade change to 52%/F?

_____

_____

_____

- Now it's time for you to measure your own grade calculations.

_____

_____

_____

Good work calculating ... *but now what?* Are you satisfied with all of your current grades? If your answer is yes, then continue reading the next study skills sections, *communication's assessment and interpretations.* If you not satisfied, then use a few of the *Super Six Theories* to help you come up with a plan to get back on track (a path to success). If needed, consider different forms of tutoring or cutting back on the number of school organizations and clubs to which you belong. Consider additional study time and less time hanging out. Sometimes your path to success could simply be going to bed earlier and eating healthy in order to keep your mind and brain fresh. Whatever the roadblock or obstacles might be, you need to *identify and remove it (or them) immediately.*

If the above solutions do not remove or properly address the roadblock(s), then skip ahead to Chapter IV, **Generating Motivation and ~~Time~~/Self-Management** and **The Taxonomy of Goal-Setting.** Both sections are designed to help you assess your situation and plan out a path for success.
Moving On...

Study Skill: Communication's Assessment and Interpretations

Workforce Skill Acquisition: Effective Communication

Three Domains of Learning Assessed for Visual and Written Interpretations

When I think of *communication*, I tend to consider the roots of communication, and that leads me to our senses: to hear, to see, to touch, to taste, and to smell. Each sense, when working properly, receives information from the outside world; however, it's up to you, the individual, to successfully interpret and act upon such information. Whether at school, work, a social function, or at home, you can frame or clarify accurate interpretations of expressed ideas through a number of theoretical frameworks. But to master the *Super Six Theories,* we will use the *Three Domains of Learning, Bloom's Taxonomy,* and *The Elements of Thoughts* (not excluding its *Intellectual Standards*).

As you know, the *Three Domains of Learning* explains that learning takes place in three specific areas: cognitive (thinking); affective (feelings); psychomotor (doing). If you agree, then let's further suggest that all communications are either influenced by, or were influenced by, one or more of the *Three Domains of Learning,* thus providing you, me, and/or anyone else with the framework needed to interpret written, oral, and/or verbal expressions. Further, if you will, I would like to suggest that for accurate expressions, each of us should employ *Bloom's Taxonomy* and *The Elements of Thought.*

Let's examine two different expressions or communications using the above theories. One of them we will walk through together; the second expression you will engage in on your own.

Let's Examine Together

Figure 3.08: *Visual Communication and Interpretation*

- *Task*
  - o Use *CHOP®* to support your developed interpretation of the given artwork.

- *Student Learning Outcome*
  - o *The SLO is to use CHOP®*
    At the end of this task, you should be able to construct a synthesized theoretical approach to learning that leads to mindful developments and deductions in academia via reading, notetaking, dissecting instructions, **communication**, and empirical and quantitative reasoning.

- *The Super Six Theories Used for CHOP®*
  - *Three Domains of Learning*
  - *The Elements of Thought w/ Intellectual Standards*
  - *Bloom's Taxonomy*

The first thing I try to do is rely on *Domains of Learning* to frame my thinking. That's simple enough. So, imagine me looking at the picture and asking myself three questions:

1. What do I <u>think</u> about this figure?
2. How does this figure make me <u>feel</u>?
3. What <u>reactions</u> do I have as a result of this figure?

To answer these three questions, I am going to employ the level of *analysis* in *Bloom's Taxonomy* to evoke concepts (*concepts*, if you will remember, are from *The Elements of Thoughts*). So, here is my attempt at synthesizing theories and working through these three questions framed by the *Three Domains of Learning*:

- **What do I *<u>think</u>* about Figure 3.08 using the *Three Domains of Learning*?**
  - My first <u>thought</u> is, "I think this picture is very difficult to interpret because there is very little information to interpret." To help me, I use *Bloom's Taxonomy*.
  - *Bloom's Taxonomy*
    - *Knowledge*: In the picture, there are two people facing each other. The one on the left has a thought bubble pointing to that person.
    - *Comprehension*: I understand that this person is attempting to communicate.
    - *Analysis* and *Evaluation*: In my examination of the image, I interpret it as the person on the left is formulating a thought, while the other person waits to receive his information. The evidence support I used to make such judgment or interpretation is the thought bubble. The bubble is present but empty and assigned to only one of the two people. The emptiness to me says he is formulating a thought and that it will appear in his thought bubble when the thought is actually conceived. Because the other person has no thought bubble at all, I conclude that he is waiting to process what's to come.
  - *The Elements of Thought* and the *Intellectual Standards*
    - *Logicalness, Clarity, and Significance:* I look at the picture one more time. I do this to be sure that the evidence I used to support my answer is actually in the picture and that my explanation is written in a clear, logical fashion, and is significant and relevant to the picture.

- **Using the *Three Domains* as a reference, how does Figure 3.08 make me *<u>feel</u>*?**
  - My initial feeling was frustration. But, I quickly moved to feeling comfortable because I realized I could use the theories to help me think and come up with a good answer.

- Second, I noticed the colors in the picture. Because I thought to use *Bloom's Taxonomy* to guide my thinking, and also because the colors were light and bright, I moved from feeling frustrated to feeling happy.
  - ○ *Bloom's Taxonomy*
    - *Knowledge*: The colors in the picture are orange and white.
    - *Analysis and Evaluation*: In my examination of the image, I realize that there is a relationship between colors and feelings. Therefore, I conclude that the communication between the two people in the picture is pleasant. The color white in general means pure and orange generally means bright.
  - ○ *The Elements of Thought* and the *Intellectual Standards*
    - *Logicalness, Clarity, and Significance:* Again, I look at the picture one more time. I do this to be sure that the evidence I used to support my answer is actually in the picture and that my explanation is written in a clear, logical fashion and is significant and relevant to the picture.

- **Using the final domain within the *Three Domains of Learning*, what _reactions_ (behaviors) do I have as a result of Figure 3.08?**
  - My initial behavior was in the form of a facial movement: My face contorted, communicating my frustration.
  - Second, I talked myself into not giving up and to continue the task.
  - After employing *Bloom's Taxonomy* to help me, I became alert and began to write down my thoughts.

As a result of using the *Three Domains of Learning* to frame my thinking, then using *Bloom's Taxonomy* to guide my thinking, and finally, using *The Elements of Thought* with its *Intellectual Standards* to double-check my thinking, my interpretation of Figure 3.08 is:

- Figure 3.08 demonstrates pleasant communication between person A (on the left) and person B (on the right). Person A is taking time to think, while the other person waits to receive information.
- To support my concluded interpretation, I present the colors and the thought bubble. The lighter colors are commonly known to communicate happiness. The thought bubble is commonly known for illustrating thoughts. The empty bubble shows that it is assigned only to person A. Because the thought bubble is blank, it communicates to me that person A's thoughts are not quite formed yet but will appear in his thought bubble while person B waits.

What do you think? Do you think you can use *CHOP®* to help you interpret information? As with other examples given in this book, what I have done is shown one of many ways in which this picture could be interpreted. With that, how would you interpret this next picture? Could you, like I did, support your own conclusions by using evidence directly from the picture? Well, here is your chance to practice.

Let's Engage...

Figure 3.09: *Written Communication and Interpretation*

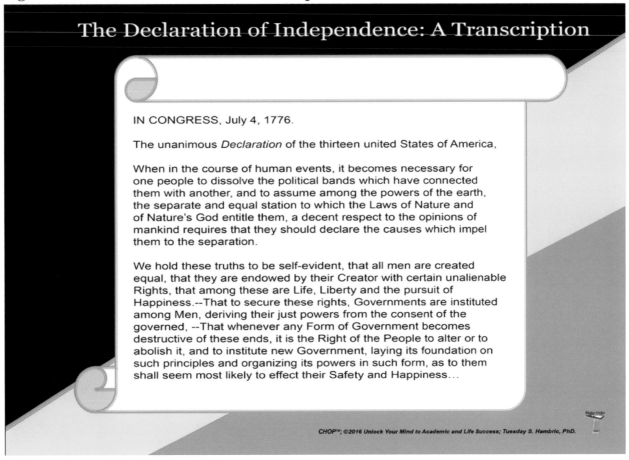

- *Task*
  - o Use *CHOP®* to support your developed interpretation of the written literature.

- *Student Learning Outcome*
  - o *The SLO is to use CHOP®*

    At the end of this task, you should be able to construct a synthesized theoretical approach to learning that leads to mindful developments and deductions in academia via reading, notetaking, dissecting instructions, **communication**, and empirical and quantitative reasoning.

- *The Super Six Theories Used for CHOP®*
  - o *Three Domains of Learning*
  - o *The Elements of Thought w/ Intellectual Standards*
  - o *Bloom's Taxonomy*

First, frame your thinking using the *Three Domains of Learning* by asking and answering the following three questions:

1. What do I think about this written communication?

2. How does this written communication make me <u>feel</u>?

3. What <u>reactions</u> do I have as a result of this written communication?

Remember, to answer these three questions, you must use *Bloom's Taxonomy* to guide your thinking.

- **Using Figure 3.09 and the *Cognitive Domain*, what do you *think*?**
  - *Three Domains of Learning*
    - My first <u>thoughts</u> are

    _____

    _____

    _____

  - *Bloom's Taxonomy*
    - *Knowledge:* <u>State</u> what you see.

    _____

    _____

    _____

    - *Comprehension:* Based on what you see in Figure 3.09, what do you <u>understand</u>?

    _____

    _____

    _____

    - *Application:* How can you <u>apply</u> what you understand to current events to gain deeper understanding?

    _____

    _____

    _____

    - *Analysis:* <u>Examine</u> what you see and state the <u>implications</u> of the written material.

    _____

    _____

    _____

    - *Evaluation:* <u>Critique</u> Figure 3.09 by explaining its <u>value or importance</u>.

    _____

    _____

    _____

  - *The Elements of Thought* and the *Intellectual Standards*
    - *Logicalness, Clarity, and Significance:* Look at the picture one more time to be sure that your answers are supported by information that comes directly from the

literature, picture, or audio (e.g., whatever source you are interpreting from at the time).

- **Now using the *Affective Domain,* how does Figure 3.09 make you *feel?***
  - *Three Domains of Learning*
    - My initial <u>feelings</u> about this written document are

    _____

    _____

    _____

  - *Bloom's Taxonomy*
    - *Knowledge and Comprehension:* <u>State</u> if there are certain words that bring forth strong or calm feelings.

    _____

    _____

    _____

  - *The Elements of Thought* and the *Intellectual Standards*
    - *Logicalness, Clarity, and Significance:* Look at the picture one more time to be sure that your answers are supported by information that comes directly from the literature, picture, or audio (i.e., whatever source you are interpreting from at the time).

- **Using the *psychomotor domain,* what *reactions* do you have as a result of this Figure 3.09?**
  - *Three Domains of Learning*
    - What are your <u>behavioral responses</u> to Figure 3.09?

    _____

    _____

    _____

    - Now, as a result of your synthesized thinking or *CHOP®*, summarize below your overall interpretation of Figure 3.09.

    _____

    _____

    _____

Great work! Now might be time to take a break. In our next section, we are going to do something a little different. So, before you move on to the *"Writing with Bloom's Taxonomy in Mind"* section, be sure to revisit and complete—if you have not already—the section on *analytical reading.* This section will help you jump right into the *Bloom's Taxonomy* and the writing section.

Workforce Skill Acquisition: Creativity and Multitasking

If you took a break, welcome back. If you did not take a break, that is okay, too. We'll move forward together. In this section, we are going to focus on creating one VERY flexible approach to writing. That way, regardless as to what the "written" need may be, you will always have an approach to writing or a writing process to get you started. Well, that's the plan anyway. ☺

Okay, I am going to give you a set of instructions and an empty picture of *Bloom's Taxonomy*. I want you to use the picture of *Bloom's Taxonomy* to help you create a writing process. You will notice that in this section you are getting way less of me. ☺ That is a good thing. Remember when I said there comes a time when the pupil moves on to become the teacher? Well, we are not quite there yet, but hey, let's try anyway. Who knows, some of you are more advanced than others and may have already become the teacher. ☺ I welcome this.

Let's Engage...

In this section, you are going to successfully demonstrate your ability to recall, apply, and transfer important skills and concepts learned from the analytical reading section to create a comprehensive reading plan. By doing this, you will have also demonstrated that the teaching and learning techniques' *repetition* and *assimilation* actually work. ☺

- *Task*
  - Use *CHOP®* to devise a universal approach to writing, one that will aid you in most college-level writing assignments (including research papers and essays).

- *Student Learning Outcome*
  - *The SLO is to use CHOP®*
    At the end of this task, you should be able to construct a synthesized theoretical approach to learning that leads to mindful developments and deductions in academia via reading, notetaking, dissecting instructions, ***communication***, and empirical and quantitative reasoning.

- *The Super Six Theories Used for CHOP®*
  - *Bloom's Taxonomy*

Here is the picture I promised. Remember to use what you know and understand about *Bloom's Taxonomy* and also what you know and understand about dissecting instructions. Use that information to help you *write down clear and coherent steps that you would take to write any given paper.* You may capture your work on the lines provided. I will jump back in at the completion of your task. *Many blessings or good luck—whichever you prefer.*

Figure 3.10: *Writing with Bloom's Taxonomy in Mind*

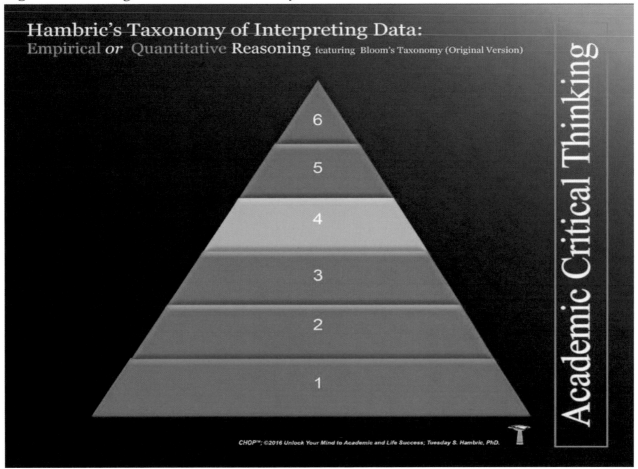

Using Figure 3.10

- What steps would you take at the level of knowledge in order to <u>prepare</u> to write a paper?

  _____

  _____

  _____

- What steps would you take at the level of comprehension in order to <u>prepare</u> to write a paper?

  _____

  _____

  _____

- What steps would you take at the level of application in order to <u>prepare</u> to write a paper? (It is this part of the paper as well as the level of analysis that can make any given paper fit most college-level papers.)

_____

- What steps would you take at the level of analysis in order to <u>prepare</u> to write a paper? (It is this part of the paper, as well as the level of application, that can make any given paper fit most college-level papers.)

_____

- What steps would you take at the level of synthesis in order to <u>prepare</u> to write a paper?

_____

- What steps would you take at the level of evaluation in order to <u>prepare</u> to write a paper, when your first draft is complete, and when your document is complete?

_____

How did you do? This was simply enough, right? Well, if you struggled with this, please do not hesitate to simply ask your instructor for help. I know that I am asking a lot from you in such a short period of time, but if my students and I can do this, so can you. ☺ Hang in there.

Study Skill: Empirical & Quantitative Reasoning

Workforce Skill Acquisition: Quantitative and Critical Reasoning

Math… Numbers… Statistics… Data… Do any of these words bring you anxiety, frustration, or fear? If no, great! But if you said yes, know that you are not alone. In this section, I will talk a bit about understanding data and then give you some examples where you can further explore that understanding. I will then give you some exercises in which you can apply your understanding in the hope that you will gain confidence for future analyses and applications.

We'll get started with brain *assimilations*, and, where needed, you will have to make the necessary adjustments for brain *accommodations*. Does that make sense? Good, let's talk data.

As I see it, *data* are just like a language: They are *a form of expression that is achieved through numbers, symbols, and text*. And, just like any other language, data—to include mathematics—cause you to think, to feel, and to behave (*Three Domains of Learning*). Some people think deeply about data by analyzing them; as a result, they draw conclusions ranging from minor decisions to life-changing decisions. Others might look at data and noticeably experience a range of emotions, like when a college-level baseball player finally makes it to the major league and sees his paycheck for the first time or when someone frees themselves of debt and is finally able to live debt-free. This person is excited because of what the data are communicating. And yet, some people can simply be overwhelmed and afraid when they first walk into an accounting or a math class; although it's just data, they conclude out of fear or from past negative engagement with numbers that math and accounting are intimidating data. Nevertheless, in all of these examples, there were *activating events* in the form of data engagements that allowed each individual to formulate beliefs, which resulted in positive or negative consequences (*ABCD Theory*). Okay, follow me here…

If my statement "*data are a language*" is true—and it is ☺—then we can better understand and relate to data by working within a certain set of assumptions or beliefs. These assumptions are **(1)** because data can be viewed as their own language, then like a language, data also have a period of time called a critical period. It is during that time that proper stimuli must be present for specific things to be learned: case in point, language. Now, if people are not properly stimulated during a critical learning period, then specific learning will require extensive training. Therefore, it stands to reason that people in middle school and beyond will have a difficult time learning the language of data, numbers, math, and statistics if they are not properly introduced and developed within a specific timeframe (Shaffer & Kipp, 2013). With that said, the words "difficult time" does *not* mean doing so is impossible. For example, adults learn new languages every day. What those words *do* mean, however, is that the adults may have plenty of work ahead of them.

The second assumption regarding data as a language is **(2)** as with all languages, there are specific rules, formulas, and theories that govern that particular language. Data's language is no different—and that's a good thing: As a result of the rules and structure that come with languages, people can be successful when they apply these rules and structures properly.

And that leads to the third assumption **(3)** *if* people are able to memorize the appropriate rules, formulas, and theories, explain them to someone else, and analyze them for possible implied meaning, while properly applying them, *then*, with a bit of hard work, they can learn *to master data*. (Or at the very least, they can enhance their current skills.)

Now after reading that third assumption, you might be thinking, that sure is a lot of "ifs." Well, you're right: It *is* a lot of "ifs." But while you were taking note of that, I hope you also noticed that each "*if*" represents a different level of thinking in *Bloom's Taxonomy*, and you should be familiar if not comfortable with *Bloom's Taxonomy* by now. ☺ (Don't you just love these *Super Six Theories*?) I will show you a visual of that shortly, but, for now, let's check in and then refocus on our intended purpose and task.

Checking In…

- I overtly used one teaching technique and two theories to help you understand how data work. I spoke of the teaching technique at the beginning of Chapter III, and the *Super Six Theories* throughout Chapter II. So, *which one technique did I use and which two theories?* BTW, I ask you these types of questions because it is just as important to remember *what* you are doing as it is to remember *how* you are doing things. Recall that we are attempting to be successful *on purpose*—not by accident. ☺ So again, which one technique did I use and which two theories?

_____
_____
_____

- According to *empirical and quantitative reasoning* section of this chapter, how are data like a language?

  _____
  _____
  _____

- When you learn to communicate in a new language, is there some basic information that you need to know? Yes or no? What might that information be?

  _____
  _____
  _____

- List the three assumptions that will frame our thinking as we remove some of the barriers and anxieties related to data.

  _____
  _____
  _____

Good job engaging. Now let's further assimilate by showing you how to use *Bloom's Taxonomy* as a tool to guide your interpretation of data and how to use *Bloom's Taxonomy* as a tool to process mathematics. Let's look first at Figure 3.11, *Hambric's Taxonomy of Interpreting Data: Empirical or Quantitative Reasoning.*

Figure 3.11: *Hambric's Taxonomy of Interpreting Data: Empirical or Quantitative Reasoning*

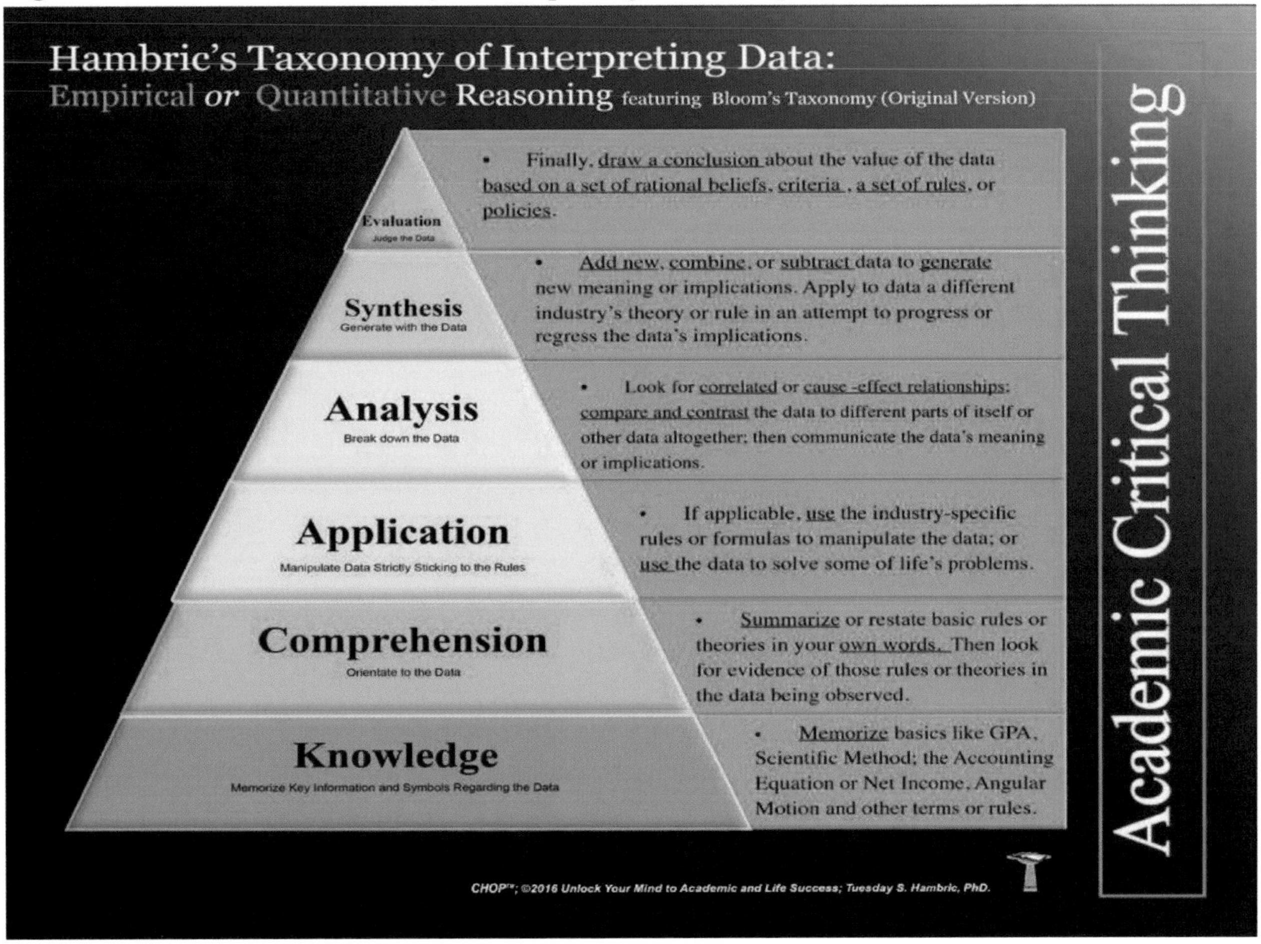

The first thing I want you to notice is that this *basic* method of interpreting data can be used to interpret empirical and quantitative data via inductive and deductive reasoning. In other words, you will be able to examine observed data and numerical data. You will further be able to use your examinations to draw broad conclusions or specific conclusions. Let me break it down even further. Whenever you are given a court transcript or information in a chart, graph, columns, or rows, for example, and are asked to draw some specific or broad conclusions, you will be able to use this method to help you do just that.

Of course, there will be times where you will be asked to go "beyond the basics." Well, by mastering the use of this method—or your own variation of it—you will find that moving from basic data interpretations to advanced data interpretations is just a matter of adding more rules, industry theories, or analytical tools to your intellectual toolbox. ☺ So again, keep in mind this is just one of my many ways of creating a system for interpreting data. You, too, can use any one of these *Super Six Theories* to develop your own method for interpreting data. This is simply a start.

Let's Engage at the Level of Evaluation in Bloom's Taxonomy…

Examine the previous figure, Figure 3.11, one level at a time. Be sure to take note of your thinking because I am going to have you compare and contrast the *Taxonomy of Interpreting Data* with the *Taxonomy of*

Mathematics. Hopefully, you will be able to determine the ease of both methods and gain just enough confidence (*a mustard-seed's worth*) to ward off any anxiety you may have about understand and expressing data. Remember, examine the figure *one level at a time* and then place your ***assessment*** of the *Taxonomy of Interpreting Data* here:

_____

_____

_____

That wasn't so bad, right? Now take a look at Figure 3.12, *Hambric's Taxonomy of Interpreting Empirical Data*. It is an interpretation example that is explained. The full explanations are expounded upon immediately *after* the image. Let's look at the image, read the level of knowledge next to that image, and then compare that with the expanded text explanation of what I actually did that follows. We will do the same thing for each and every level. Okay, here goes…

Figure 3.12: *Hambric's Taxonomy of Interpreting Empirical Data*

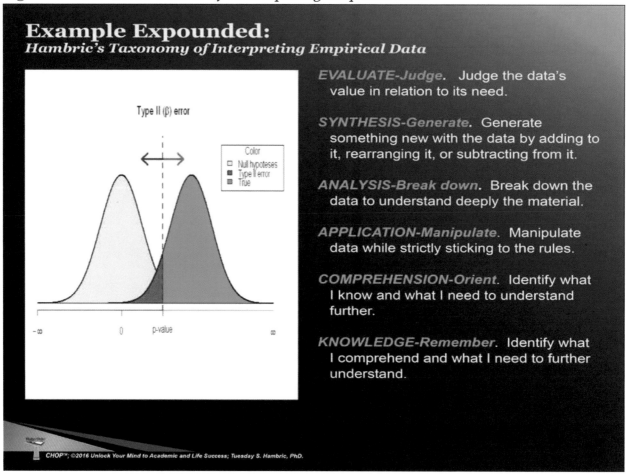

KNOWLEDGE: *Remember.* The image says, "Identify what I know and what I need to know further." So, I did. For example, I am familiar with everything in the given image, like the symbol for beta (ß). But, while I <u>know</u> what the symbol stands for, I also need to understand the implications of beta and how it interacts with the null hypothesis. Additionally, I need to further understand the position of one symbol or image in relation to the other symbol or image and how those positions represent the rules that govern beta errors, etc.

So, what did I end up doing?

- I looked up the implications of a beta error.

- I researched the term *p-value* and found out the rules surrounding *p*-value.

- I looked up the actual meaning of *infinity (∞)*.

- I looked up the term *null hypothesis* and then was led to look up the term *alternative hypothesis* as well. I did this so I can, at the level of *analysis*, compare and contrast the two to gain critical insights.

- *I put in a lot of work, but it was worth it. Now I am more clear and confident.*

COMPREHENSION: *Orient*. The image says, "Identify what I comprehend and what I need to understand further." So, I did. I am now able to explain both the image and its rules in my own words. For example, I fathom the colors and what they represent. I understand the null and the type II error and the infinity sign. However, this happened because I moved to the level of application when I *rearranged the large amounts of information I gathered from the level of knowledge and placed it in a logical and visual form that best fit me*. I rewrote things in bullet-point format and then redrew the picture, so I could add labels accordingly (see Figure 3.13). Because I better understand and am now interpreting at both the levels of *knowledge* and *comprehension*, I am able to move to more advanced levels of learning.

APPLICATION: *Manipulate*. The image says, "Manipulate data, while strictly sticking to the rules." There is nothing to manipulate here, except where I personally had to rewrite newly learned material and place that material on the chart. So, by adding my notes to the picture, the image became easier for me to understand. You can find my add-ins in Figure 3.13: *Hambric's Examples with w/ Written Notes for Greater Understanding*.

Figure 3.13: *Hambric's Taxonomy of Interpreting Empirical Data w/Written Notes*

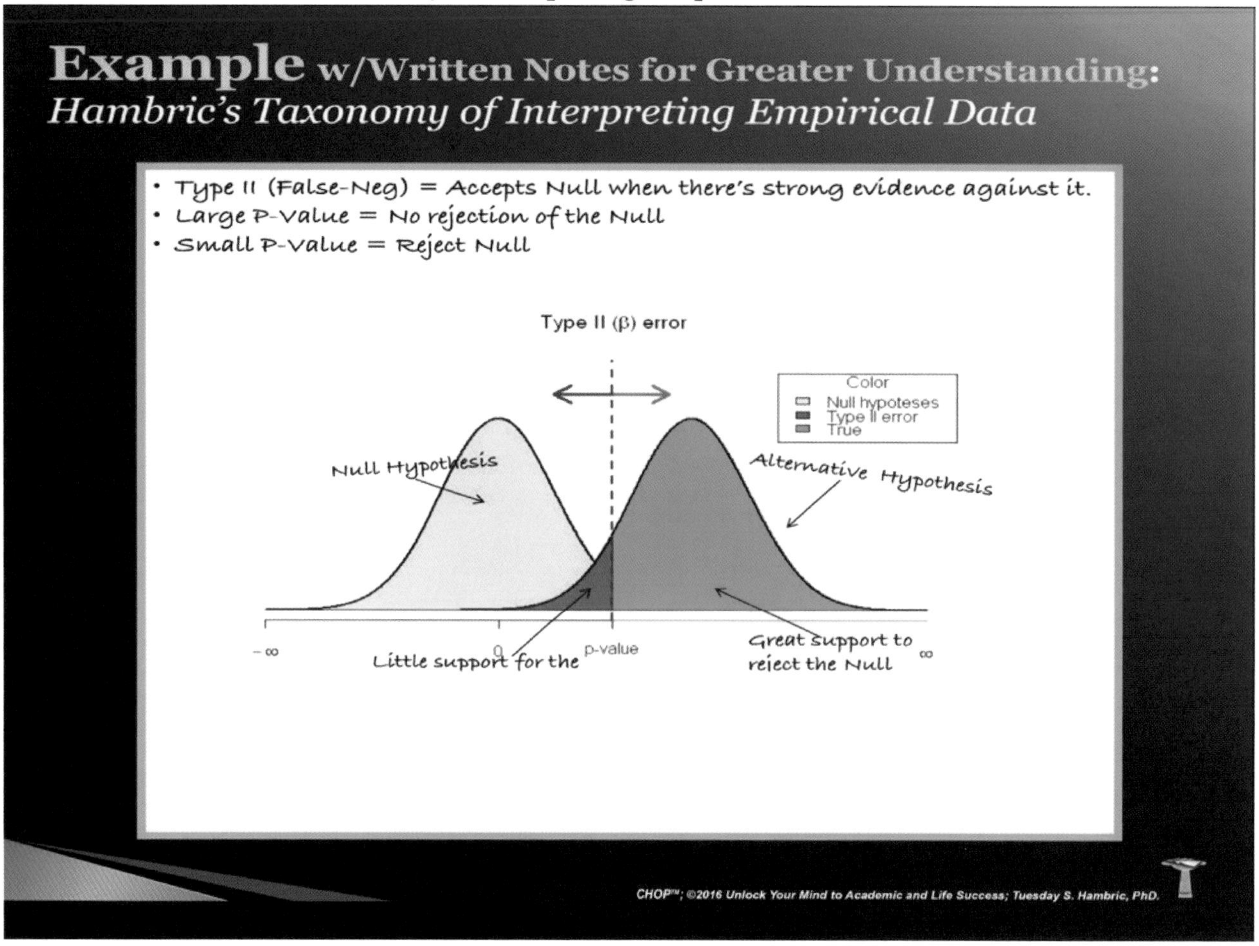

Let's now engage at the levels of *analysis*, *synthesis*, and *evaluation*. See Figure 3.12, *Hambric's Taxonomy of Interpreting Empirical Data*.

Figure 3.12: *Hambric's Taxonomy of Interpreting Empirical Data*

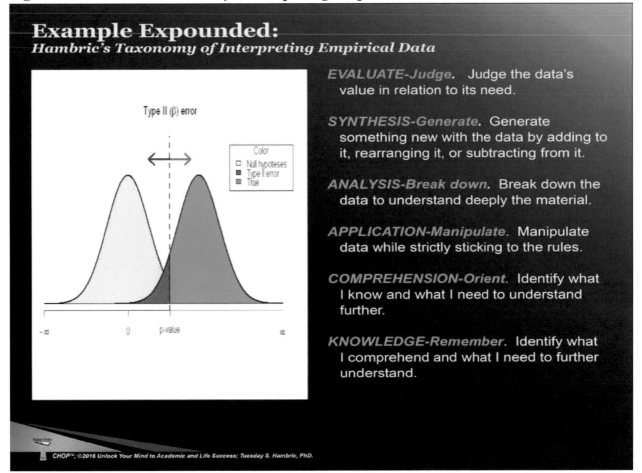

ANALYSIS: *Break down.* The image says, "Break down the data to understand the material deeply." So I did. Because of the work performed at the levels of knowledge, comprehension, and application, I now understand clearly what the symbols mean and their implications. At this point, I am able to look deeper at the relationships between the elements within the image and their meaning. For example, the green area indicates there is significant evidence against the null. Because there also is little evidence in support of the null (the red area), the researcher should reject the null. This basic information allowed me to understand that the relationship between the null hypothesis and the alternative null hypothesis is a correlated relationship. One does not cause the other, but, as the alternative shows to have greater support, by default the null will have less support and therefore be rejected. With that said, for this image to be a type II error, it means that the researcher actually accepted a false null hypothesis, resulting in the type II error or a false-negative.

SYNTHESIS: *Generate.* The image says, "Generate something new with the data by adding to it, rearranging it, or subtracting from it." This level of thinking shows creativity. So, I simply added text to the image in Figure 3.13 to generate a new understanding of the material.

EVALUATE: *Judge.* The image says, "Judge the data's value in relation to its need." So, here I am going to give my overall thoughts about the data and its usefulness…. Well, this image was great! Why? **1)** It allowed me to use my own process to relearn something with which I was vaguely familiar. **2)** This image allowed me to experience what my students may experience when using this method of interpreting data on their first try. **3)** This image gave me just the right amount of data to help me help myself to learn … and what and how I learned led me to experience *coherent* learning instead of *mimicked* learning. My self-esteem grew a bit as a result. ☺

Let's Engage…

- What do you think? Is this a method you can use to help you interpret non-numerical data? Yes or no and why?

  _____

  _____

  _____

Well, now I am going to ask you a few more questions. The purpose of asking these questions is to make sure you are constantly referring back to the intellectual tools (and in this case, the images) to help you learn ON PURPOSE and mindfully. Be prepared, if needed, to look back to earlier chapters. Use Table 3.03 *Hambric's Go-To Bloom's Taxonomy Verbs* and the information you just read regarding interpreting empirical data to answer the following questions:

- Other than identify, what else did I do at the level of knowledge to familiarize myself with Figure 3.13?

  _____

  _____

  _____

- What level is the word *paraphrase* associated with in Table 3.03: *Hambric's Go-To Bloom's Taxonomy Verbs?* **Also** explain how I used that level of thinking to *paraphrase* Figure 3.13.

  _____

  _____

  _____

- In Table 3.03, the word *problem-solve* is associated with the level of application. How did I use the information in Figure 3.12 to help me problem-solve?

  _____

  _____

  _____

- At the level of synthesis, what word did I use in Figure 3.12 to bring about additional clarity and learning? Explain.

_____
_____
_____

- Choose an action word other than *judge* from the level of evaluation in Table 3.03 and explain how I used Figure 3.13 to complete that action.

_____
_____
_____

Outstanding work! I strongly suggest you take a break now because *The Taxonomy of Mathematics* is next. I am not suggesting the break because the reading is difficult or because the work is difficult. I am suggesting the break because you just completed a lot of reading and work. So, if you need the break, take it. If not, move on to *The Taxonomy of Math*.

Welcome back if you took a break. We are jumping right in where we left off. Last, we were using *Bloom's Taxonomy* as a tool to help us interpret non-numerical data. Well, it only fits that I show you how to use *Bloom's* with numerical data as well

Now let's get started examining Figure 3.14, *Hambric's Taxonomy of Mathematics*. This figure illustrates how to process all kinds of mathematics using *Bloom's Taxonomy*. I want you to analyze, interpret, and then evaluate Figure 3.14 for its usefulness. Shortly after, you will be asked to express those thoughts. So, let's do that now.

Figure 3.14: *Hambric's Taxonomy of Mathematics*

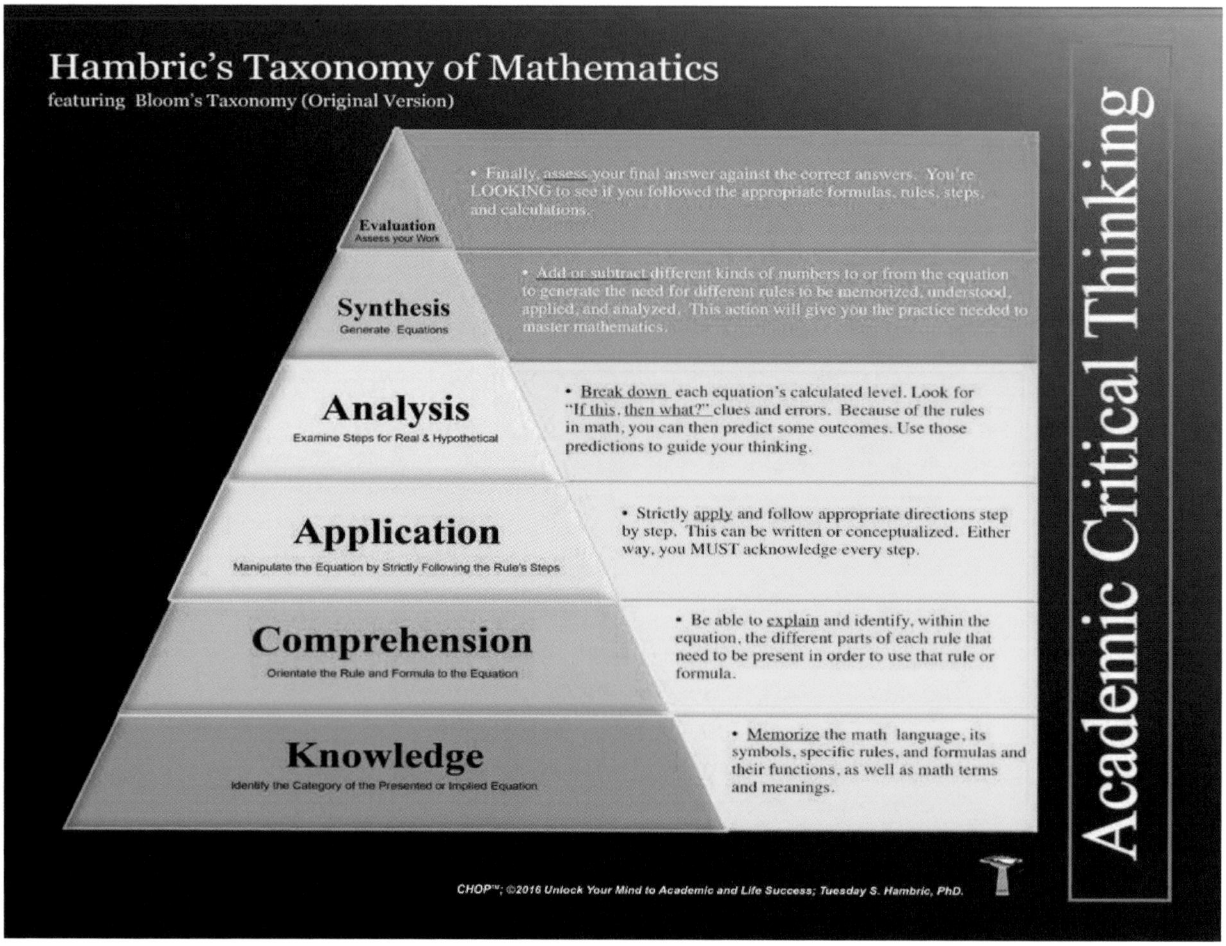

Let's Engage at the Level of Analysis in Bloom's Taxonomy…

Again, examine the chart, one level at a time. Be sure to take note of your thinking. This time, though, I want you to compare and contrast Figure 3.14: *Taxonomy of Mathematics* with Figure 3.12: *Taxonomy of Interpreting Data*. Once finished, place your analysis of the *Taxonomy of Mathematics* here:

_____

_____

_____

Good work! Now that you have spent time studying both methods, here is an example of how I applied the *Taxonomy of Mathematics* to a real math problem. As with the interpretation example, the full explanations of the *Taxonomy of Mathematics* are given immediately after the image.

We will look first at the level of knowledge within the image and then compare that with the expanded explanation. We will do the same thing for each level. Okay…

Figure 3.15: *Hambric's Taxonomy of Mathematics*: Familiar Elementary Algebra

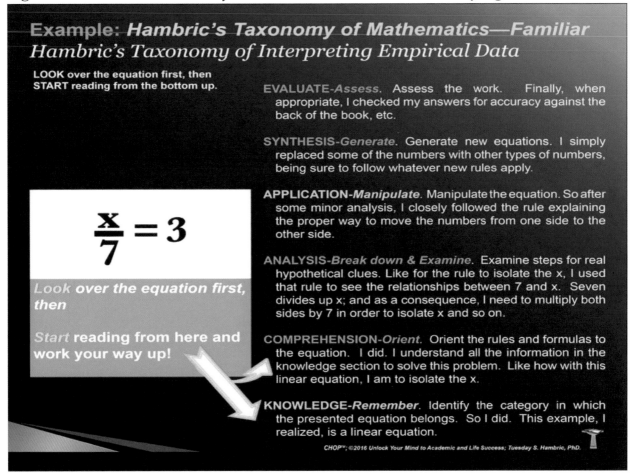

KNOWLEDGE: *Remember.* The image says, "Identify the category in which the presented equation belongs." So, I did. For example, I look to identify the equation type, and I realize it's a linear equation. I know one of the rules here is that I need to isolate the *x*. I know that, to isolate the *x*, I must apply another rule called *Inverse Operations*, which means to mathematically do the opposite operation and the rule called *Multiplication Property of Equality*, which means that, whatever number you multiply on one side of the equation, you multiply the same number on the other side of the equation. For example, if the function states that *x* is divided by 7, then I would apply the inverse operation and multiply that side of the equation by 7 instead. Further, I would apply the multiplication property of equality rule by multiplying the other side of the equation by 7 also.

COMPREHENSION: *Orient.* The image says, "Orient the rules and formulas to the equation." In this case, I understand all the information needed at the level of knowledge, and here is where my comprehension comes in. Because the current equation is communicating that *x* is divided by 7, then I need to multiply the fraction *x*/7 by 7 and then do the same thing on the other side, which means I have to multiply 3 by 7.

ANALYSIS: *Break Down & Examine.* The image says, "Examine steps for real hypothetical clues." (You may have noticed that this level is visually out of order according to *Bloom's Taxonomy*. That is because, with math, I personally sometimes analyze before I manipulate.) But let's continue…. Now that I know and understand what type of equation this is and what rules to apply, I then take one rule at a time, like the rule to isolate the x and use it to look at relationships between the elements presented in the data. For example, I see how the 7 is in a divisible relationship with the x and how, when the x is divided by 7, it is equal to 3. I use these as clues to help me further calculate the answer. For example, because the 7 and the 3 are low numbers, I may be able to make some predictions about how high or how low the answer should be.

APPLICATION: *Manipulate.* The image says, "Manipulate the equation." So, I did, and after some minor analysis, I applied what I know, understand, and have analyzed. For example:

Knowledge	$(x/7) = 3$	Original Equation
Application of Comprehension	$7(x/7) = 3$	Applying the Inverse Operation Rule
Application of Comprehension	$7(x/7) = 3(7)$	Applying the Multiplication Property of Equality
Application of Comprehension	$x = 3(7)$	Applying Multiplication Rules
	$x = 21$	Solved for X

SYNTHESIS: *Generate.* The image says, "Generate new equations." This level of thinking shows my creative side. Here, I am simply going to replace some of the numbers with other types of numbers. For example, I can replace the number 3 with the number negative 21 squared (-21^2). Then, I would apply all the same rules as before. But because I changed the nature of the positive 3 to a negative 21, I need to reassess the lower levels of thinking (LOTs), like the level of knowledge and comprehension, for new rules, a good understanding of those rules, and new relationships between the numbers and the rules. Thus, by making the earlier mentioned changes, I now have to add the rule PEMDAS (which means to compute in this order: parenthesis, exponents, multiplication, division, addition, and then subtraction) as well as any other rules that govern negative numbers, radicals, etc.

EVALUATE: *Assess.* The image says, "Assess your work." Here at this level in mathematics, I simply can check my answers for accuracy by simply replacing the x in the original equation with my final answer 21. In doing so, the left side of the equation should equal the right side of the equation. Because it does, then I know my answer is correct. If it did not, then I would redo the equation and seek help if needed. If the answers are supplied in the back of the book, I can check my answers against the book's answers. Another way I can assess my work is by comparing and contrasting my methods to the methods of the students in my study group (whenever appropriate). Further, I can compare my answer with the tutors' answers (whenever appropriate). Finally, I can always check with the instructor.

Let's Engage. What do you think? Is this a method you can use to help you process mathematics? I hope so. But as you can see, this is a lot of work, mainly at the levels of knowledge and comprehension. So, let me quickly show you an example of just how much work is needed when *you don't know how to do a*

particular math problem, and you are using this method.

Here is an example of me using this method with a quadratic equation. You will quickly see that, although I know a lot at the level of knowledge, there are important rules that I still do not know or understand— and because of that, I really can't move forward. See Figure 3.16: *Hambric's Taxonomy of Mathematics— Unfamiliar Quadratic.*

Figure 3.16: *Hambric's Taxonomy of Mathematics: Unfamiliar Quadratic*

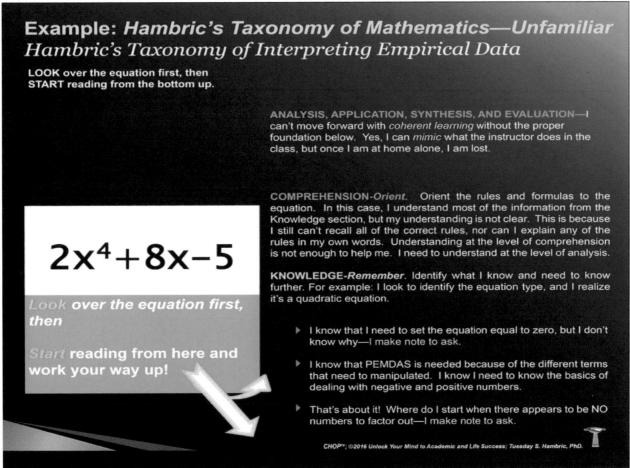

**KNOWLEDGE*: Remember.* The image says, "Identify what I know and need to know further." So, I did. For example, I look to identify the equation type, and I realize it's a quadratic equation. I know one of the rules is that anytime x is raised to an exponent, and that exponent is a multiple of 2, then it is a *quadratic equation.* I know that I need to set the equation equal to zero, but I don't know why. So, I make a *note to ask.* I know that PEMDAS is needed because of the different terms that are in need of manipulation. I know that I need to know the basics of dealing with negative and positive numbers. I also know I need to factor, but that's about it. Where do I start when there appears to be *NO* numbers to factor out? I make a note to ask.

It seems like I am stuck, but, because I love a challenge, I push forward to see what I can do at the level of comprehension. I hope that maybe I will understand enough of the rules to help me get started.

COMPREHENSION: *Orient.* The image says, "Orient the rules and the formulas to the equation." Here, I need to identify what I comprehend and what I need to understand further. In this case, I understand most of the information I stated within the level of knowledge. But it is *nowhere near enough* to get me started in the right direction. Honestly, I can fumble around a bit and actually solve this. But what happens when fractions and decimals are used, and denominators are replaced with a binomial, and so on and so forth? At this point, I realize that, when it comes to quadratic equations, I need to put some real time in at the level of knowledge and comprehension. Moreover, I need to commit those rules and formulas to my memory, so that I can coherently move up the levels of thinking in *Bloom's Taxonomy* and master this type of mathematics.

Now, do you see what I mean about the amount of work and time you have to put into learning mathematics? But guess what? I also want you to understand that, when you do *commit*, you get to reap the rewards and see just how sweet your accomplishments can be.

ANALYSIS, APPLICATION, SYNTHESIS, AND EVALUATION: I cannot move forward with *coherent* learning without the proper foundation. Yes, I can *mimic* what the instructor does in the class—but once I am at home alone, I am lost, frustrated, and stressed out. Don't let this be you! Put the time in at the level of knowledge and comprehension to coherently move to the higher levels of thinking in math.

Now, let me also offer this: You may need to use the ABCD Theory at this point to help you develop a positive mindset when you find yourself living out the Hambric's Taxonomy of Mathematics: Unfamiliar Example. Because it is easy to quit and just do what is needed to get by. Always give 100%, and, if you fall short of your goals, then you have done WELL because you did the best YOU could do at that time and place in your life. Hey, we can't ask for more than that. ☺

Let's Engage…

I want you to do just two things here because I think you got this—and if you don't, this is not a problem. This exercise should help.

- Compare and contrast Figure 3.14 *Taxonomy of Mathematics* with Figure 3.16 *Taxonomy of Mathematics: Unfamiliar Quadratic.*

  _____

  _____

  _____

- Compare and contrast Figure 3.12: *Taxonomy of Interpreting Empirical Data* to Figure 3.14: *Taxonomy of Mathematics.*

  _____

  _____

  _____

So, what do you think? Do you think you will give either of these methods a try? Or, do you think you will use a different one of the *Super Six Theories* to help you interpret data or to process mathematics? Again, all of the *Super Six Theories* are tools for you to use to sharpen your skill set or to add to your intellectual toolbox for later use.

Finally, keep in mind that mathematics and interpreting data can be frustrating **or** fun. As with all other *activating events*, we experience in life what we allow ourselves to think about these events will make all the difference in the world.

Study Skill: Generating Motivation and ~~Time~~ / Self-Management

---

Workforce Skills Acquisition: Self-Motivation and Self-Regulation

Motivation and ~~time~~/self-management go hand-in-hand. Oh wait … did you notice that the word *time* has a line drawn through it? I did that on purpose. You see, I wanted to get your attention. I am going to make two statements shortly. Some of you may believe only one of these statements; others of you may believe both of them or neither. Either way, I am going to attempt to present a compelling argument in support of both statements. ☺ So here they are:

1). NO ONE can motivate you but you… and I mean *no one*.

2). There is NO SUCH THING as time management.

First, we will explore the implications of my initial statement on motivation; then, we will explore my second statement regarding time. *Quick note*: As I explore these two concepts—motivation and time—my tone will change from "in general" to "targeted," as though I am speaking directly to you. Please don't take offense. Whether you do or do not have a problem with motivation or ~~time~~/self-management, try to use the information as self-help or to help someone else.

Motivation

I have read plenty of books on motivation, from the father of motivation himself, Abraham Maslow, *Maslow's Hierarchy of Needs*, to my most recent read by Daniel H. Pink called *Drive: The Surprising Truth about What Motivates Us*. Out of all the books I've read so far regarding motivation, Maslow and Pink's were by far the most interesting and the most relevant.

Dr. Maslow's theory of motivation talks about six distinct stages of needs or desires, which are driven by deficiencies within any given stage of development. The six stages, from the most basic to the most advanced stage, are *physiological* (eating, sex, etc.), *safety and security*, *love and belonging*, and *self-esteem*. These four phases are considered the basic stages that house our most rudimentary desires. The fifth stage is called *self-actualization*. This stage represents our motivation to become our best selves after we have reach homeostasis within each of the other four junctures of development. The sixth stage is called the *self-transcendence* stage. This phase of development represents our desire to connect to a greater cause or state of being. Further, Dr. Maslow claims in his *Hierarchy of Needs* theory that, when the lower stages of desires are unfulfilled or deficient, that stage then dominates the energy needed to fulfill the higher stages (Maslow, 2012).

Now, Daniel Pink in his book, *Drive*, presents his theory of motivation via two commonly known types of motivation: internal and external. Internal motivation is labeled as people's personal drive to achieve something; external motivation is presented as people being motivated by what others are doing or saying; BUT, then he adds a twist to the conversation. Mr. Pink adds the notion of "motivated, people types— *Algorithmic* and *Heuristic*" (2009). Pink says that *algorithmic* people are motivated by *routine actions that rarely require "off-script" feedback*, whereas *heuristic* people are motivated by *exploratory experiences and creativity* (Pink, 2009).

Now each of these theorists, of course, has much deeper ideas regarding motivation, but these concepts that I just mentioned are the ones that, in my opinion, add the most to this field of study. With that stated, however, even these two great authors still directly and indirectly focused on motivation as something that can be controlled by someone other than the person actually "being motivated." (And for a while I, too, believed that someone else could motivate me and that I could motivate others.)

Now, allow me to give a quick note to Dr. Maslow's credit: In *Maslow's Theory of Motivation*, each level of desire or need was described as being internally initiated by the person in need of motivation (Maslow, 2012). However, according to his theory, "love" and the "need to belong" place an implicit focus on *the external actions taken by others* versus places emphasis on the person in need of motivation having the ability to alter their own such needs or desires (Maslow, 2012).

Well, after many years of pondering Maslow's theory of motivation, learning and teaching Dr. Ellis' theory called Rational Emotive Behavioral Therapy or the ABCD Theory, I came to believe that the power to generate motivation comes from a person's system of beliefs and values. Motivation is generated and controlled within oneself. Again, motivation is the act of consciously or subconsciously, assessing, applying, and sometimes altering one's own beliefs to stimulate actions and reactions. The best means of strategically generating motivation is to alter and renew your own mind through self-assessment, prioritizing actions, and follow-through via your own system of beliefs and values.

As blessings would have it, just today (June 14, 2016), I found an article written by Dr. Daniel David, a professor of psychology and psychotherapy at Babes-Bolyai University of Romania. Dr. David, an expert in *Rational Emotive Behavioral Therapy*, expressed in his article some of my very same thoughts regarding motivation and the impact of conscious and subconscious thinking as it concerns motivation (David, 2014). This is SO awesome. This is good because, for so many years, I have conceived and considered such thoughts, and then to have an expert practically echo my opinions is an honor, to say the least. Anyway, here is my case.

No one else can motivate you, and here is why: According to *ABCD Theory*, events in life are simply experiences that trigger you to think and then assign meaning. As you do so, you then act or react to the meaning you've assigned to the event. The key here is *the meaning that YOU have assigned*. In other words, *Activating Events* can come with some intended meaning; yet still, no one else can motivate you unless *you* disagree or agree with the meaning and deem it so. Let's take a look at my diagramed version of the *ABCD Theory* before going further (see Figure 3.17).

Figure 3.17: *The ABCD Theory w/Disputing*

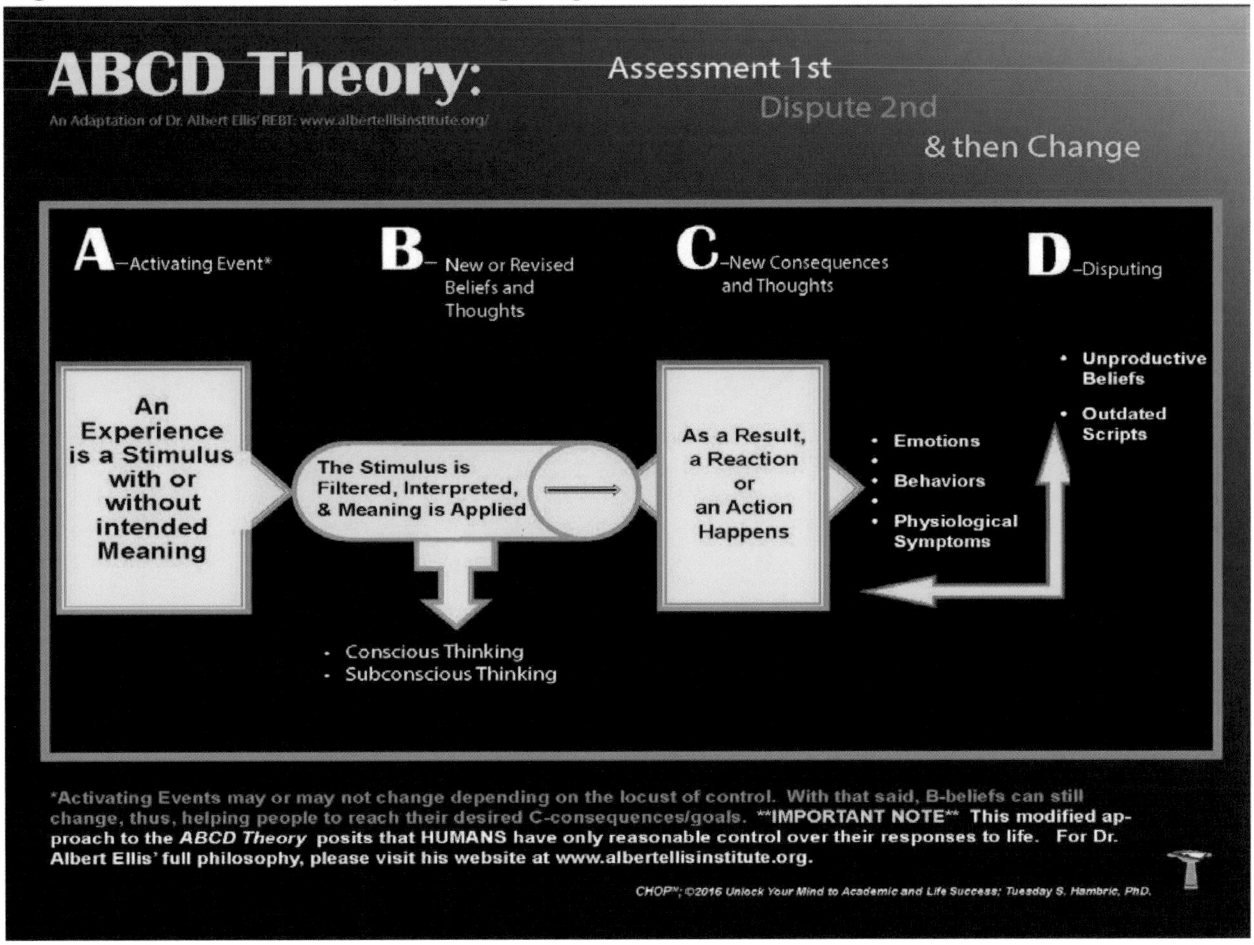

As you can see, the image illustrates the *activating event* as one that may or may not have intended meaning. Further, the image illustrates the activating event as being filtered through a person's thought processes. As a result, emotional, behavioral, and/or physiological consequences occur. So, if *you* say I'm motivated by my mother's hard work and strength, then *her* hard work and strength become *your* motivation. But make sure you understand the forces that are at play here.... Your mother's **work** is simply an *A-Activating Event*. Notice that I removed the descriptive terms "hard" and "strength." That's because both are your interpretations of what you believe best describes your mother's work. Your *conscious* description that the work is hard and that the work takes strength has reiterated or added to your subconscious beliefs that both the terms *hard* and *strength* are positive attributes. Again, both are representative of your *B-Beliefs* surrounding your mother's work. As a result of your *B-Beliefs*, your *C-Consequences* present themselves as actions or reactions; thus, *you* become motivated.

Do you see what I am revealing here? If you are closely following my logic, you may be saying, "But Dr. Hambric, this is just a play on words." Well, if you are thinking that, then you would be thinking correctly. But this isn't just *any* play on words; this is a **POWER PLAY** on words. Follow me here...

When you believe that you need something or someone, that belief immediately becomes *your* truth and also *your* confines. *Your beliefs or truths act as motivation that leads you to act or react within the confines of said beliefs:* You move toward your goals, away from your goals, or do nothing (and keep in mind, doing nothing can be positive or negative). Now, depending upon the urgency or priority that you place on your truths or beliefs, you will assign more energy to certain truths versus others, thus causing you to procrastinate on some beliefs and to feverishly work toward the success of others. This is somewhat similar to what Dr. Maslow believed, i.e., that, as you naturally find lower levels of desires unsatisfied, you would then work hard to satisfy that level of needs (Maslow, 2012). Again, with that, Dr. Maslow also claimed that you could not satisfy or concentrate on higher levels of need when one of the lower levels was unsatisfied (Maslow, 2012). I disagree.

I find that, because of the power of the mind, and the beauty of multiple perceptions or points of view, you are able to take a basic need and use that as fuel to motivate yourself to work toward greater levels of satisfaction. For example, in an experiment I conducted, one of the participants stated that she sometimes worried about having enough food to eat or whether or not they would have to a place to live due to her parent's divorce and her mom's low wages. She said that she saw how hard her mother worked and that her hard work still sometimes was not enough. She further stated the reason why her mother struggled so was that she was uneducated. This young lady said she did not want to be like her mother.

Now, here is a young woman who worried about her next meal and her shelter. Both of these worries could be considered a physiological need and safety and security need. Yet, this young lady perceived/developed the notion that both the unsatisfied and lower level needs were a burden (according to Dr. Maslow's Theory) to her. As a result of the burden, she aimed to accomplish what Dr. Maslow would call *an act of self-actualization*—the highest of all motivational levels—her best self (Maslow, 2012). She saw and aimed for her best self as a way of achieving her *physiological* and *safety and security* needs. In essence, she used demanding worries as fuel to generate motivation to graduate from college.

I believe this is the power of the mind being **resilient**. My participant could have given her power to *her circumstances*. For example, she could have believed that she had to drop out of school and get a job to help her mother right then and there, thus falling victim to a narrow confine, caged by a rigid set of beliefs. Instead, she believed that getting an education would better serve her and her family in the long run. As a result of that belief, she is now in a position to help her mother go back to school and learn to take better care of herself. My participant decided to *retain control of her power by broadening her beliefs, therefore her confines and her opportunities and, thus, her circumstances*. She chose to identify and function from a perspective that generated victory versus a perspective that would generate defeat.

What about classroom settings? How does all this have an impact on learning? Think about your professors for a moment. If you think that it is your professor's job to motivate you, you are sadly mistaken. And, for all of my colleagues out there who think they can motivate students, they, too, are sadly mistaken. Here is the danger in such thinking. Professors who think their job is to motivate you are actually *taking away your responsibility and giving it to themselves as a sense of responsibility, authority, and power*. Professors who think it is their job to motivate you, don't realize that they have adopted a false sense of responsibility, authority, and power.

Your professors have *no* control over whether or not you will enjoy what they present. They are attempting, however, to do their part of the teaching and learning process but your part as well, while you sit back waiting on "_____" (fill in the blank). These professors tend to burn themselves out when their students do not achieve their desired results. They blame themselves and then eventually become dull, frustrated, and sometimes angry teachers. But this is just one-half of the story.

When you relinquish *your* power to your professors by expecting them to think they can motivate you, you stop acting as a *Generator*. A ***Generator*** *is someone who identifies or discovers the present energy and then utilizes that energy to form new opportunities for success.* Basically, it is someone who is ***resilient.***

According to one of the leading student success authors, Skip Downing, if you have relinquished your power to your professors and let them think they can motivate you, you are acting instead as a victim (Downing, 2012). A ***Victim*** *is someone who runs away from ownership and responsibility and blames others for his or her failures.* If this is you, then you often make up excuses for not following through on your responsibilities; as a result of your faulty beliefs, you are choosing to be a victim.

Can you see the danger in such thinking? When the teachers act contrary to what you believe, discomfort or stress is induced in you and then vice versa. When professors assume false power, they burn out trying to reach a goal to control students' motivation—a goal that was doomed to fail in the first place. Teachers can't control students, and students have no control over teachers.

In essence, what both groups have done is misconstrued their own responsibility regarding the teaching and learning process and created a teaching and learning environment that is prone to failure.

Well, if all of that is true, then what should we do to create success in the classroom, and what is the teacher's responsibility? I'm glad you asked. Believe it or not, there is a simple answer to that question: We—teachers and students—are to bring our best selves to the teaching and learning environment. Each one of us is to do 100% of what we can do to monitor, assess, and alter our own belief system where needed. Remember, your beliefs are what drive you as well as what confines you. So, please work hard to give your different beliefs different priorities, which will more appropriately shape the boundaries from which you work and play.

So, ***for teachers***: We are to present relevant and applicable content via methods that deliver the highest rate of success. This technique is presenting statistical *best practices*. That means that we, as professors, have to stay abreast of the latest research *so that, as students, information, and technology change, we, as professors, should change as well (within reason).* We have to present *best practices*. It's our job.

Now, needless to say, a happy professor brings about a happy classroom. But what happens if and when you, as a student, do not get a happy professor? Do you play the ***Victim***? This is where you, the student, have yet another opportunity to give 100%.

Your job ***as a student*** is to mindfully and intentionally monitor and maintain your beliefs. If you find that something in class is not working for you, then it is your job to be *assertive*—assertive with yourself first, that is. It is your responsibility to think like a participant—like a ***Generator***. Remember, the power to generate rests within ***your*** beliefs. You have to see your circumstances from a perspective that generates victory versus a perspective that generates defeat. So, if clarification from the instructor is needed, seek it. If tutoring is needed, seek it. If group study is better for you, seek it. ***Seeing how and where you can*** *generate the energy that brings about positive thoughts allows you to find out that success is right around the corner.*

In summary, no one else can motivate you. It is <u>you</u> who decide, by your prioritized beliefs, what meaning to assign to any given situation. Hence, you decide whether or not something or someone is motivating. It is critical that you understand this **POWER PLAY ON WORDS.** Because, if you do not take ownership of your actions and learn to renew your mind, you lose the ability to discern, change, prioritize, and maintain your own belief system; thus, you are left at the mercy of those to whom you have granted your power.

Checking In...

- What is your overall reaction to the presented case on motivation?

_____

_____

_____

I hope by now, you understand the social science behind motivation. In this section, the *Student Learning Outcome* for the end of this lesson is that you will be able to self-motivate and self-regulate via reasoning. Let's put that to the test right now.

The following reading is an *Insights: Penetrating Below the Surface* scenario. I want you to use your *Values-Based Motto* and *The Elements of Thought* to explain how you would personally motivate **and** regulate yourself in the given scenario. My advice would be to also use the *ABCD Theory* or the *Three Domains of Learning* to guide your thinking. But of course, you can use ANY of the additional *Super Six Theories* along with your *Values-Based Motto* to accomplish this task.

Insights: Penetrating below the Surface: Application of Theories...

Living Resiliently

You are now a freshman in college, and life could not be more different than you had expected. You are taking five classes ... and each teacher acts as though *his or her* class is the only one you're taking. Right now you have three exams and a five-page paper due in one week. On top of that, the fencing coach scheduled a mandatory team sleepover (to promote team-building efforts) at his house. The sleepover starts at 10 p.m. the day before your assignment, and exams are due and last until 7 a.m. the next morning. To make matters worse, you have made no efforts to meet anyone new outside of your teammates ... who, incidentally, are not taking any of the same classes as you. Again, you have one week to finish all your work, but so far all you can think about are your parents' high expectations for your success, the mounds of work and research you have to do—and the upcoming party.

- *Task*
    a. To use your *Values-Based Motto* and *The Elements of Thought* to explain how you would personally motivate and regulate yourself to complete all homework and studying—and make the team's sleepover.

- *Student Learning Outcome*
  a. *1st SLO is to use Values-Based Reasoning*
     At the end of this task, you should be able to communicate via oral, visual, and/or written means, a self-developed values system that ethically frames personal decisions.

  b. *2nd SLO is to use Self-Manage & Teamwork*
     At the end of this task, you should be able to use meta-cognitive skills and *The Elements of Thought* to achieve **individual** and/or as a team cognitive, emotional, and behavioral success.
- *The Super Six Theories Used for CHOP®*
  a. *Values-Based Motto* and *The Elements of Thought*

Hint: While you attempt to accomplish the earlier mentioned task, use the same approach or method that we used in the *Dissecting, Deeply Understanding, and Prepping Instructions* section. That should help guide you through this process and ensure that you completely address the task below.

_____

_____

_____

How did you do? Are you able to confidently add the skills of self-motivation and self-regulation via reasoning to your résumé? The key here is *via reasoning*. Anyone can react, but can *you* mindfully and reasonably act when it's needed? That is what leaders do; that is what families need, and that is what employers are expecting from family members or students who graduate. Just thought I would plant the seed once again. Now on to my second statement: *there is no such thing as time-management.*

~~Time~~/Self-Management

The claim, "there is no such thing as time-management," is an easy one to present. Can you stop time, speed it up, or slow it down? No, right? Then, I think it is safe to claim there is no such thing as time-management. To manage time, we would need to influence time or change it—and we cannot do this. With that said, why do we find ourselves making statements like, "I just did *not* have enough time or time got away from me"? Both of these statements are ***Victim*** statements (Downing, 2012).

So, why is this important? Well, we established the notion that, if you believe that someone else can motivate you, then that would be you giving *your* power to that person, so the idea that you "did not have enough time" or that "time ran away from you" personifies time and empowers it ... thus making *time* the reason you missed your deadlines—and not you. Again, you are giving away your ability and responsibility to be in control of your actions. Time becomes the thing you blame. It would be better for you to take responsibility for your actions because, by doing so, you properly place the responsibility to change on you, thus empowering and claiming yourself capable of making plans to avoid such situations in the future.

Now, add language to this conversation. Language is one of many ways in which we reveal our *B-Beliefs*. As long as you use language that avoids or keeps you from taking responsibility, then you will continue to develop beliefs that confine and restrict you to *Victim* cognitions, emotions, and behaviors or *C-Consequences*. **You have to change your language**—and instead of saying "time-management," say, "*self-management.*" But, of course, time still would be one of many frameworks you'd use to govern yourself.

Now don't get me wrong ... I know this will be a difficult shift. I still find myself saying "time-management" because it is a part of my upbringing and larger culture. So now, when I do slip and say, "time-management," I strive to make a mental note that I really *mean* self-management.

Making the Shift...

Self-management outplays the idea of ~~time~~-management. The idea of self-management sets the tone: It communicates right away that *you* have power, and *you* are responsible for your successes and failures. Remember I stated in Chapter I that every chapter promotes taking ownership of your life's outcomes? Well, as you can see, the subject of ~~time~~/self-management is no different. For example, *generators* and *victims* can both share this belief: "I did not have enough time to finish my project." However, *Generators* can take that belief and say, "I need to better plan my activities in the future so I can finish assignments within the time allowed." In other words, Generators use their power and take responsibility to assess the situation, identify that time is simply a framework in which to manage themselves, and then plan accordingly. *Victims* can take that belief, "I did not have enough time to finish my project," and own it without critical thought, therefore, hardwiring into their brains the idea that "having little time" is the reason for their incomplete work. And just like that, time becomes the guilty party.

If this is you, you may want to consider changing. You may want to consider adopting the *Generator's* mindset, which can be accomplished by strategically using *CHOP®* and the *Super Six Theories*.

Optimizing Self-Management within a Framework of Time

When it comes to self-management, several elements are at play here. Still, there are three theories that not only account for these elements but that integrate very well to bring about optimized self-management within a framework of time. Now for self-management, we must keep in mind the *Three Domains of Learning* (see Figure 3.18).

Figure 3.18: *The Three Domains of Learning*

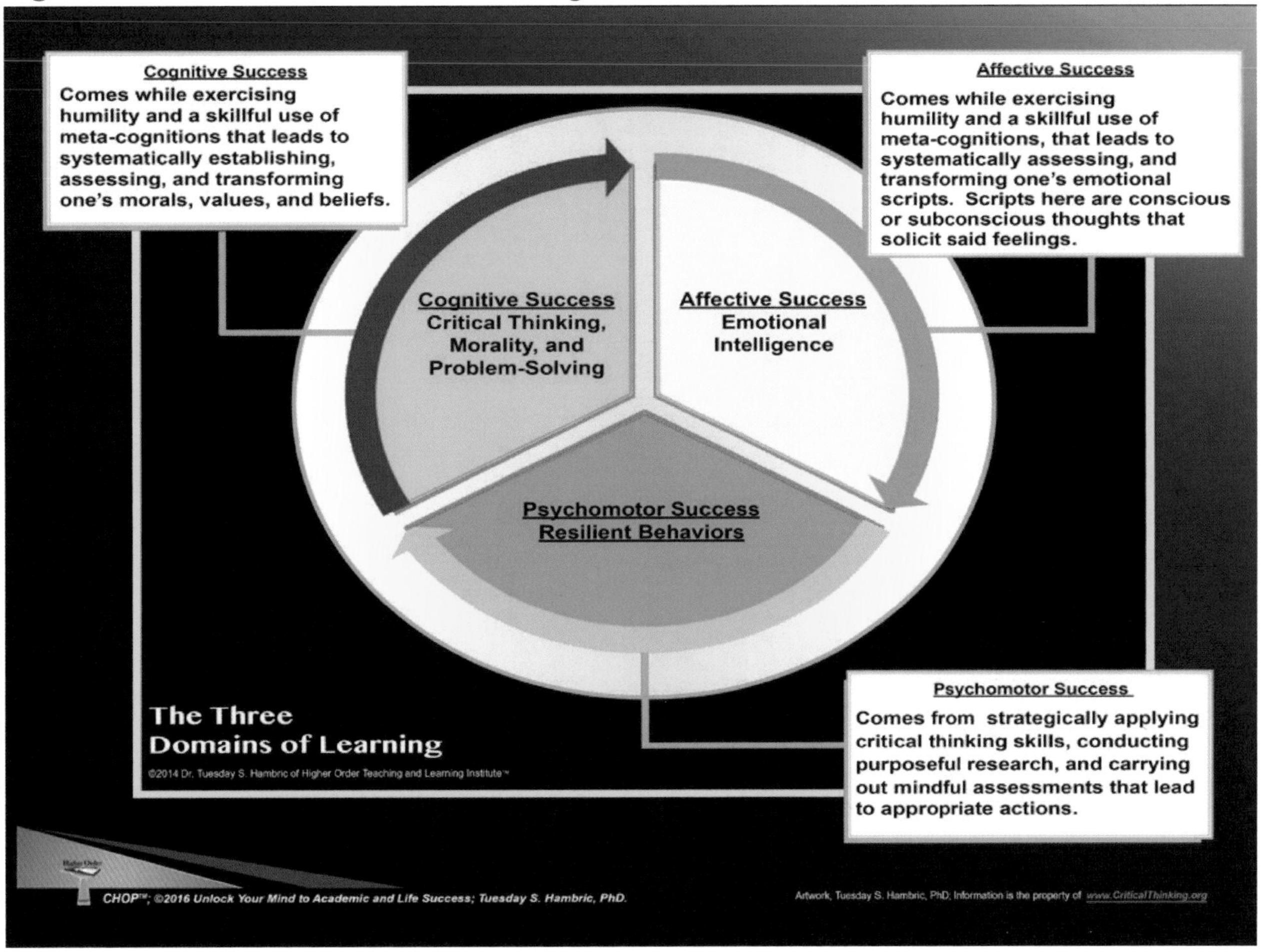

This theory helps us to understand that we, as humans, are cognitive (mind), psychomotor (body), and affective (spirit). The *Three Domains of Learning* and *Maslow's Theory of Motivation* further help us to understand that, *for us to mindfully succeed, we must achieve homeostasis or balance in each of the three domains.* The *ABCD Theory* helps us to assess and moderate each of those areas *by our becoming aware of our conscious and subconscious beliefs* and then further helps us to restore homeostasis when needed by using *reasonable disputing techniques* (see Figure 3.17).

Figure 3.17: *The ABCD Theory w/Disputing*

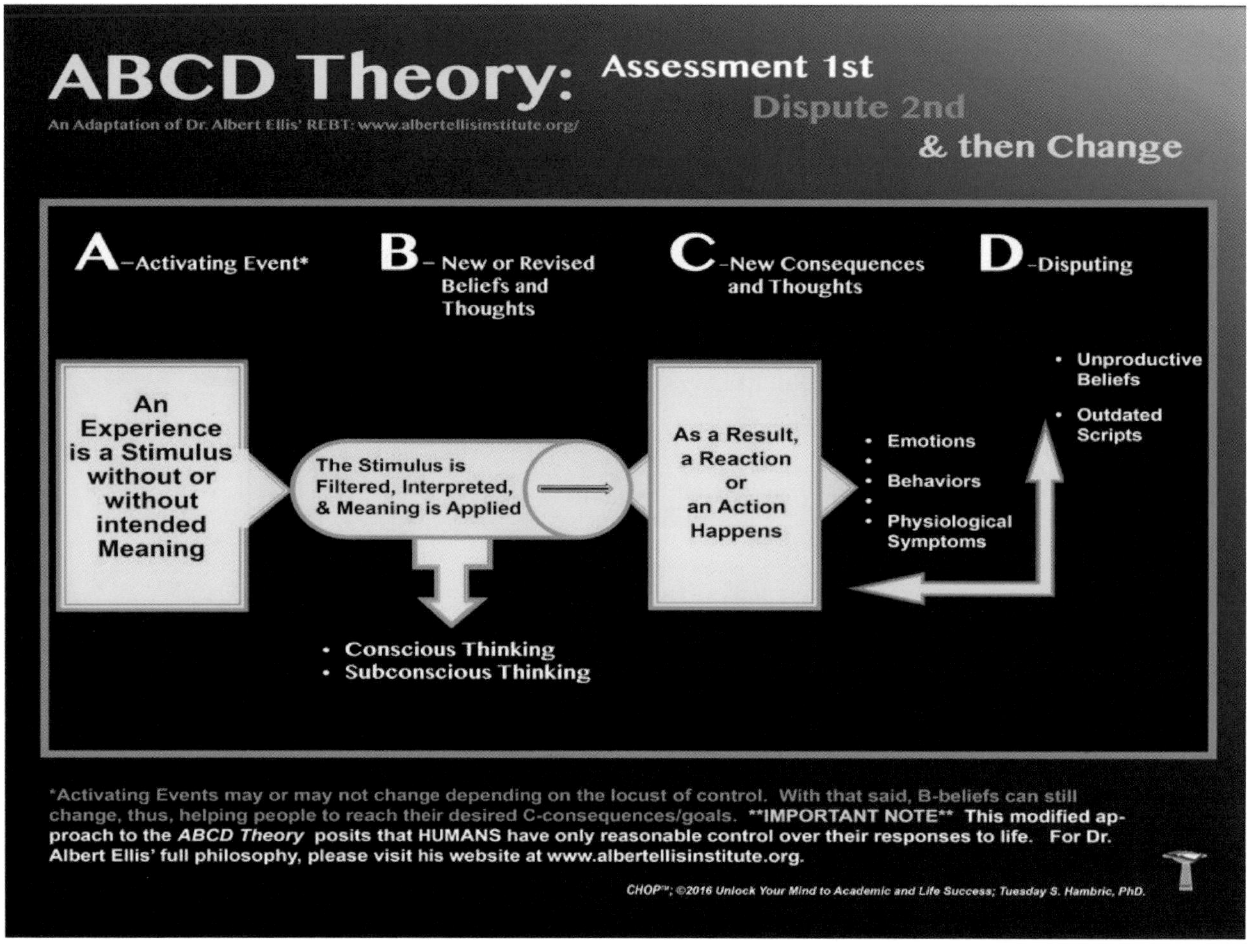

Now let's add another theory, *Steven Covey's Theory of Time Management*. We will use the overall concept that applies to his theory as our *framework for time*. But we will keep with our original premise to use *CHOP®* to optimize Steven Covey's approach. With that, we will add an important ingredient that appears to be missing from his theory: the ability to rationalize about the different *A-Activating Events* we encounter in life within our framework of beliefs.

In Figure 3.19: *Steven Covey's Time Quadrant System, Now Optimized* illustrates two rows, two columns, and four quadrants. You will see how each row has one label different from the other and how each column also has its own label. Finally, you will then see how each quadrant is given meaning by sharing one label from its corresponding column and one label from its corresponding row.

Figure 3.19: *Steven Covey's Time Quadrant System: Now Optimized*

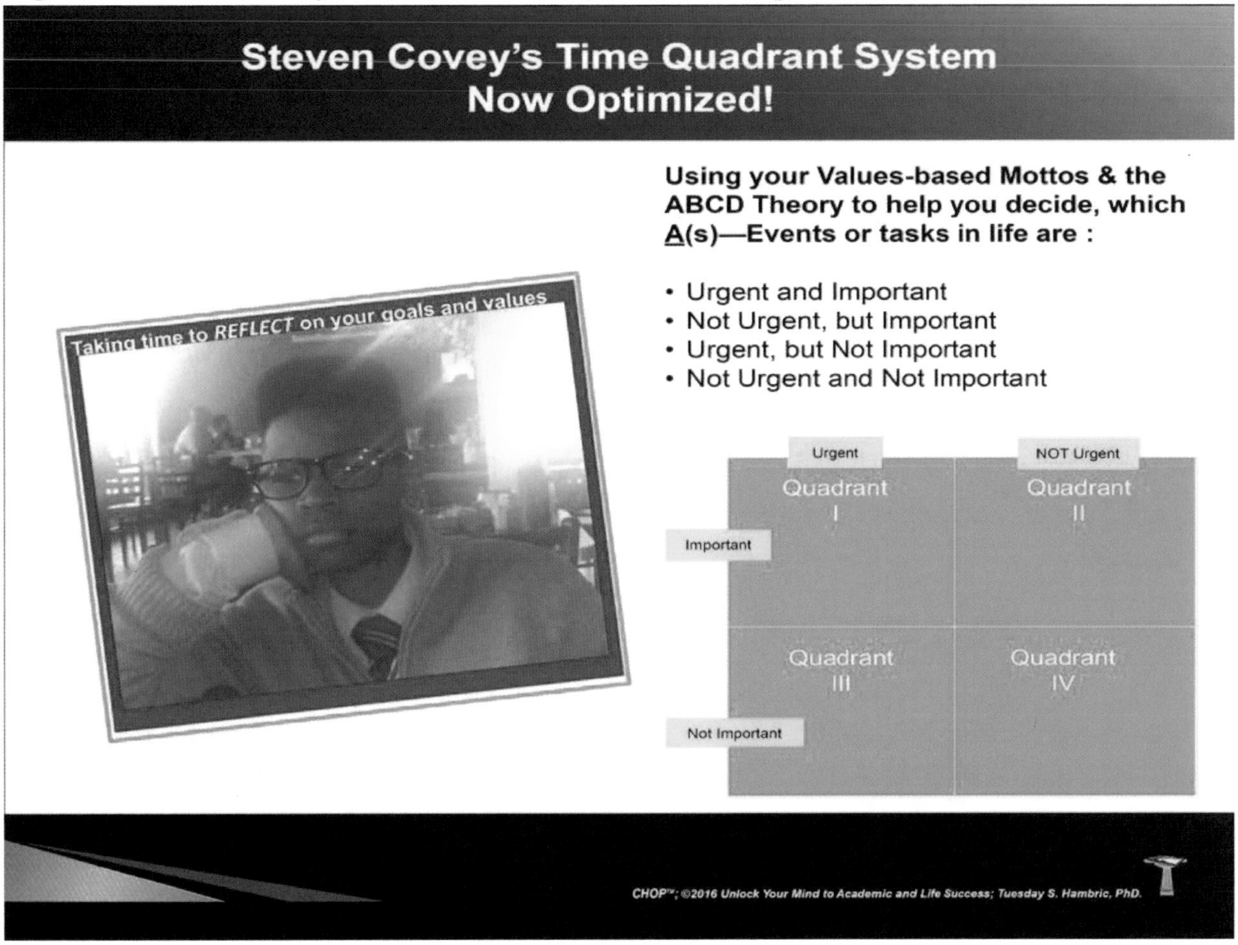

The goal of Mr. Covey's time-management system is to place all of a person's tasks, be it homework or daily to-do list items, into one of these four quadrants (Downing, 2012). Then, from there, they are supposed to assign an appropriate amount of time to plan and complete the task as the quadrant dictates.

For example, most people would put "browsing social media" into Quadrant III or IV. However, some people would say "browsing social media" is urgent and important because they want to immediately know what is happening in their friends' lives and in the lives of celebrities; therefore, they would designate Quadrant II as appropriate. Others would say cruising social media is neither urgent nor important—that it's just a big waste of time—and thus would place it in Quadrant IV.

Well, believe this or not, for me browsing social media is something that I place in Quadrant II. It is not urgent, but it *is* important. It's not urgent for me because I *strategically assign time to it* by *purposefully scheduling downtime*. It is important to me for business reasons, so that I can communicate with family, friends, and past students. For business reasons, I use social media to stay abreast of what's trending in my industry, in science, and in the world of finance. These things are important to me because, if I am totally unaware of industry changes, scientific advances, and financial trends, then I would be limiting my ability to make essential business decisions. Furthermore, I would not be in the best position to relate to my students and other educators around the world. As for my closer relationships, I love to see how my family and friends are doing and how well my past students are maturing and progressing in their life. So again, for me, I would place "browsing social media" in Quadrant II.

Now, this was just an example of how *Steven Covey's Time Management System* works: You pick a task, and you place that task into one of the four quadrants. Then, you assign an appropriate amount of time to design and complete that task. But my questions to you are these: "How is it that one task—social media—can be placed in more than one quadrant, and who gets to say which one quadrant is correct?" And, "What about the big things in life? How do you decide where to place the *A-Activating Events* in life?" Those questions bring me to this point. *Steven Covey's Time Management System* is great, but it only gives *the framework*, and it operates from the assumption that we all know how to make the best decisions when in difficult situations. For example, which quadrant would we place the following *A-Activating Event*?

Let's say … your sister is in need. She suddenly needs a ride from band practice; she is 30 minutes away, and she missed the bus. Conversely, you have a final exam in 15 minutes, which takes on average two hours to complete. Now, just like that, you have two events that both appear to be *important* and *urgent*.

Some of you would immediately place your sister's needs above your own. You would leave to pick her up and miss the final exam without thinking twice. For example, you might be saying, "There is no way I would leave my sister for two-plus hours alone waiting for me to finish a test. That could prove to be dangerous." And, that would be noble of you but not responsible regarding your education.

Now don't get me wrong, if you are thinking like that, know that I agree with you; I wouldn't leave my family waiting either, unless … see, this is the part where we all could use some help (all of us … *include me as well!*). Whenever we are in an emergency situation, sometimes we let our emotions take over, and we suddenly become out of balance (referring to the *Three Domains of Learning*). *We must use our cognitions to keep our emotions in balance; therefore, we must think twice.* **We must think to be RESILIENT.**

In moments like these, you have to be mindful AND strategic—not completely emotional nor completely logical. I suggest you quickly reflect on your values and your goals. In my case, I value family, intelligence, and education, and my immediate goal would be to pass my final exam AND to pick up my sister immediately. Then, I would ask myself, how can I honor *all* my values and *both* my goals? By asking myself this question, I am forcing my brain to seek several solutions that will help me place each item in a more appropriate quadrant and to choose from the many possible solutions. By doing this, I am *thinking twice*. I am mindful of my values and strategic in how I carefully place thoughts and possible solutions in their appropriate quadrants. This will help me choose the one that will bring me optimal results.

But, if for some reason, I cannot think of any viable solutions, then I would seek out *resources*. My immediate resources, in this case, would be other family members and my instructor. I would immediately inform them of the emergency and ask them to help me brainstorm solutions. After that, I would decide and then act. Regardless as to what decision I make, I would be okay with it *because it would be a decision that I strategically thought through and one that truly honored what I believed to be the best thing to do at that time*—so there would be no regrets.

I hope this helped and that you are now able (provided you were not able to before) to see the importance of not only having a framework of time but also having the ability to think critically within that framework.

I hope you are now able to see that picking up your sister from band practice at the exact same time that you have a final exam is an *A-Activating Event* that can be placed in Quadrant I or Quadrant II. (Any task or event large or small can be placed in either of the quadrants.) But it all depends *on how well you can mindfully react, how well you can brainstorm according to your values and beliefs, and how well you can act in ways that maintain balance in your three domains.*

As you can see, it does not matter the subject or the context of which we speak. What does matter is how you prioritize your *B-Beliefs* about such subjects, contexts, or experiences because those beliefs will determine your *C-Consequences*—your reactions and actions. So, **to gain the most control or power over your life outcomes, you must develop a "go-to" systematic way of assessing your small tasks and your big A-Activating Events in life; place them in the appropriate quadrant, and assign them an appropriate amount of time and energy.** Ah! The *Super Six Theories* never seem to fail us. ☺

Checking In ...

Self-Management & Teamwork

In our last exercise, I had you explain how you would self-motivate and self-regulate to accomplish a particular or an individual goal. Now I want you to do the same, but this time you will also have to assess the verbal and nonverbal communications of your team members to accomplish a team goal.

Insights: Penetrating Below the Surface; Application of Theories...

One Body Made Up of Many Members

You are a senior in college, and you are attending one of the top two schools in London. Each summer for the last three summers, you have returned home to Texas to work as an ambassador for the American Heart Association. Every summer so far, you earned a performance excellence award—but this summer you expect more: This summer you hope that your internship will evolve into a permanent career with the American Heart Association (AHA) and be the start of your new life.

It's been three weeks now since you graduated and returned home to the state of Texas and your AHA internship. In those two work weeks, the days were the same as before—uneventful; but today—today took a surprising turn. The supervisor announced something you never did before. She announced a team task.

> Guys,
>
> We are falling behind on our charitable funds, and I want you all to come up with a campaign that will raise $200,000 for our Children's Healthy Heart Foundation. The proceeds will go to underprivileged children and their families to help with medical expenses and to assist with temporary housing for the families during the children's surgical procedures. Now, I handpicked each of your members because of your individual attributes and experience. So, let's pull together and work as one body. We have three weeks left to do this, so let's plan well and get to work.

Upon hearing this, you thought to yourself, "This is great! I double-majored in both health science and marketing, and I once raised $200,000 by myself to help with a similar campaign for the March of Dimes. This should be a piece of cake."

Once your supervisor left the room, you and your team introduce yourselves to each other. Here are the group demographics and qualifications:

- Conner: 44-year-old white male from the US. scientist.
- John: 44-year-old white male from the US, health science, computer technician.
- Deepak: 40-year-old Indian male from India, medical doctor and artist by trade.
- Lagos: 42-year-old African male from Africa, health science engineer and philanthropist.
- Cindy: 25-year-old white female from Europe, volunteer and well-connected.
- You: You are in this scenario as a 28-year-old _____ [insert what you associate yourself with, your race, gender, and country of origin]. You graduated with double-majors in health science and marketing, and you have excellent nonprofit experience.

At the end of the introductions, Conner takes the lead and asks for initial ideas. Quickly, everyone begins brainstorming aloud. After a round of sharing, you notice that your ideas do not receive the same respect as that of others in the group. In other words, the team is ignoring your ideas.

For example, when your four male colleagues spoke, everyone had both positive and negative responses that were mutually respectful and valid. When Cindy spoke, all the men listened to her ideas as well, even though none of them were relevant to the campaign. For example, she would say things like, "Well, I will be sure that we have food each time we meet," and the men on the team responded with such gratitude. Then, when you spoke, your ideas were shunned. You shared with the team your experience raising money for the March of Dimes campaign, and they all just sat quietly. Some of the men would not give you eye contact when you spoke, and others would ask questions that tested your knowledge of the task at hand. Lagos even made a joke about how some of the men's combined years of experience ran circles around the average intern's time of service.

At the end of that meeting, all you could think about was *how the team was rude, but also this team experience could either increase or decrease your chances to become a career employee.* What do you do? Because the time you have left is really short (three weeks).

You decide to earn your team's respect and to be an important part of the campaign results. You believe that, if you do well, you will get a job offer. You also believe it is next-to-impossible to earn the respect of your team in a mere three weeks. But you are a *Generator* and decide to *go for it*.

- *Task*
    - b. To use *The Elements of Thought* and at least one other of the *Super Six Theories* to explain how you would:
        - i. Think like a *Generator* to change your negative judgments about your colleagues' verbal and nonverbal behaviors to judgments that promote a positive understanding of their cognitions, emotions, and behaviors.

ii. Think like a *Generator* to become an *important* part of the campaign's success.

iii. Think like a *Generator* to earn your colleagues' respect.

iv. Think like a *Generator* and use time as a framework.

- *Student Learning Outcome*
  a. **The SLO is to use self-management & teamwork**

    At the end of this task, you should be able to use meta-cognitive skills and *The Elements of Thought* to achieve individual and/or as a team cognitive, emotional, and behavioral success within a condensed period of time.

- *The Super Six Theories Used for CHOP®*
  a. *Three Domains of Learning*
  b. *Bloom's Taxonomy*
  c. *Stage Theory*
  d. *The Elements of Thought*
  e. *ABCD Theory*
  f. *Values-Based Motto*

Hint: While attempting to accomplish the aforementioned task, use the section on *dissecting, understanding, and prepping instructions* as guidance for preparation. That should help you through this process and ensure that you completely address the task.

- Use the space given to explain how you would accomplish the given task.

_____

_____

_____

How did you do? Are you able to confidently add the skill teamwork to your résumé? Good!

After all, we are always, in some shape or fashion, a part of a team. Whether we are collaborating in the classroom, a part of a family, at work, or unintentionally being lumped in a group for statistical purposes, we are always a part of some team. It is our job—or I would like to think so, anyway—to affect the team in positive ways, but positive impacts require great skills.

Moving On…

In summary, *The Elements of Thought* teaches us to see things from more than one perspective and to look at the depth and breadth of any given event. Whether we are refining information, calculating and interpreting data, dissecting instructions, or collaborating as a team, I suggest we choose a positive perspective that can be supported by viable evidence, complements our *Values-Based Mottos*, and allows us to truly embrace and carry out such a perspective.

Last, but not least, when all else fails—have faith.

Chapter IV

CHOP®

Personally and Socially

Customized Higher Order Processing©

An Applied Integration of Cognitive Frameworks, Self-Tailored to Develop Your Academic,
Social, and Personal Skills for Success

Overall, Chapter IV gives you opportunities to use *CHOP*ᴿ personally and socially. Chapter IV helps you strengthen your personal and social skills using the *Super Six Theories*, but, more specifically, you will further develop and master your critical thinking, doing, and **emotional** profile, thus further understanding what it means to become a *healthy autonomous learner.*

Chapter IV explores topics that will help you further solidify and act upon your core values and beliefs. You will use again your *Values-Based Mottos* to help guide your thinking as you ponder, discuss, and possibly debate ideas surrounding *responsibility.* Then, you will extend those ideas to society needs via *STEAM trends, careers,* and *goal settings.* The chapter ends with what I hope is a great discussion about your values and *fiscal responsibility.*

MENTAL NOTE

Please keep the following in mind as you turn the page to continue your reading:

- Remember you are to use *CHOP*ᴿ, *Customized Higher Order Processing.*
- Practice using the ***critical thinking and doing profile*** you developed in Chapter II and reinforced academically in Chapter III.
- Focus on both your critical thinking and doing profile, but now intentionally learn emotional intelligence.
- Remember the goal is in this chapter is to add personal and social responsibility to what it means to become a *healthy autonomous learner.*

Let me be the first to say, great academic work thus far. However, we still have a ways to go. Remember in Chapter I that I spoke of *resiliency.* Allow me to recap, if you will. In Chapter I, I said ***resiliency*** is *the ability to intentionally see things from more than one perspective and to create or find **and** achieve opportunities for success* (Hambric, 2011). After that, I gave you this key formula:

TP + TAˢᴸᴼˢ **= Intentional Academic and Life Success.**

Spelled out, it reads: theories processed, plus theories applied, powered by student learning outcomes, equal academic, and life success—or the premise of this course. ☺ But, we've only used our *Super Six Theories* to complete the *intentional academic* part of the equation. Now it is time to work on the *life success* part of the equation using the *Super Six Theories.* With that said, from this point forward, *Life Success* will be referred to as *Personal and Social Success,* or P&S success. Okay, now that we've revisited our overall purpose and course premise, let's move on...

At the heart of *Life Success* or *P&S success* is **RESILIENCY—period! Achievements are driven by those who intentionally and reasonably establish and then use their core values to filter successful outcomes.**

Lucky for us, you've already established these core values and have been intentionally using them since Chapter II. Your core values reflect the very essence of who you are: your thoughts, your feelings, and your behaviors (the *Three Domains of Learning*). In other words, your values reflect how you identify yourself. So, if you pursue any kind of success without aligning it with your core values, then you could very well be in opposition of your own beliefs, creating internal conflict or cognitive dissonance, which can lead to misery—and we don't want that.

Personal & Social Success: Determining Responsibility

Personal and Social Success (P&S success) is very near and dear to my heart, just like *Academic success*. With *Academic success*, the professors, teachers, and standardized test(s) determine whether or not you will succeed. But with P&S success, who gets to decide if you are successful or not? Is it you, society, or both? This is just one of many questions we will briefly explore. However, you will have to answer this question—and a few others like it—for yourself.

To get started, let's set up a context in which to explore P&S success via responsibility. When I think about success, I think about the things that govern success … and, as a result of that thinking, what I realized is that, within all categories of success, there is a sense of responsibility being fueled by our prioritized beliefs and values. It all comes down to whether you think you are responsible to yourself only, or to others, or to both, and then you act on those relevant beliefs and values until you succeed. P&S success is no different: As with any other category of success, responsibility lies at the roots.

So, let's generate and justify the parameters for our discussion and activities. Let's define *personal* and *social responsibility*. According to the *Merriam-Webster Dictionary*, **responsibility** *means to carry out a duty or an obligation that requires or expects physical accountability, reliability, and trustworthiness* (2015). It also means *to be morally, legally, and mentally accountable*. The definitions for **personal** *mean to belong to a particular person; first-hand experience or the action of an individual;* and *a private matter, not one connected to one's public or professional career* (*Collins English Dictionary*, 2016).

Now that we've defined both of those terms, let's combine the two to make one definition for personal responsibility. **Personal responsibility** *means to develop, maintain, and trust oneself morally and mentally and to be reliable while holding oneself accountable for one's own actions.*

What about *social responsibility*? Let's define that as well. *Social responsibility* is slightly different than that of *personal responsibility*. According to *Merriam-Webster Dictionary*, **social** *means relating to people or activities with the intention of doing enjoyable things with each other*. As you can see, the term **personal** focuses on yourself only, whereas the term **social** focuses on harmony between you and others. So, similar to what we did with *personal responsibility*, we will combine the definition of *social* and *responsibility* to develop our own working definition of *social responsibility*.

Social Responsibility means to develop, maintain, and trust oneself morally and mentally and to be reliable while holding oneself and others accountable for intentional and enjoyable interactions. The parameters are set; we now have working definitions for both *personal* and *social responsibility*.

With that said, affective (i.e., emotional) practical wisdom is needed as well. It's a kind of wisdom that can be used to help foster *enjoyable interactions* and help to fulfill what it means to be personally responsible and socially responsible. According to both definitions, you need to be able to *develop, maintain, and trust yourself morally and mentally and be reliable while holding yourself and others accountable for desired outcomes*. Well, in order to develop <u>and</u> maintain your moral and mental health, be it personally or socially, you will have to not only establish and incorporate your beliefs and values, but you will also have to improve your thinking skills, your affective skills, and your behaviors with experience over time. By doing this, you will be able to define who you are, live who you are, and generate safe boundaries for when you interact with others. With that stated, make note that I am *not* saying you should abandon or be rigid about your core values. What I am saying, though, is that insightful people mature and improve over time as they encounter different experiences.

For example, if you are reading this book, then you are in several relationships: one with your teacher and or other students, one with your family and or friends, one with co-workers, and/or even one with God (or whomever or whatever you believe in). In each of those relationships, there is a spoken and unspoken set of cognitive, affective (emotional), and psychomotor (behavioral) responsibilities and expectations. So, if you *value* relationships, you may think in the beginning that a relationship simply involves mutual respect, respect for things that's been stated, and respect for things that are assumed. But, as you progress and develop different levels of maturity, you come to quickly learn that in order to have consistently positive relationships, you must develop *emotional intelligence* (IQ).

Throughout this entire resource, we learned different cognitive and behavioral tools paired with different marketable skills; however, we must address the final component of the *Three Domains of Learning*—and that is *affective skills*. Without emotional intelligence, we may find the executive function of our brains hijacked by our extreme emotions, thus causing us to behave in undesirable ways. So, *we can learn all the intellectual and behavioral skills we want, but without emotional intelligence, it all falls apart*. Therefore, emotional intelligence will serve as our affective practical wisdom.

According to author and psychologist Daniel Goleman, ***Emotional Intelligence** is being able to identify and manage our own emotions and the emotions of others* (1995). Goleman lays out ***Four Components of Emotional Intelligence***, i.e., *emotional self-awareness, emotional self-management, social awareness,* and *relationship management*. Within these four components, you have key information that can help you take *Personal responsibility* for your actions and behave in *socially responsible* ways.

According to Goleman, the first two components of Emotional Intelligence addresses *Personal responsibility*:

1. ***Emotional Self*-Awareness** is being able to identify self-defeating feelings. Here, Goleman is saying you need to know "what" you are feeling (Goleman, 1995). I agree, for if you can't identify, "what" you are feeling, how can you personally address it?

2. *Emotional Self-Management* is being able to control self-defeating feeling(s) in order to avoid irrational decisions (Goleman, 1995). Again, you must first be able to identify and label the feeling(s). Once you are able to do that, you can then use *The Elements of Thought* or *The ABCD Theory* to manage and change, if needed, feelings that are undesirable. Remember we explored this during the Jason and Elka exercise (Chapter II).

In addition to Goleman's basic premise on emotional self-management, I suggest you be able to *identify and manage things that trigger your self-defeating emotions prior to them surfacing.* That way you can work to avoid those thoughts or situations that trigger your undesired emotions. Also, this means you can choose to safely work through your exposure to certain events prior to you being exposed. Back to the four components of emotional intelligence.

The last two components *Emotional Intelligence* focus on *Social Success*. So, when we think about *social responsibility*, we are striving to master the following:

3. *Social Awareness* is being able to accurately empathize or relate to other people's emotions (Goleman, 1995). That's good, right? But then what? The big question, then, is what do you do once you are able to relate to or understand another person's feelings? (Good question. *You then manage the relationship!*)

4. *Relationship Management* is being able to handle emotions in relationships with the intentions of achieving harmony (Goleman, 1995). Remember, to be socially responsible, we try to generate intentional and enjoyable interactions. Therefore, we must be skilled in identifying and labeling emotions, be it our own or someone else's—and we must also be able to manage those emotions.

Checking In...

- Define *Personal responsibility*.

  _____

  _____

  _____

- Using the definition of *Personal responsibility*, the information on relationships, and your values, answer the following question. Who gets to determine if you are personally successful or not? Be sure to explain your answer.

  _____

  _____

  _____

- Define *Social responsibility*.

  _____

  _____

  _____

- Using the definition of *Social responsibility*, the information on relationships, and your values, answer the following question: Who gets to determine if you are socially successful or not? Be sure to explain your answer.

_____

_____

_____

Let's Talk Personal Responsibility

My teaching philosophy is, "I am here to help you help yourself." It falls along the same lines as, "Give a man a fish, you feed him for a day. Teach a man to fish, you feed him for a lifetime" [*unknown*]. When you look at these statements' implied meaning, on the surface they look like statements for *Social responsibility* only. But look deeper… for me, it is a statement of *Personal responsibility* as well.

Here is how I see it: Yes, by teaching a person how to fish, I am helping that person to develop a skill (fishing); thus, I am helping a member of society. However, I am also working to protect myself. I value independence and interdependence when needed. I also value education and intelligence. So, in teaching someone to fish or in helping someone to help him or herself, I am teaching independence through interdependence, for I am educating. I am advancing the depth of my values by reinforcing them personally *and* extending them to a social setting as well.

You have to protect yourself. You personally have to set boundaries to protect your cognitive, emotional, and physical self. If you don't, you will find yourself in unhealthy relationships or ***toxic relationships***, *where people violate what you have established as personal, healthy boundaries, and take you far beyond your comfort zone.* You have to be aware of when this is happening and be able to identify it and manage it—and, yes, sometimes that means cutting people out of your life.

What's interesting though, is that typically we don't discover that our values and boundaries have been violated until *after* we FEEL uneasy. It's usually not our cognitions that consciously say, "Hey, wait a minute, he just crossed me, or she just disrespected me." No. It's usually *our emotions* that give us the first clue. Our thoughts are linked to our feelings, but they are usually subconscious thoughts. Let's check in.

- When and what was your last personal conflict (i.e., internal struggle)? Please explain.

_____

_____

_____

Use your *Values-Based Motto*, the definition of *Personal responsibility*, and the information on relationships, values, and emotional intelligence to answer the following questions.

- What values were violated in your last personal conflict? What part of *emotional intelligence* did you use—part one, part two, or both—to resolve or work through your conflict? Please explain your answer.

_____

_____

_____

- As a result of your personal conflict, do you think you matured cognitively, emotionally, or behaviorally? Please explain.

_____

_____

_____

Good work so far. Now I am going to ask you a few thought-provoking questions regarding *social responsibility* using one of my personal *Insights: Penetrating Below the Surface*. After that, you will have another opportunity to apply your ideas. I will provide you with a second scenario, *Insights: Penetrating Below the Surface*, and you will get to put your beliefs, values, emotional intelligence, and decision-making skills to the test. ☺

Social Responsibility

Social responsibility to some extent raises the question, "Am I my brother's [or sister's] keeper?" This is a famous line from the Book of Genesis that is commonly used in movies or by people when they want to sarcastically make the point that they are not responsible for others (Genesis 4:9, NIV). However, according to the definition of *social* and the definition of *responsibility,* or even our combined definition of the two, we *are* our brother and sisters' keepers.

But to what extent are we our brother or sisters' keepers? What happens when we come from different cultures? And let's be clear here: Our cultural differences don't have to be as apparent as an Asian working and living in Africa or a Brazilian attending school in the United States. It can be as subtle as the few similarities and great differences that may exist between two African-American women, one of whom grew up in an affluent suburb and the other in an affluent urban area. So, whether the cultural differences are apparent or subtle, we must be able to recognize and use intercultural factors to create harmony … hence, being able to fulfill the ideas surrounding *social responsibility* and being our brothers' or sisters' keepers.

Let's look at the following example…

Insights: Penetrating Below the Surface; Application of Theories…

Attack on U.S. Soil: Fight, Flight, or Freeze

On September 11, 2001, I was a little more than 40 minutes from my home and about 10 minutes away from my job, when I took note of the broadcast. I was listening to the radio when the message came: "A terrorist attack in progress on US soil!" New York's Twin Towers were being destroyed, along with the Pentagon. At that moment, everything that I believed and valued triggered my fight, flight, or freeze response. As ex-military and a combat veteran, I naturally decided to fight—except this time semi-automatic and automatic weapons were not my choice of munitions.

As a mother, a wife, and an educator, my first concern was for my family and my students. I lived and worked more than five states away from New York, and I knew that both of my boys were in very capable hands; so naturally, my thoughts stirred to my next concern—my husband. But just as before, familiar and comforting thoughts surfaced. I knew we were more than five states away from the terror, and my husband, who is also a combat veteran, was also trained to think critically in these situations. At ease with those thoughts, I settled in my mind that things would be fine (although my husband and I checked in with each other to be sure). At this point, my only concern was my students. I was concerned with how they would react to the broadcasts and to each other. You see, some of my students physically looked as though they came from the same region as the terrorist group initiating the attack, and I knew this because speculations about who the terrorist might be were being aired throughout all the radio and news outlets. As a result of these dynamics and the media frenzy, I knew my students would be filled with anxiety …

So, on that same fatal morning of September 11, 2001, I entered my classroom prepared to engage in my normal way, with my regular class of college freshmen and sophomores. My students were from all over the United States as well as the world. They were between the ages of 17 and 24. Out of those 25 students, the population consisted of Americans, Palestinians, Israelites, Neapolitans, Koreans, Saudi Arabians, and Africans (in that order of from many students to fewer students).

All things considered, the majority of my students had never received any type of "emergency" critical-thinking training or crisis-management training; to make matters worse, there was a "be scared, be offended, and be angry" propaganda campaign being broadcasted on every radio station and every television station throughout our entire college campus.

Now, I could have given in to the propaganda myself and responded with fear, anger, and offense. But, I had a job to do, and that job involved staying true to my values and beliefs and serving my students. I value education and intelligence; I also value trust and what that does for people. In addition, I value transparency and security (among other things). So, what did I do? *I acted accordingly, in accordance with my core values*—I taught.

I did not teach my planned curriculum, however. I taught from the material that was most current and pressing: the broadcasts. I allowed the students to listen. Then we dialogued, and we dispelled any faulty thinking. Each of us exposed our own irrational thinking and feelings, and *we helped each other to see things from different perspectives.* Most of all, we sorted through the facts and the opinions of the commentators and analysts. We engaged in *Customized Higher Order Processing (CHOP®)* to identify the broadcasters' *perceived* fears and how those fears may have colored their commentary.

Each of those actions exercised and polarized my values and beliefs as well as those of the students. By taking the students through this exercise of critical thinking, my students were able to engage in seeking clarity and accuracy of data. They were able to get to the depth and breadth of not only their own thoughts and beliefs but also the thoughts and *perceived* beliefs *of those who were telling them what to think.* The students were able to see me model transparency and came to trust me even more. As a result of this process, the students ended up feeling a bit more secure.

My job as an educator is a <u>social</u> one; therefore, I have social responsibilities I must fulfill. On September 11, 2001, I needed *to develop, maintain, and trust myself morally and mentally. I needed to show my students that they could rely on me, but, at the same time, I had to hold myself and my students accountable for intentional and enjoyable interactions* (the definition of *Social responsibility,* if you recall).

For that crisis, I did what I always do: I taught. But I did something more: ***I mindfully decided to fight— and not to retreat/flight or freeze. I intentionally planned my attack.*** Except this time, the battle did not call for fists or weapons of destruction. This battle called for *critical thinking and love.* And with that—I am my brother and sisters' keeper!

Let's Engage. Use your *Values-Based Motto,* the definition of *Social responsibility,* and the information on relationships, values, and *emotional intelligence* to answer the following questions about what *I* just did:

- What values did I rely on ***to develop a plan of action?*** What element(s) within the theory of *emotional intelligence* did I use: part one, part two, part three, part four, or some combination thereof? Please explain your answer.

  _____
  _____
  _____

- Did I use *emotional intelligence* and the ideas surrounding *social responsibility* ***to solve*** a problem or ***to foresee*** a ***potential*** problem? Please explain your answer.

  _____
  _____
  _____

- Do you think I matured cognitively, emotionally, and/or behaviorally as a result of the presented conflict? Please be sure to explain your answer.

  _____
  _____
  _____

Now, use your *Values-Based Motto,* the definition of *Social responsibility,* and the information on relationships, values, and *emotional intelligence* to answer the following questions about *you*:

- What are your values, ***and*** how might you have used them ***as a student during that 9/11 crisis*** to develop, maintain, and trust yourself morally and mentally and to show your peers that you can be reliable while holding yourself and others accountable for intentional and enjoyable interactions (definition of *Social responsibility*)? Please explain your answer:

  _____
  _____
  _____

Thank you for engaging.

Next are two scenarios under *Insights: Penetrating Below the Surface.* Use the information you just learned, along with your *Values-Based Motto,* and any of the other *Super Six Theories,* to help you complete the task.

Task

    a.   After reading the following two scenarios, choose *ONLY one* to identify and weigh relevant personal and social factors that influence civic responsibility, ethical decision-making, and effective cultural engagement.

Student Learning Outcome

    b.   **The SLO Is to Determine Responsibility**

        At the end of this task, you should be able to use your *Values-Based Motto* and one or more points of view to articulate and justify your *personal* and *social responsibility.*

The Super Six Theories Used for CHOP®

    c.   *Values-Based Mottos*

    d.   *Etc.*

Insights: Penetrating below the Surface...

Scenario One

Public Bathroom Debate Sparks Discrimination Toward All Genders

You are in your second year of graduate school and your professor, Professor McFarland, is eliminating the last two weeks of assignments. Professor McFarland's rationale is to integrate current events into the classroom in order to facilitate learning that is more relevant and time appropriate. Here is the scenario:

> "Dia duit," he says as he walks into the room and places his work on the computer table. "As you know, I have elected to change the latter part of our semester, and here's why. President Taha has decided to give a $500 award to the governing teacher and a $5,000 award to the team of students who come up with the best solution to the current public debate." Because you and your peers are familiar with the recent debates, you all perk up as Professor McFarland continues.

> "I want you all to propose the most effective way to resolve the issue of transgender access to bathrooms. I want you to decide which bathroom they should be allowed to use—the one that they associate with or the bathroom that corresponds with their birth certificate? With that being said, please be creative and think of solutions beyond the barriers that I framed for you."

Here is the task and the parameters: You are to pair up into teams of five, then come up with the best proposed solution that includes the following:

    a.   ***Civic/Social Responsibility:*** Provide a mission statement that explains and outlines your civic responsibility regarding this issue.

---

b. ***Personal Responsibility***: Provide a brief list of ***each*** team member's values ***and*** *Values-Based Mottos*. Be sure to explain how your values influenced the team's final proposed solution ***and*** how your values were not violated as a result of the proposed solution.

c. ***Social Factors***: Provide a list of ***and*** explain the major social factors that influenced your team's final proposed solution.

d. ***Multiple Perspectives***: State and explain the different categories of perspectives used to influence your team's final proposed solution.

e. ***Ethical Decision-Making*** (moral, decent, right, or just decision-making): Include in your final proposal a *conclusion statement* that explains how your team's proposed solution is an ethical solution. **Be sure** that this statement is supported by your team's collective values, beliefs, and mission statement.

Insights: Penetrating Below the Surface...

Scenario Two

Healthcare Costs, The Financially Able vs. the Not Able vs. the Disable

You are in your last year of medical school when your professor, Dr. Chyphes (C-fiss), decides to eliminate the last two weeks of your classroom format and assigned work. Here's the scenario:

"Hello, class," he says as he stands in the front of the science lab. "As you know, I have decided to change the latter part of our semester assignments, and here's why. Soon you all will enter into the world of medicine, and you will find that the cost of healthcare and your means to financially manage your private practice are out of control. So, to combat these problems, I've decided to place you all in groups of four or five and then have you develop and implement a persuasive campaign. It is my hope that this activity will encourage you to be a part of the solution and not the problem." Dr. Chyphes pauses anticipating a response. Appropriately adjusting to his read of the class' blank stare, he quickly says, "Here's the catch!"

"The winning team will receive their ***PREFERRED*** residency/practicum assignment." Immediately, every student perks up and starts to chatter about how the changes would bring forth greater opportunities and how the fact that only a specific group of five out of the 20 residencies guarantees the best training and the best job offers after that training. Dr. Chyphes lets the news soak in for a moment, and then he continues.

"So, you all will pair up into teams of four or five, and then your teams are to come up with a proposed solution that will lower the cost of healthcare and increase the number of doctors willing to accept Medicare and Medicaid patients. With that said, your solution has to include the following":

a. ***Civic/Social Responsibility***: Provide a mission statement that explains and outlines your team's civic responsibility regarding this issue.

    b.   **Personal Responsibility:** Provide a brief list of **each** team member's values **and** *Values-Based Mottos.* Be sure to explain how these values influenced the team's final proposed solution **and** how these values were not violated as a result of the proposed solution.

    c.   **Social Factors:** Provide a list of **and** explain the major social factors that influenced your team's final proposed solution.

    d.   **Multiple Perspectives:** State and explain the different categories of perspectives used to influence your team's final proposed solution.

    e.   **Ethical Decision-Making** (moral, decent, right, or just decision-making): Include a *conclusion statement* that explains how your team's proposed solution is an ethical solution. **Be sure** that this statement is supported by your team's collective values, beliefs, and mission statement."

Now that you have read through both scenarios, chose only one scenario that you will address. There are two ways to experience the following engagement: **1)** you can work alone; **2)** you can work in teams. Hopefully, you will be required to work in teams. Because I am so optimistic, all of the following questions are written as if you are a part of a team.

However, if you are reading and working in solitude, no problem, simply answer the questions accordingly. Be sure to use the lines below to capture your thoughts. This will help you better understand the material; and it will help you better express yourself when working with a group. It will allow you to comfortably participate and present your thoughts with no problem. Either way, team or no team, just be sure you use the section on *Dissecting, Understanding, and Prepping Instructions* to guide your preparation.

Civic/Social Responsibility: Provide a mission statement that explains and outlines your team's civic responsibility regarding the issue proposed problem.

_____

_____

_____

- ***Personal Responsibility:*** Provide a brief list of yours and/or **each** team member's values **and** *Values-Based Mottos.* Be sure to explain how your values influenced your team's final proposed solution **and** how your values were not violated. In other words, how did you compromise without violating your values?

_____

_____

_____

- ***Social Factors:*** Provide a list of **and** explain the major social factors that influenced your team's final proposed solution.

_____

_____

_____

- ***Multiple Perspectives:*** State and explain the different categories of perspectives used to influence your team's final proposed solution.

_____
_____
_____

- *Ethical Decision-Making* (moral, decent, right, or just decision-making): Include a *conclusion statement* that explains how your team's proposed solution is an ethical solution. **Be sure** that this statement is supported by your team's collective values, beliefs, and mission statement.

_____
_____
_____

How did you do overall? Are you now able to use your *Values-Based Motto* and one or more points of view to articulate and justify your *personal* and *social responsibility*? Are you able to confidently add the characteristic of *cultural awareness* to your résumé? What about *personal* and *social responsibilities* … are you able to establish healthy personal boundaries that are grounded in your values and beliefs? Are you able to use those values and beliefs to make ethical decisions when being socially responsible is necessary?

My hope is that you were able to say yes to all of these questions, but I also know that this is a growing process. So, however you answered those questions, most of all I hope you said, "I will strive to answer yes to each of those questions." I want you to remember *we have to know who we are, what we will stand for, and for what are we willing fight, flight, or freeze—because every single one of our A(s)—Activating Events—in life gets filtered through that perspective respectively.*

Moving On…

Hambric's Five-Step "Optimized" Career Inquiry & Design

Okay, let me be very **UPFRONT**: This topic—career exploration—is ideal for some students and annoying to others. It's annoying for some students who have already committed to their career choice but is usually ideal for those students who are undecided. If you have not committed to a career choice, please pay special attention as you read the soon to follow career exploration material; most of the time, it will seem as though I am communicating only with students who have already confirmed their career choices. Well, it will seem that way because it's partly true. In the next few pages, all the career information is directed towards those who have already decided on a career. However, I am talking to those of you who are undecided as well. I will be indirectly speaking to you vs. directly.

Now to both groups (decision-makers and non-decision makers), when you read the career exploration material, you will quickly realize that I'm making assumptions regarding the steps taken by those that have already chosen a career. That's on purpose. However, during this section of reading, I want both groups to please accept the next bit of career exploration information as a guided checklist; and jot down things you might need to do to explore and find your career-purpose. That way, I can walk you through whichever steps you deem most interesting and your notes can serve as a quick reference. This exercise will take place during the *"Checking In"* section.

Finally, if you've decided on a career, I want you to know I respect your commitment to your early choices; and here is why. I decided at 12 years old that I would be almost exactly the person I am today. I made some tweaks along the way, but mostly I am who I imagined I'd be. So, yes, I respect your early commitment. Having stated that, perhaps some of the career exploration steps you've already taken are the same as some of the steps I've listed in the *career inquiry and design* process. If the steps you've already taken are different than the ones I listed, again use this information as an additional guide.

Now, when it comes to exploring careers, I chose to put forth *optimized* time and *Optimized* research efforts. This way, you choose a career and find your *purpose*. So, let's assess the career exploration decisions you made so far, using the *Hambric's Five-Step Optimized Career Inquiry & Design*.

Let's Engage...

Have you already completed the following five steps?

- ***Step One:*** *Identify, Understand, and Apply Your Core Career Beliefs*
  - ☐ Perhaps you conducted an exploration of your values and beliefs to ensure that your career selection fulfills your natural desires and values. For example, you may desire to be *challenged* because you value **competition** or you may have a desire to *serve* because you value **purpose** or because you value **justice**, you may value **knowledge** and **wisdom**, inspiring you to *teach*. So, step one is to identify, understand, and apply your core beliefs.

- ***Step Two:*** *Investigate and Create Your Optimized Work Profile*
  - ☐ It is possible that you have already taken ***one excellent*** inventory that served several purposes. The inventory that you've already taken, may have ***summed up your overall personality, your primary characteristics, and your relevant work factors***. I'm sure that same inventory provided you with an excellent list of personalized career choices and further used that same data to create your *optimized work profile*. Finally, that same inventory explained how you would perform best within each career choice. If you have an inventory that can do all of that, then you have ONE EXCELLENT inventory. If not, then in step two-to investigate and create your optimized work profile, you will find a link to *Unlock Your Mind's Career Fitter's Inventory* that does ALL of what I mentioned and some. So, if you've completed steps one and two already, then you are off to a great start.

- ***Step Three:*** *Identify and Create a Plan A <u>and</u> a Plan B*
  - ☐ Have you researched reliable and credible resources, such as a government website, to find credible, reliable, and relevant information? Did you concerned yourself with finding different career descriptions, their requirements and their required personality traits? If yes, make sure to picked <u>two</u> careers that best fit the *optimized work profile* you discovered in step two.

  - ☐ Looking ahead to the future, you probably looked for the different skills that are needed to prepare you in advance of your college graduation and future interviews. I'm sure you were careful to find the salary ranges and projected growth for both your career choices. *If you did not*, be sure to go back and do this because this is super important for a couple of reasons. **1)** You don't want to spend two to 12 years in school and, at the end of all that time, find out that your career industry has downsized, and very few jobs are available or even exist; **2)** You do not want to attend school for all that time and later realize the pay for your career choice does not and cannot support the lifestyle you imagined yourself living. If you haven't completed any of this, no worries. Remember, I will walk you through all five steps, shortly, during the *"Checking In..."* section.

- **Step Four:** *Find a Degree that Matches or Best Fits Your Career Choices*
  - ☐ So, again, if you've already committed to a career, then you may have completed this part already. You may have used your current school as a starting point to make sure your current educational requirements fit your *two* selected career choices, and that's okay. Be sure to double-check all your requirements to include the *specific math and science classes* needed; these are reportedly quitting points for some students. If you need to make a few changes, no problem. Your advisor can help with that.

  - ☐ Now for those of you who need to transfer, if you haven't explored transfer degrees, then make sure your transfer schools offer appropriate degree plans to match your two career selections as well. If you haven't already, make sure that your past credits and your current credits are accepted at your transfer school(s). With that mentioned, be sure to think about the idea of possibly earning a double-major or a major and a minor. That way, your *Plan A* and your *Plan B* are tracking for success. If needed, your advisor can help you with that.

- **Step Five:** *Develop a Self-Management Plan Guided by Time*
  - ☐ Finally step five. You probably used one or more of the *Super Six Theories* to assess your beliefs and motivation levels and to develop and apply appropriate study habits. By now, you all should know to add your learned classroom skills to your resume as transferable workforce skills. Think about it. It doesn't make sense to earn a degree and still have *no* skills that can help you in the workforce. So, step five says to develop a self-management plan guided by time; a plan that helps you be self-directed, a team leader, and an excellent follower. Also, by using timed deadlines as motivation to increase your speed and accuracy, you will develop into a more valuable employee.

----------------------------------*Making Sense of It All via Goal Setting*----------------------------------

Now, perhaps as a result of taking this class or reading this entire resource, you realize the importance of committing to *optimized* time and *optimized* research efforts. I hope you see that this is not only good for career purposes, but for other key areas of your life as well. I hope you set goals with deadlines in five major goal categories. Then, break those categories down into "Necessary Steps" as we did throughout the career exploration assessment. For example, you may consider if you haven't already, creating, developing, and monitoring an *Academic* goal; a *Career* goal; a *Spiritual* or *Personal* goal; a *Fiscal* goal; and a *Fitness* goal.

Now, as a final motivating act, I would love to know that you have created a vision board, one that represents all of your goal categories. Conceivably, you added to the top of your vision board your *Values-Based Motto* and then pictures and other art as daily reminders to help keep you focused on your future. *Whew!* If you've already completed all five of these steps, you are truly acting as an *Advance thinker* (from *Stage Theory*) and are on your path to success.

So, there you have it. You just conducted an assessment of your current career goals using the *Hambric's Five-Step Optimized Career Inquiry & Design*. If you used *CHOP®* to complete ALL five steps *AND* made an appointment to meet with your current and transfer advisors, with the intention of double-checking all of your findings and your plans for accuracy and practicality, then "It's a Wrap!" Now, all you have to do is follow the steps **you** created for each of your goals, making sure to assess your progress, use appropriate resources like advising, study groups, internships, spiritual readings, mentors, etc., make appropriate adjustments as needed, and follow your plan through to success.

Now, to everyone else, if you did NOT complete ALL of the *optimized career inquiry and design* steps, then you have a choice to make. **1)** you can go back and complete the entire list; **2)** you can add to what you've already completed, only the things that you've missed; or **3)** you can decide that exploring careers this manner is *waaaaay* too much work" and simply wing it. You know, let life happen to you verses helping life happen. Again, it is your choice. But, *there are only a few things that you will ever do in your life that are more important than choosing a career.* With that stated, please know that having the most popular piece of technology or wearing the latest fashion is not one of them. 😊 I use these two examples because today more than ever, people tend to engage in superficial matters **over** significant matters. It seems to be more important for people to give significant thoughts, feelings, efforts, time, and their money to purchasing the latest technology or the latest fashion gear than it is for them to think, feel, act, and use their time and money to discover their future security and self-fulfillment.

Finding the right career can be the same as finding your purpose in life; finding your purpose in life is both a personal and social responsibility. It's *personal* because your career is an extension of who you are and a representation of what you value and believe. *For me*, I believe my gift is teaching, and I value God. As a result, my values are manifested through my teaching service and my call to "plant seeds." With that stated, careers also extend out into our social beliefs and responsibilities as well. Careers are social because, in order for us to fulfill the very definition of *Social responsibility*, we must contribute to society and do it with the intentions of creating joyful engagements.

So, I see being happy and working as two of many *Social responsibilities*. Being happy is implied in the definition of *Social responsibility*, and working is a *Social responsibility* for several reasons, but here is the rationale. **1)** The act of working, in and of itself, contributes to society directly. For example, careers such as teachers, police officers, firefighters, nurses, and doctors contribute to society simply because of the nature of the career. These professionals all render social service. **2)** The act of working contributes to socieity indirectly. For example, librarians educate, gardeners balance the ecosystem, and artists provide beauty; further, each of these professions contributes to the tax system, and those taxes are then redistributed to help those society members who are in need of food, water, shelter, and so on. **3)** Working contributes to society not only locally, as previously established, but globally as well. Working has a positive impact on the world's financial systems. For example, when we have low unemployment rates, we also have improved stock market trends. When we have improved stock market trends, consequently, we have improved borrowing and lending interest rates, individual finances, and individual spending. So, you see, finding your purpose via your career not only makes you happy, but it is your, get this—*personal, social responsibility.*

So, with all you've read so far, surely you can see how finding your career and finding your purpose is an important *personal* and *social responsibility.* As individual members, you and I can work within society while at the same time serving the whole body. So, by me exercising my gift in ways that develop and maintain moral and ethical standards, while holding myself and my students accountable for intentional and enjoyable interactions, *I transform my job into a career where I become socially responsible and a valuable part of society. Thus, I use my values and beliefs as a foundation from which I serve.* Austrian neurologist and psychiatrist—and Holocaust survivor—Viktor E. Frankl states it this way (Life Principle "#7: *Extend Beyond Yourself*): You should manifest the human spirit at work by relating and being directed to something more than yourself" (Frankl & Winslade, 2006).

Checking In. For those of you who have already committed to a career, what have you decided regarding your career? Will you add to what you've already explored? Now, to all of you who are undecided, will you carefully follow *Hambric's Five-Step Optimized Inquiry & Design Process?* Or have some of you decided to do nothing? Well, to ALL of you who have decided to do something, let's revisit your values and motto—but this time, let's add a twist and briefly revisit the five steps.

Discovering Your Workplace Values…

Step One: *Identify, Understand, and Apply Your Core Career Beliefs.* This exercise will help you complete the first step in *Hambric's Five-Step Optimized Career Inquiry & Design*:

- I want you to think about your overall values and list them below. (In Chapter II, you compiled a list and used them to create a *Values-Based Motto.* If you want, you can use those values here as well.)

  _____

  _____

  _____

- Now, examine Table 4.01. Once you are finished, use that same table as an example to help you brainstorm about your own values and beliefs as they relate to your desired or ideal work environment.

Table 4.01: *Jatory's Career Motto Exploration*

Jatory's Example: My Values, Thoughts, & Attitude Toward Working…		
Thoughts About Work	*Attitude Toward Work*	*Work Values*
I think knowledgeable and experienced supervisors are easy for me to trust.	*I feel happy at work when I trust my supervisors, and this helps work to flow easier.*	*I value **Expertise***

I think it is important to lower my risk of being harmed and to live a healthy life.	*I feel anxious about working late hours.*	*I value my* **Safety** *and* **Leisure Time**
I think working under pressure helps me concentrate and makes me a better employee. *I think goals are good because they help me achieve; this helps me improve my self-esteem, even when I fail at reaching my goals. I have to have a positive attitude.*	*I feel good about training under pressure. I feel happy when I exceed goals and challenged when I don't. I feel accomplished when I receive accolades.*	*I value* **Competition** *I value being* **Self-Driven** *I value being* **Appreciated**

- Now, using Jatory's example as a guide, I want you to develop *your* thoughts and feelings about work, and then use that information to discover and showcase your career values and beliefs. Please place your answers in the following chart. See Chapter II for a list of additional values if needed.

Your Name and Title:		
Thoughts About Work	*Attitude Toward Work*	*Work Values*
I think…	*I feel…*	*I value…*
I think…	*I feel…*	*I value…*
I think…	*I feel…*	*I value…*

Next, I want you to craft your very own *Career Exploration Motto—acronyms or sentences made up of a person's chosen values and beliefs as it relates to work and work environments, used as guidelines to maintain a state of homeostasis or balanced living.* Jatory came up with this as his career motto: CLASS-E. He values Competition, his Leisure time, being Appreciated, Self-Driven, Safety, and working with Experts. So, as Jatory explores different types of careers and different companies to work for, he can readily keep his values in mind and search for employment that offers CLASS-E careers. ☺ How cool is that?

Now it's your turn. The motto you create can do the same for you as it does for Jatory. Your motto can serve as a guide as you search for your desired career choices. Please be sure it is grounded in your values and your beliefs about careers and your positive attitude toward work. Also, do not limit yourself in your thinking here.

Write your *Career Exploration Motto* on the following lines:

_____

_____

_____

_____

Perfect! Because you've taken *personal responsibility* regarding your career, you now have a much better chance of identifying a career and school that will aid in your future security, self-fulfillment, and overall social responsibilities.

Step One is now complete. Let's do steps two through five. I don't know if you noticed, but each outlined step in *Hambric's Five-Step Optimized Career Inquiry* gives one or more reasons to seriously consider that step and sometimes subsequent steps. In that same spirit, please give serious consideration to completing the other four steps needed to complete your career exploration.

Step Two asked you to take one personal inventory that will provide you with comprehensive, accurate, and targeted advice that is easily outlined in one report. With that said, an optimized assessment, including a detailed report, costs money. Now I'm sure you can find a free assessment somewhere online, but I must say—with all confidence—that in my numerous years of living, ☺ I have never had a more accurate and motivating self-assessment than the one I have prepackaged in this resource/book at a _**huge**_ **discounted rate**.

So, to take advantage of the discount, simply go online to the *Career Fitters* website at www.careerfitter.com/free_test/careerbuilder?afid=176. Once there
- First, read the entire page from left to right.
- Then scroll back up to the top and click the large BLUE start button.
- Next answer the 60-question survey. Be sure to answer each question within the context of a work environment.
- Once you are finished, you will get a short summary of your results. HOWEVER, the *optimized work profile* will provide you with a comprehensive report that is in FULL color and thoroughly explained in text and visual charts. This includes but is not limited to
  a. An Expanded Summary
  b. Personality Chart and How It Relates
  c. Personalized Career Choices
  d. Occupational Factors That Matter to You
  e. Primary Characteristics to Maintain and Possible Weaknesses for Improvements
  f. Communication Methods
  g. Ideal Environment and More
- Once you are finished, move on to step three.

Step Three requires that you access the most reliable, trustworthy, and widely used career resource to research and select two career options. I recommend the *Outlook Occupational Handbook* (OOH). It can be found at http://www.bls.gov/ooh/, which is a government website; therefore, the information in the *Outlook Occupational Handbook* will contain information that is considered reliable, creditable, and accurate. It is here that you should look to find the job descriptions for *two career choices, as well as their skill requirements, their salary ranges, their life expectancy, and their growth forecasts.* Go back and read **step three** again (a few pages back), if you need to know why you need this information and how to use it for decision making. Once you are finished with this, move on to step four.

Steps Four: Now you are set to find and analyze degrees and colleges for their appropriateness. You are seeking to match the schools to your career choices. There are all kinds of websites that will help you do this, but I recommend using *Peterson's,* which can be found at https://www.petersons.com/college-search.aspx. Once there, you can search colleges by majors, school names, locations, and keywords. Revisit my earlier information in **step four** if you need to know more about what to do with this information. Once you have appropriately matched your career choices up with degree plans and schools, then move one to step number five.

Step Five: Set goals and then create a plan for whatever steps you need to accomplish your goals. Then, simply follow through! Use one or more of the *Super Six Theories* to assess your motivation levels. In other words, if you find yourself losing motivation or the will to carry out your planned steps; then, use the *ABCD Theory* and *The Elements of Thoughts* to identify any **victim** language and thoughts that are preventing you from acting positively. Then, use *D-Disputing* element of the *ABCD Theory* to dispute all faulty thinking and replace it with the language of one who is a ***generator****—*a go-getter. Then, revisit Chapter III: *CHOP®* if needed. By recommitting to the different study skills, you learned or reinforced in Chapter III, you are simply helping to ensure your success. Finally, create a vision board to serve as a daily reminder of the commitment that you made to yourself. Heads Up: You may have to present this in class.

Learning who you are and matching that to your future purpose and sense of security requires a significant amount of positive thinking, feeling, acting, time, and possibly, in the long run, money. But isn't doing this worth more than simply purchasing the latest technology and gear? Just keep in mind if you decide to use *Hambric's Five-Step Optimized Career Inquiry & Design,* you will have to **commit** to the work. You will only get optimized results if you **use** your **Career Exploration Motto,** your *Values-Based Motto,* and your *optimized work profile* to guide your thinking and final decision-making.

Whew! Excellent work exploring. Now remember, to be happy and healthy, you have to live true to your life philosophies. With that said, the risk of not doing so leaves you pursuing success without aligning it with your core values. Please do everything you can to ensure you do not live the rest of your working career in opposition to loving beliefs, feelings, and desired behaviors—thus creating internal conflict, as this can lead to misery.

The Taxonomy of Goal Setting

HOTL® In step five of *Hambric's Five-Step Optimized Career Inquiry & Design,* I used foreshadowing to introduce the idea of setting goals in more than one area of your life. So, let's explore that further. In order to successfully set and follow through on categorical goals, you'll need a "go-to" approach to goal-setting. I really like using *Bloom's Taxonomy,* so I will share with you my approach to goal-setting. Notice that, in Figure 4.01, *Bloom's Taxonomy* is in a different order. We will discuss this in more detail a bit later, but I rearranged the order on purpose to make this point. There are several ways to approach goal-setting; so please, if this approach doesn't work for you, you can use one or more of the *Super Six Theories* to create your own approach or you can choose one from the web that works best for you.

Figure 4.01: *Taxonomy of Goal-Setting*

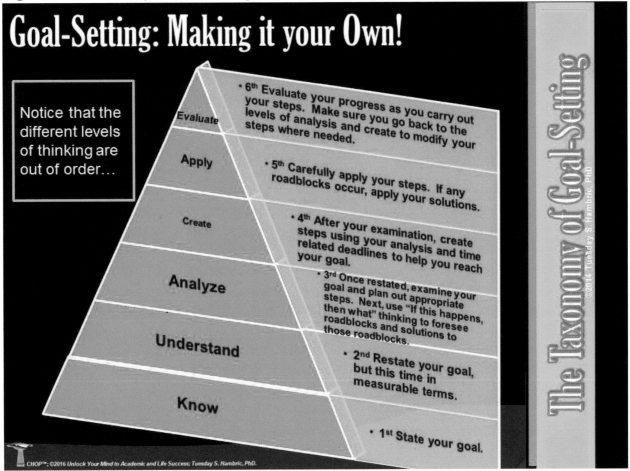

Now, let us go back to the arrangement. Look again at how the levels of thinking are out of order; look at how this order implies that I can analyze and create before I apply. Well, I can't, although on the surface it seems like I can. "Well, why not?" I am glad you asked. This diagram is illustrating the more pronounced thinking that I am doing—and not the less evident thinking. In other words, in order for me to move from the level of understanding to the levels of analysis and creation, I must first understand and use, be it subconsciously or consciously, pieces of information related to my desired level of thinking in order to process that information at the higher levels. In this case, I would have to understand some piece of information like what a goal is, in order to process the goal at the levels of analysis and creation. Does that make sense? You see, as of today, no one has ever been able to prove to me that he or she can process at higher levels of thinking without processing at the lower levels first. This line of thinking is disputed because the lower levels of thinking **_are_** taking place subconsciously. In other words, they are less apparent when the intensions are to evaluate or synthesize and so on. There is more to be said here, but I won't. It's for another day and another time. ☺

Let's see what setting a goal looks like using a modified version of *Bloom's Taxonomy* as *The Taxonomy of Goal-Setting.*

Table 4.02: *Rachel's Semester Goal*

Rachel's Semester Goal		
Know	State your goal.	*My goal is to earn a B or better in all my classes.*
Understand	Restate your goal in a measurable way but be sure to use every day language.	*My goal is to have earned a B or better in all of my classes this semester. A grade of B for me means an 80% or higher not a 79.5%. Some professors do not round up. My currently classes are Math, English, Science, and Psychology.* *This restatement of my goal allows me to do an overall measurement of my victory or defeat so on the last day of class I can see if I achieved my goal.*
Analyze & Create/Synthesis	First, conduct an analysis of your goal and then write a "Statement of Rationale" that tells why you chose this goal and whether or not it is rational and beneficial to you and those you represent. Second, examine your goal or goals for potential roadblocks. Do this by using the, *"If this, then what?"* For each problem, plan out steps that will prevent those problems, as well as, steps to help you reach your goal.	***If college is harder than high school, then what?*** *My goal is reasonable. In high school I was a straight-A student and, because this is my first semester of college, and college should be more difficult than high school, I will leave room for error by going for As, but setting my goal to earn Bs or better.* ***If my mom is running late for work, and she cannot take me to school, then what?*** *I will find out tomorrow how to catch the bus to school just in case I need a ride to school or home.* ***I am really good at science and math, but only okay in English. If I fall behind, then what?*** *Well, I know the school offers a writing lab. They talked about it during orientation, and we walked by there during the tour. I plan to use it at the first sign of me not understanding the material, so that I do not fall behind.*

		Using time as a framework, my other steps are to study: Math and science for one hour each, at 1 p.m. on Mondays and Wednesdays, and to study psychology and English for one hour each, at 1 p.m. on Tuesdays and Thursdays. *Any additional study time is during Mondays–Thursdays. Fridays and Saturday are fun time. Sunday is reflection and worship time.*
Apply	Carefully carry out your planned steps.	*It's 1 p.m. on Tuesday. Yesterday I studied math and science for one hour each. Now today, I am starting my first hour of studying. English it is!*
Evaluate	Evaluate your actions looking for progress and **Generator** thoughts and actions to build on; or, for defeat and **Victim** thoughts and actions to analyze and plan to change.	*My steps are working out well—BUT I am not doing so well in math. Out of my two classes, I am making an A in English, and I am making a C in math. Math is harder than I thought. So, back to the level of evaluation to assess the situation. I will use the ABCD Theory. It can be used to help me with this problem.* *Thinking … Okay, I see the problem. I got cocky because I was great at math in high school, but I am quickly realizing that, in high school, I was doing what Dr. Hambric calls mimicked learning.* *To fix this, I will stop acting too proud to get help, study harder the taxonomy of math, and then seek tutoring. NO MORE MESSING AROUND FOR ME!* *New Step:* *I am going to study the taxonomy of math today, then read the math textbook for additional understanding and analysis, then I will go to the "Math Mania" tutoring lab tomorrow and every Tuesday after that until I catch up.*

Connecting the Dots

1. Using the *Taxonomy of Goal-Setting* as your reference, explain the difference between the level of *knowledge* when stating your goal and the level of *comprehension* when restating your goal.

   _____

   _____

   _____

2. Demonstrate that you understand the difference between stating a goal and restating a goal by creating a financial goal for yourself at the level of *knowledge* and then restating it at the level of *comprehension*. Use the *Taxonomy of Goal-Setting* as a guide to help you.

    _____

    _____

    _____

3. Using the *Taxonomy of Goal-Setting* as a reference, demonstrate that you understand the levels of analysis and create/synthesis by writing an appropriate *"If this happens, then what?"* statement regarding your financial goal *and* one step to follow regarding that financial statement.

    _____

    _____

    _____

4. According to the Taxonomy of Goal-Setting, what do you do if your goal and steps are not going according to plan?

    _____

    _____

    _____

Very good! So, what do you think about using *Bloom's Taxonomy* this way? Remember this is just one more tool to add to your intellectual toolbox. The ability to analyze, set appropriate goals accordingly, and then follow through is a *very* sought-after academic and workforce skill. So, if you do not have your own go-to method of setting goals, please consider using my method or creating your own, so you can add that skill to your résumé. You cannot go wrong if you do.

Developing a Fiscal Mindset

Let me start this section by saying I am *not* an expert in money matters. However, before I wrote this book, I learned to live and am currently living financially stress-free. So, I can honestly report, with all confidence, that what I'm doing is working and working well. It has not always been like this, so *when*, I am excited that I changed my fiscal mindset!

You do *not* want to be the person saying, "Man! If only someone had told me this when I was…" I used to be that person, and one day I just said, "No more!" After seeing so many people lose their retirement funds, their homes, and their lifestyles due to mismanaged money and the stock market crash of 2008, I decided to become financially savvy. With that said, I just believe that, when you have good fortune, you should share your experience with those who will listen. I pray you will listen to me.

Okay, the sole purpose of this section is to encourage each of you to look deep within yourselves to find out if you have *any faulty or outdated beliefs or values* that may keep you from achieving your own idea of financial freedom. Notice I said *your* own idea of financial freedom, and that is because we all need to live a balanced life. Life should NOT be about money only. So, with that said, let me be clear, as clear as I can be: I am by no means teaching you to be driven by the almighty dollar. (The rest of this resource bears witness to that.) What I am trying to get across is that it does not make any sense at all to earn a college degree, get a great education, and land the greatest career fit for yourself, only to have matters possibly fall apart because of a defeating fiscal mindset. So, let's jump right in.

According to Dave Ramsey, one of the few self-made financial moguls in the United States, if you save $1,995 per month for 15 years, you will have earned (through investments) $1 million; and in just five additional years, your $1 million will have doubled into $2 million (2013). Now initially, especially at this juncture in your life, that may sound like an enormous amount of money for you to save each month. But hear me out, and *really listen*. Don't allow victim language to block your hearing. *Right now, there is no time for negative self-talk.* Relax and let me tell you a story to help guide your financial reflections and exploration.

Insights: Penetrating below the Surface; Application of Theories...

Financial Excuses or Financial Investments

Brian is 21-years-old and will graduate in less than six months with a bachelor's degree in communications. In his three and a half years in college, Brian lived by a strict code, and that was that Mondays through Thursdays he spent most of his time at work or at school. Fridays and Saturdays, he dedicated to his girlfriend and his friends. From time to time, Brian would hit the party scene, but most of his leisure time he spent attending the school's basketball and football games, bowling, and shooting pool with his girlfriend and friends. When it came to money, Brian was just like the average college student. For the most part, he lived check to check and saved very little if anything at all. But one day Brian heard Dave Ramsey on the radio and decided to change his fiscal mindset.

Brian decided that, because setting goals and following them to completion worked out so well in his past, he would do that same thing again but this time with his finances. So, he used the *Taxonomy of Goal-Setting*, and he set financial goals for himself. He started out with a small goal and then planned bigger goals the closer he came to completing his smaller goal.

About three months before Brian graduated, his career exploration, preparation, and interviewing paid off. He was offered a position at a local news station paying him $38,000 a year.

Now, Brian has no children and is not married. His household expenses include $560 monthly rent for his apartment, $200 for his car payment, and about another $800 for his standard monthly living expenses. Together those total $1,560—give or take a few dollars, depending on the month. With his new job, Brian projects his bring-home pay, after taxes, will equal $2,691.66 per month. Brian is excited about the job offer but bummed out about not being able to invest the monies that Dave Ramsey's recommended—$1,995 per month.

But being the **Generator** that he is, Brian decides to commit to investing $1,000 per month. He knows it will be tight, but he feels it is worth it. Brian thinks to himself, "I will get a better paying job in the near future; and even if I keep investing only $1,000 per month—never adding more to it—I still will have at least $500,000 in investments or at least $241,000 in the bank without investments, by the age of 41. Hey, that's WAAAY better than having nothing like most 41-year-olds I know."

Brian commits to this line of thinking—and is now well on his way!

Checking In...

1. When it comes to money, I use Bible Scriptures to guide my financial thoughts and actions. What do you use to govern your thoughts and behaviors when it comes to money?

   _____

   _____

   _____

2. After knowing how much money you could earn from saving and having the potential to live financially stress-free, would you commit to saving $1,000 per month if you were in Brian's shoes? Yes or no? Why?

   _____

   _____

   _____

3. Looking at Brian's household expenses, imagine different things that Brian can legally do with his current bills and new income to create more available cash flow—again, only using his current bills and his bring-home pay as parameters?

   _____

   _____

   _____

4. What values and beliefs do you have that would stop you from setting and/or carrying out financial goals?

   _____

   _____

   _____

5. Are you willing to start paying off all of your bills now, so that you can freely create an emergency fund of $1,000 and begin investing? Yes or no? Why? If you are, pick up Dave Ramsey's book, *The Total Money Makeover!* In my opinion, it's a great financial read, but you have to do what is best for *you* according to *your* overall goals, values, and beliefs.

   _____

   _____

   _____

Believe it or not, budget management is also a great skill to add to your résumé, but to really enhance that skill and to make yourself that much more marketable, take a Microsoft Excel class, if you haven't already, and learn to create and maintain budgets using that software. You can practice by creating your own personal budget, debt payoff plans, and investment plans. There will be a minimum number of calculations on your part because the computer does it all for you after you initially set things up.

With all of that said and done, please allow me to leave you with a few philosophical examples that shape Dr. Hambric's—MY fiscal mindset. ☺ Again, these are just my examples; you can come up with your own fiscal philosophies in which to further develop and shape your own financial mindset:

1. Tithe first (for those who believe in God).
2. Save and invest.
3. Never live on more than 55% of your income. If you can't do this from the start, set it as a goal and work towards it.
4. Use MS Excel or some other budget to help with the 55% rule and financial goal setting.
5. Live debt-free most of the time. In other words, if you don't have the money—wait, save it, and then buy.
6. If you have to have credit, use no more than one credit card and pay it off every month. You can pretty much do everything you need to do with a debit card.
7. Money is a blessing. Give to charity or a cause that you believe in, but be sure to use careful discernment when someone is asking you for money.
8. Try to avoid loaning money; of course, this depends on the circumstances. But if you think (NOT FEEL) you should loan someone money, NEVER loan money to anyone if you can't afford to give it to them. That way, if they don't pay it back and it turned out to be a mistake, the relationship is not severed, and you know then not to make the same mistake twice. ☺

Break: Monitoring Your Academic Progress...

Monitoring Your Academic Progress

It's time *again* to stop and measure your academic progress. Next, you will see a familiar set of instructions, but this time the calculations will be slightly different than those in Chapter II. So, follow these instructions closely to see how well you're finishing the semester and how well you are advancing toward your academic goals. Remember some instructors will have all of your work calculated and posted in Blackboard, Moodle, or whatever ePlatform your school is currently using. As I stated in Chapter II, if your work is already calculated and available to you, I suggest you still follow these instructions for each of your classes, one class at a time, to confirm your understanding of the calculations, and so that you don't miss your chance to make changes where they are needed.

Instructions for Calculating Your Current and Overall Grades

1. The example we will use this time will be as though you are in a *government* class, and the class grades are calculations are *based on a straight point system.*
2. Now, the same as before, you look for the grading criteria in the given chart and notice that, although the assignments are broken down into categories, no percentage points are assigned to each category, indicating this is a straight point system.
   a. Here is an example:

Government Grade Breakdown... 640 Total Possible Points	
Tests worth 400 points Notice how this class uses a straight point system	Test One: 92/100
	Test Two: 85/100
	Test Three: 94/100
	Final Exam: NA/100
Attendance 100 points	1 Absence: 90/100
Discussions worth 40 points	Dis1: 10/10
	Dis2: 10/10
	Dis3: 10/10
	Dis4: 10/10
Group presentations worth 100 points	N/A/100

3. Now if this was your class, you would calculate your grades in ***government*** according to the number of points earned and the total number of possible points. With that said, still keep in mind that there are two overall grades in which you want to be concerned. They are

    a. **Micro-grade:** A report of your grade progress, using <u>only</u> your earned attempted points and <u>only</u> your total, possible, attempted points to calculate your final numbers as a weighted point system or straight point system.

    b. **Macro-grade:** A report of your final class grade; the grade you would earn if you turned in all of your assignments **or** if you stopped turning in assignments without officially withdrawing from the class. The macro-grade is calculated by using <u>all</u> of your earned attempted points as well as <u>all</u> of your non-attempted points (replaced by and calculated as zeros if applicable) in order to calculate your final numbers as a weighted point system or as a straight point system.

Government Grade Breakdown... 640 Total Possible Points	
Tests worth 400 points. Note how this class uses a straight point system. This class is broken down by categories AND points—not categories and percentages. As a result, you do <u>not</u> have to calculate averages and percent of averages per section. You simply add up all of your earned points and divide them by the total number of possible attempted points for the "micro-grades" or the total number or possible points (attempted or not) for "macro-grades."	Test One: 92/100
	Test Two: 94/100
	Test Three: 94/100
	Final Exam: N/A/100
Attendance 100 points	1 Absence: 90/100
Discussions worth 40 points	Dis1: 10/10
	Dis2: 10/10

	Dis3: 10/10
	Dis4: 10/10
Group presentations worth 100 points	N/A/100

      c. Your *micro-grade* **would equal** <u>**410/440 or 93% out of 100% or a grade of A.**</u>

          1. Tests equals 92 + 94 + 94 = **280**
          2. Attendance equals **90**
          3. Discussion equals 10 + 10 + 10 + 10 = **40**
          4. Group presentation = not due yet
          5. Grade as you go equals 280 + 90 + 40 = 410 then 410/440 equals 93.1 or A

Your turn. First, orient yourself to the chart and the bullets following the chart.

What do the numbers 280 + 90 + 40 = 410 represent? *Also,* what does the number 410 represent? Why did I divide that number by 440?

_____

_____

_____

Now let's calculate your ***macro-grade*** in ***government.*** Using these same numbers, let's see what your grade would be if you decided to stop turning in your work without officially withdrawing from class.

Government **Grade Breakdown…** **640 Total Possible Points**	
Tests worth 400 points. Note how this class uses a straight point system. This class is broken down by categories AND points—not categories and percentages. As a result, you do <u>not</u> have to calculate averages and percent of averages per section. You simply add up all of your earned points and divide them by the total number of possible attempted points for the "micro-grades" or the total number or possible points (attempted or not) for "macro-grades."	Test One: 92/100 Test Two: 94/100 Test Three: 94/100 Final Exam: N/A/100
Attendance 100 points	1 Absence: 90/100
Discussions worth 40 points	Dis1: 10/10 Dis2: 10/10 Dis3: 10/10 Dis4: 10/10
Group presentations worth 100 points	100/100

4. Your *macro-grade* would equal <u>510/640 or 78% out of 100% or a grade of A.</u>
   a. Tests equals 92 + 94 + 94 + 0 = **280**
   b. Attendance equals **90**
   c. Discussion equals 10 + 10 + 10 + 10 = **40**
   d. Group presentation = **100**
   e. Your grade if you decided to stop attending class without officially withdrawing, and you missed the final exam; this would leave you with grades of 280+90+40+100=510, then 510/640 equals 79.6. The 79.6 is then converted into a letter grade that **solely depends on the teacher and letter grade he or she assigns.** Some teachers round up and some teachers do not. If the professor rounds up, you earn a grade of B. If the professor does NOT round up, you earn a grade of C.

You try. First, orient yourself to the chart and the bullets following the chart.

1. Using the *government* class grades as an example. What happens when you get the grade of A on all of your assignments and miss the final exam?

   _____

   _____

   _____

2. What is the benefit of calculating your grades throughout the semester and right before you go into the final exam?

   _____

   _____

   _____

3. If you don't like what you have earned in one or more of your classes, what should you do?

   _____

   _____

   _____

Now it's time for you to measure your own grade calculations.

   _____

   _____

   _____

Great work and be sure to hang in there. We are *Generators,* and if that means you have to tap into your resources for help, *then so be it.* You may still have time to talk to the teacher for extra credit or makeup work. Think about what you have to lose besides faulty pride—and if that's the case, we all can afford to lose that. ☺

Chapter Conclusions

At the heart of *Life Success* or *Personal Success* are your ***beliefs, your values, and your ability to be resilient—period.*** Achievements are driven by those who intentionally and reasonably establish and then use their core values to filter successful outcomes. Remember, your values reflect how you identify yourself.

Throughout this entire resource, we've learned different cognitive and behavioral tools paired with different marketable skills. Let me say again, GREAT WORK! But, hey, we have one final chapter. Let's see if we can go out with a bang.

Chapter V

Finish Strong!

Reflecting & Closing on Your Terms

Chapter V: *Finish Strong!*

Chapter V is designed to help you reflect on your learning. Take some time to look back on who you were before you started the class and who you are now that you are finished with the class. Hopefully, you have met all my challenges and those that you may have placed on yourself...

In this chapter, you will have an opportunity to assess your academic performance and to make any plans for last minute changes, if needed.

Whew, Look at Me Now: Shining Bright or Dimmed Light!

Integrative Learning and Expectations!

It is expected that from this point forward, you will use *Customized Higher Order Processing (CHOP®)* to integrate the theories and skills you learned or reinforced in this class with every other class you take, within every social setting, and with all the big *A-Activating Events* in life. So, in the spirit of that statement, let's do that. Let's put out any remaining dim lights and continue to shine bright from now on.

Reflecting on the Journey...

Take a few moments to reflect back on who you were before you started this journey and who you are at its completion.

Who were you *personally* before you started reading this resource, this book?

- Did you know that, in order to be successful, you had to *define* success?
- Did you know that the quality of your thinking dictated your success and your failures? Do you now know if you are a challenged thinker or higher on that scale? Why does it matter?
- Did you call to mind your values and beliefs in order to develop a foundation in which to live? Can you now explain why this is important to your success?
- Did you know that you needed to *mindfully practice thinking* in order to get better at achieving success on purpose?
- Did you know that your *Three Domains—cognitions, affective, and psychomotor* OR mind, body, and emotions—all need to be balanced in order to bring optimal success?
- Did you know there was such a thing as a **Generator**—or a **Victim?** Why would this matter to you?

Who were you *academically* before you started reading this resource, this book?

- Did you know how to *CHOP®?*
- Did you know how to refine your notes or deliberately think at six different levels when the time was needed?

- Did you know that it is just as important to *dissect and prep instructions* before you start to complete the work?
- Did you know how to support your interpretation of visual, written, or oral communications? What's the problem with NOT knowing how to do this?
- Were you comfortable with empirical and quantitative data analysis or financial planning? Do you now see the importance of both and how one relates to the other?
- Did you know that no one else can motivate you or steal your motivation without your permission? Do you now see the correlation between power and motivation?

Who were you *socially* before you started reading this resource, this book?

- With what thoughts or issues were you mostly concerned?
- Did you allow media and others to dictate your values and beliefs? Have you now decided to dictate this for yourself?
- Were you the person who read the headlines and ran with the story without researching the story further? Do you now know the dangers of doing this?
- Did you take the time to learn about other cultures and use that information to better relate to others?
- Did you strive to do onto others as you would have them do on to you? Do you now know that this famous saying really means, to treat a person the way he or she wants to be treated because isn't that what you want? With that said, you strive to do this without compromising your own personal beliefs because; if you don't, that defeats the whole statement all together. A compromise will always happen, but we look for win–win opportunities, always.

Who were you *industrially and skillfully* before you started reading this resource, this book?

- Were you skilled in critical reasoning, analysis, planning, development, and implementation; effective communications, creativity and multitasking; quantitative reasoning, self-motivator, self-regulator, and goal-oriented; teamwork and interpersonal, problem-solving, and humility?

Let's Engage. Please use your reflections to complete the following questions:

1. Write a well-organized statement explaining your experience in this class and what the class has taught you.

   _____

   _____

   _____

2. Briefly explain two or more workforce skills you have strengthened or learned as a result of this class.

   _____

   _____

   _____

3. Do you plan to use the _Super Six Theories_ that you learned in this class, in future classes, your personal life, your social life, and/or your work life? Yes or no? Why?

_____

_____

_____

In an effort to improve the class, please briefly answer the following four questions:

1. What do you like about the class?

_____

_____

_____

2. What do you dislike about the class?

_____

_____

_____

3. What do you like about the book?

_____

_____

_____

4. What do you dislike about the book?

_____

_____

_____

FAREWELL & BLESSINGS:

LET THOSE WHO HAVE EARS HEAR

Hello, Everyone!

It has truly been my pleasure engaging with you. From the time I wrote the first word of this book to the last, *I had you in mind.* I want to thank all of you that took the time to read this material and *learn deeply.* Thank you. Because of *you*—those of you who cared to learn and pass that learning on to others—I have hope that our society of people will continue to grow and flourish. I would love to hear your thoughts on the different subjects presented in the book or any updated information that you've learned in your studies. After all, I am a lifelong learner. ☺

With that stated, my fear is that, with technology dominating our experiences each day and how we learn, our brains have and will continue to evolve in ways that prefer *less* instead of *more.* Many of us are settling for, or have settled for, less than quality information and, as a result, prefer hashtags and superficial soundbites as our way of, "being in the know." Now don't get me wrong; I know that some people are capable of taking a little information and, with that information, can learn and create *a lot.* So, to them I say, "Kudos for being self-driven and curious!" To the rest of us, STAY CURIOUS, DEEPLY LEARN, and APPLY WHAT YOU'VE LEARNED AT QUALITY LEVELS—*because each time you engage in this manner, you are ever changing and unlocking your mind to academic and life success.*

Stay balanced everyone. "Do not conform to the patterns of this world but be transformed by the renewing of your mind. Then you will be able to test and approve what God's will is—his good, pleasing, and perfect will" (Romans 12:2-3).

To All, Many Blessings _OR_ Good Luck, whichever you prefer,

Dr. Tuesday S. Hambric
a.k.a. Mrs. Tuesday

Appendix

ABCD Theory is a complex assessment of a person's cognitions, emotions, and behaviors (Ellis, 1973, 2001). It is also a means for self-assessment and lasting change. The *A* or *Activating Event* is an experience that has no meaning until the person experiencing it gives it (the *Activating Event*) meaning. The *B* is the meaning (or *Beliefs* or *Thoughts*) about *A* that is applied. The *C* or the *Consequences*, within the *ABCD Theory*, naturally follow a person's *B*, *Belief*. The *D* or *Disputing* is a critical thinking technique that serves as a way of reasonably and logically changing one's unproductive beliefs and outdated scripts to productive beliefs and more relevant scripts.

Academic Success *the act of using relevant critical thinking skills to meet all the requirements to graduate or all the requirements to attain an artifact that illustrates all educational goals were met.*

Accommodation is when the brain and mind process new material by making room for storage in the brain (Siegel, 2015; Shaffer & Kipp, 2013).

Accomplished thinkers are those who encompass the forward-moving characteristics of the practicing and advanced stages. They constantly and consistently work at controlling life outcomes by monitoring and revising their conscious thinking strategies for continued improvement. Paul and Elder would disagree; they claim that accomplished thinkers are consistently successful even at the subconscious levels because their thinking about their thinking has paid off. Their diligent and consistent intellectual monitoring has created successful scripts or habits that lead to positive outcomes, and, due to their consistent self-assessment, they tend to quickly identify outdated scripts and move to change them. At this stage, any egocentrism is managed well with little room for relapse (Elder & Paul, 2013b).

Advanced thinkers refer to those who constantly and consistently refining their thinking across domains, leading to successes in several areas of their lives (Elder & Paul, 2013b).

Assimilation is when the brain bridges a connection between previously learned information and newly introduced material (Shaffer & Kipp, 2013).

Auditory learners refer to those who prefer to hear things explained (Brown, 2005).

Beginning thinkers refers to those who are aware that thinking drives behaviors, but without the use of systematic thinking, the attempt to control their success (Elder & Paul, 2013b).

Bloom's Taxonomy is a six-level illustrated hierarchy of learning, where each progressive level of thinking uses specific verbs to provoke action.

Career Exploration Motto refers to acronyms or sentences made up of a person's chosen values and beliefs as it relates to work and work environments, used as guidelines to maintain a state of homeostasis or balanced living.

Challenged thinkers refers to those who understand that thinking actually plays a role in their life's outcomes but refuse to use that knowledge to control their success (Elder & Paul, 2013b).

Coherent demonstrations are learning that demonstrates reason and discernment. It is learning that is, at the very least, paraphrased and can go beyond what someone else has already articulated or completed. **Conscious thinking** refers to explicit thoughts and beliefs of which a person is aware.

Customized Higher Order Processing (*CHOP®*) is a process by which a person gets to choose from several cognitive-behavioral frameworks, "chop them up," and integrate them in any manner they desire and then use them in order to produce a systemized way of thinking that will maximize his or her chances for success.

Elements of Thought refers to the natural process of thinking broken down into its individual parts. These parts are the basis for thinking (Elder & Paul, 2013a).

Emotional Intelligence is being able to identify and manage one's own emotions and the emotions of others (Goldman, 1995).

Emotional Self-Awareness is being able to identify self-defeating feelings (Goleman, 1995).

Emotional Self-Management is being able to control self-defeating feeling(s) in order to avoid irrational decisions (Goleman, 1995).

Generators refers to those who identify or discover present energy and then utilize that energy to form new opportunities for success.

Hambric's Notetaking Refinement System (HNRS) is a four-level in-depth conversion of lecture notes (e.g., terms, concepts, theories, ideologies, formulas, etc.) using *Bloom's Taxonomy*. It is the act of taking the definition of a word, concept, formula, etc., and progressing that word, concept, or formula from the level of knowledge to the levels of comprehension, then application, and then analysis.

Healthy Autonomous Learner refers to a learner who is self-directed and yet interdependent.

Information-Savvy is the ability to discern whether or not information or resources are relevant to the task or inquiry; whether information or resources are usable to make or support a logical premise, claim, or argument; and, whether information or resources are creditable among an audience, and/or timely, significant, or noteworthy.

Insightful Choices are choices that are reasoned and filtered through a person's core beliefs.

Intellectual Standards refers to a reasoned approach to examining and assessing knowledge and wisdom by seeking clarity, accuracy, relevance, logicalness, breadth, precision, significance, completeness, fairness, and depth of information (Elder & Paul, 2013b).

Kinesthetic Learners refers to those who gain insights from doing or performing a task (Brown, 2005).

Macro-grade is a person's final grade earn if he or she turned in all assignments <u>or</u> if he or she stopped turning in assignments without officially withdrawing from the class. The macro-grade is calculated by using <u>all</u> earned attempted points as well as <u>all</u> non-attempted points (replaced by and calculated as zeros if applicable) in order to calculate a person's final set of numbers as a weighted point system or as a straight point system.

Meta-cognitions are thinking about one's thinking.

Micro-grade is a person's grade progress, using <u>only</u> his or her earned attempted points and <u>only</u> his or her total possible attempted points to calculate the final numbers as a weighted point system or straight point system.

Mimicked demonstrations are learning that is unable to be explained or completed beyond the act of repeating or memorizing exactly what someone else has already said or done. It is a form of modeling without insightful understanding.

Motivation 3.0 is the act of consciously or subconsciously, assessing, applying, and sometimes altering one's own beliefs to stimulate actions and reactions.

Personal is belonging to a particular person; first-hand experience or the action of an individual; and a private matter, not one connected to one's public or professional career (Collins English Dictionary, 2016).

Personal Responsibility means to develop, maintain, and trust oneself morally and mentally, and to be reliable while holding oneself accountable for one's own actions.

Personal Success *the act of intentionally using one's values and critical thinking skills to make decisions that reflect his or her personal identity—desired thoughts, feelings, and behaviors.*

Practicing Thinkers are those who possess the same great qualities of the *beginning thinkers*; however, *practicing thinkers* not only believe that they have control over their thinking, but they have committed to at least ONE way of systematically assessing the quality of their thinking.

Relationship Management is being able to handle emotions in relationships with the intentions of achieving harmony (Goleman, 1995).

Repetition is when significant information is repeated or restated within more than one context or domain for easy recall.

Resiliency is the ability to intentionally see things from more than one perspective and to create or to find opportunities to achieve success; it is the ability to seek out and understand knowledge, and then, through analysis, apply its wisdom (Hambric, 2011).

Scripts are preconceived thoughts, emotions, and/or behavioral reactions to *activating events.*

Social means relating to people or activities with the intention of doing enjoyable things with each other.

Social Awareness is being able to accurately empathize or relate to other people's emotions (Goleman, 1995).

Social Responsibility means to develop, maintain, and trust oneself morally and mentally and to be reliable while holding oneself and others accountable for intentional and enjoyable interactions.

Social Success *the act of intentionally using critical thinking skills that create social advantages over others in the humblest of ways.*

Socratic Method is a style of teaching where Socrates used progressive questioning, inspired by specific verbs, to arouse deep and insightful thinking from his students (Jowett, 2011).

Stage Theory is a theory of intellectual development in which critical reasoning is improved by systematically subjecting it to intellectual self-assessment (Elder & Paul, 2013b).

Straight Point System is a system of calculating one's grade when there are no categories, and points earned are simply divided by total possible points.

Student Success courses are classes designed to help students be successful in college.

Subconscious Thinking refers to implicit thoughts and beliefs of which a person is not aware and yet is still reacting to (2015).

Super Six Theories are essential cognitive-behavioral theories that reflect human existence and can be used to monitor, assess, change, and maintain human thoughts, emotions, and behaviors.

Systemic Thinking is when you intentionally break down, examine, clarify, and reason through one's own or someone else's elements of thinking.

Three Domains of Learning is an academic tool divided into three categories where learning is demonstrated and used as a means for measuring. The domains are cognitive skills, affective skills, and psychomotor skills (Bloom & Krathwohl, 1956; Clark, 2010).

Toxic Relationships is where one or more persons violate another's boundaries and consistently cause an undesired state of homeostasis.

Unreflective Thinkers refers to those who do not consciously understand that thinking drives their behaviors and that there is a natural process to thinking (Elder & Paul, 2013b).

Values-Based Mottos are acronyms or sentences made up of a person's chosen values and beliefs, used as guidelines to maintain a state of homeostasis or balanced living.

.

Victims are those who run away from ownership and responsibility and blame others for his or her failures.

Visual Learners are those who learn best by seeing concepts, charts, and illustrations (Brown, 2015).

Weighted Point System is a system of grading that categorizes work/assignments, and each category is worth a certain percentage of the final grade, thus calculating averages, then the percent of those averages, and then finally adding each categories percent to assign a final grade.

Workforce Skills are abilities or talents that bring forth or contribute to significant economic value.

1. *Critical Thinking A Development: Stage Theory* by Linda Elder and Richard Paul at www.criticalthinking.org.

2. *Discover: The Second Coming of Freud* by Kat McGowan

3. *Drive: The Surprising Truth About What Motivates Us* by Daniel H. Pink

4. *Humanistic Psychotherapy* by Albert Ellis

5. *Overcoming Destructive Beliefs, Feelings, and Behaviors* by Albert Ellis

6. *Taxonomy of Educational Objectives: Book One, The Cognitive Domain* by Benjamin S. Bloom

7. *The Brian That Changes Itself* by Norman Doidge

8. *The Complete Works of Plato* by Benjamin Jowett

9. *The Developing Mind: How Relationships and the Brain Interact to Shape Who We Are* by Daniel Siegel

10. *The Student Bible, NIV: The book of Romans Chapters 1-16* and *John 3:16* by Zondervan

11. *The Total Money Makeover: A Proven Plan for financial fitness* by Dave Ramsey

12. *Time: The Science of Optimism, Hope Isn't Rational—So Why are Humans Wired for It?* by Tali Sharot

13. *Towards a Psychology of Being* by Abraham Maslow

References

1. Bloom, Benjamin. & Krathwohl, David. 1956. *Taxonomy of Educational Objectives: Book One, Cognitive Domains.* New York: Longman.

2. Brown. Willie C. 2005. *Reaching Your Full Potential: Success in College and in Life.* New York: Pearson.

3. Clark, David. 2010. "Bloom's Taxonomy of Learning Domains: The Three Types of Learning." Retrieved on March 28, 2011.

4. Conscious. 2015. In *Merriam Webster Dictionary.* Retrieved April 25, 2015, from http://www.merriam-webster.com/dictionary/conscious.

5. David, Daniel. 2014. "Rational Emotive Behavior Therapy in the Contest of Modern Psychological Research." Retrieved June 14, 2016 (http://albertellis.org/rebt-in-the-context-of-modern-psychological-research/).

6. Downing, Skip. 2012. *Oncourse.* Dallas: Cengage Publishing.

7. Elder, Linda, and Paul, Richard. 2013a. "An Interactive Model for Assessing Thinking" (A Graphic). Retrieved April, 20, 2015 (http://www.criticalthinking.org/ctmodel/logic-model1.htm#).

8. Elder, Linda, and Paul, Richard. 2013b. "Critical Thinking A Development: Stage Theory." Retrieved April, 20, 2015 (http://www.criticalthinking.org/articles/ct-development-a-stage-theory.cfm).

9. Ellis, Albert. 1973. *Humanistic Psychotherapy.* New York: McGraw Hill. (www.albertellisinstitute.org).

10. Ellis, Albert. 2001. *Overcoming Destructive Beliefs, Feelings, and Behaviors.* Amherst, NY: Prometheus Books. (www.albertellisinstitue.org).

11. Frankl, Viktor, and Winslade, William. 2006. *A Man's Search for Meaning.* Boston: Beacon Press.

12. Goleman, Daniel. 1995. *Emotional Intelligence.* New York: Bantam Books.

13. Hambric, Tuesday. 2011. "Community College Students Perceived Effects of their Home Environment on academic success." Ph.D. dissertation, Department of Psychology, Capella University, Minnesota.

References

14. Hambric, Tuesday. 2017. "Learning Framework: In Their Own Voices." Eastfield College.

15. Hambric, Tuesday. 2013. *Oncourse: The Remix.* Dallas, TX: Cengage Publishing.

16. Jowett, Benjamin. 2011. *The Complete Works of Plato.* Oxford, England: Oxford Press.

17. Marieb, Elaine, and Hoehn, Katja. (2013). *Human Anatomy & Physiology* (9th ed.). Boston: Pearson Publishing.

18. Maslow, Abraham. 2012. *A Theory of Human Motivation.* Start Publishing, LLC: New York.

19. McGowan Kat. 2014. "The Second Coming of Sigmund Freud." Discover: The Scientific Magazine, April, 2014, pp. 54-61.

20. Pink, Daniel. 2009. *Drive: The Surprising Truth about What Motivates Us.* New York: Penguin Group.

21. Personal. 2016. In *Collins English Dictionary – Complete & Unabridged 10th Edition.* Retrieved June 21, 2016, from http://www.dictionary.com/browse/personal.

22. Responsibility. 2015. In *Merriam-Webster Dictionary.* Retrieved June 20, 2015, from http://www.merriam-webster.com/dictionary/responsibility.

23. Ramsey, Dave. 2013. *The Total Money Makeover: A Proven Plan for Financial Fitness.* New York: Harper Collins Publishing.

24. Siegel, Daniel. 2015. *The Developing Mind: How Relationships and the Brain Interact to Shape Who We Are.* New York: The Guilford Press.

25. Shaffer, David, and Kipp, Katherine. 2013. *Developmental Psychology: Childhood and Adolescence.* Belmont, CA: Cengage Publishing.

26. Sharot, Tali. 2011. "Hardwired for Hope." *Time Magazine,* June 6, pp. 40-46.

27. Subconscious. 2015. In *Merriam Webster Dictionary.* Retrieved April 25, 2015, from http://www.merriam-webster.com/dictionary/subconscious.

28. Tinto, Vincent. 2012. *Completing College: Rethinking Institutional Action.* Chicago: The University of Chicago Press.

29. Whiteley, Rick. 2006. "Using the Socratic Method and Bloom's Taxonomy of the Cognitive Domain, to Enhance Online Discussion, Critical Thinking, and Student Learning." *Development in Business Stimulation and Experiential Learning* Vol. 33: pp. 65-70.